reading novels

reading
novels

George Hughes

Foreword by Walter L. Reed

Vanderbilt University Press
Nashville

This book is printed on acid-free paper
Manufactured in the United States of America

Library of Congress Cataloging-in-Publication Data

Hughes, George, 1944-
    Reading novels / George Hughes. — 1st ed.
        p. cm.
Includes bibliographical references and index.
    ISBN 0-8265-1399-9 (alk. paper)
    ISBN 0-8265-1400-6 (pbk. : alk. paper)
    1. Fiction—Technique. 2. Criticism. I. Title.
PN3365 .H84 2002
808.3-dc21
                                            2002001703

Contents

Foreword

George Hughes's *Reading Novels* is a unique piece of practical criticism, a comprehensive "poetics" of a genre that has not attracted a great deal of such attention, at least not on this level. It is a reader's and student's guide that reaches beyond issues of individual texts and historical traditions to essential features of the form. There are several sophisticated textbooks of this kind that deal with poetry. John Frederick Nims's *Western Wind: An Introduction to Poetry,* published twenty-five years ago and now in its fourth edition, comes to mind as a comparable volume, both for the catholicity of its examples and the intelligence of its comments. But because of the length of individual novels, perhaps, or because of the difficulty of formalizing the conventions of a genre that is always foregrounding its departure from tradition, most books on the "rhetoric of fiction," the "nature of narrative" or "structuralist poetics" that have broken important ground in the last half-century have been aimed at a scholarly, professorial audience, not at a readership of students, teachers of introductory courses, and that endangered species, the general reader. All of these more common readers stand to benefit greatly from this new book. At the same time, Hughes's engagement with a wide range of French structuralist studies of the novel, of narrative, and of language in general makes *Reading Novels* a book that ought to be informative and valuable to many American scholars as well, especially those who teach English and American literature, since this kind of criticism, once fashionable, seems no longer to be widely read in this country.

A great virtue of Hughes's approach is the way it navigates between traditional formalist approaches and postmodern theoretical ones. There was a time, it is true, when the kind of structural analysis of the novel offered here was regarded as shockingly new, unpleasantly scientistic, and decidedly foreign, but from the perspective of a new century (and from the tactful, matter-of-fact way in which Hughes is able to advance structuralist terms and techniques), it now seems eminently sane and practical, reassuringly empirical in its concern not with politics or ideologies lurking behind the text but with the way novels construct themselves as systems of significance, with the way readers can make sense of the subtleties and particularities of meaning that this centuries-old European literary art form has always been capable of conveying. The influence of Ian Watt's classic study *The Rise of the Novel* is still strong in English studies, but it has not led to the kind of classroom-level presentation that, say, Brooks and Warren's *Understanding Poetry* provided for the New Criticism of lyric poetry a generation or two earlier. Hughes brings a wide historical range of reference, a strategic preference for English and American examples in his sample passages, and a sophisticated French (and Italian) analytic perspective to bear on the novel that will be particularly welcome to teachers seeking to introduce their students to a genre that has gone well beyond its rise to literary respectability in eighteenth-century England.

Reading Novels is practical and basic in its presentation, but it is never condescending. It assumes an intelligence and curiosity on the part of its audience that, as a long-time teacher of prose fiction, I find to be quite common among my own students. But it does not assume a great deal of experience in reading novels, in perceiving the devices and decoding their significance in print narratives hundreds of pages in length. This also corresponds to my experience as a teacher, especially in the last decade. With the competition of other media so strong and insistent, few students I encounter now have spent years reading for pleasure, for escape from boredom, or for general self-improvement, as was still common a generation ago among those arriving on college campuses. Students today are perfectly intelligent and academically ambitious, but they lack the literary competence, as Jonathan Culler has termed it, that comes with long experience in novel reading. They present new challenges to teachers, and it seems to me that many teachers will see a valuable ally in George Hughes. He stands in a gap that many of us have long felt, providing a working vocabulary for focusing students' attention on ways of reading that used to go unrecognized and unanalyzed because they were so familiar, and that now go unrecognized and unanalyzed because they are so unaccustomed. At the same time, because of the lightness of his critical touch, his determination to avoid turning a toolbox of technical terms into a superstore of critical jargon, and the specificity of the examples he offers from novels of different periods and different styles, Hughes does not threaten to take over the discussion with his assistance. *Reading Novels* should be a useful supplement to any course on the novel, even those still centered (as most seem to be) on a particular period within a particular national literary history.

While this book is aimed first and foremost at the college classroom, it still seems able to serve as an intelligent person's guide to the novel as well, not (in the current fashion of publishing) "the novel for dummies," but certainly the novel for those who still read for pleasure and profit. Students and teachers as well as general readers should be pleased to be addressed neither as idiots, on the one hand, nor as initiates into the esoteric and the arcane, on the other—arguably the pitfall of postmodern literary theory. George Hughes has read widely and deeply—both in recent critical studies in "narratology," as it was once termed, in the French critical tradition and in classic studies in English and American criticism—but he keeps this learning in the background of the exposition, which comes across as attentive and imaginative but not pedantic. The counterpoint between the lists of useful critical terms and exemplary passages to which they are applied is lively—neither precept nor example dominates the discussion—and the transitions or segues from one example to another are deft. For example, the description of Darcy's sister in Austen's *Pride and Prejudice,* where we learn that she is "little more than sixteen," is followed by a description from Gissing's *The Nether World* of another "girl of sixteen." Hughes knows when not to quote as well, and how to enliven a technical discussion with an amusing but illustrative anecdote, as when he notes that Ann Radcliffe was herself much less impressed by the sight of Derwentwater in the Lake District than one of her characters in *The Mysteries of Udolpho.* He also brings in examples from novels, for instance from Beckett's *Watt,* where the particular technique under discussion is self-consciously commented on within the novel. Parodic examples enliven the more straightforward ones throughout.

From its beginnings (whenever and wherever these were, for the story is various) the novel has been an unruly citizen in the republic of letters. By the beginning of the nineteenth century in Europe it had attained literary respectability, and by the beginning of the twentieth century it had attained artistic preeminence worldwide. In the departments and curricula of colleges and universities, even at the beginning of the twenty-first century, the poetics of this prolifically innovative kind of writing, the rules and regulations of its production and consumption, are still far from achieving scholarly consensus. But it is surely time to bring some of the higher flying histories and theories of the novel down to earth, to bring some of its great traditions (plural) out of retirement, and to use both inheritances to train a new generation of readers who might otherwise miss the excitement.

Walter L. Reed
Emory University

Preface

This is a book about analysis of the novel in English. It started off, however, from discussions with teachers of French literature, in the course of which I became aware that interesting things were going on in France, particularly among a generation of academics who have absorbed the work of Gérard Genette and begun to build on it in new ways. As I came to understand it, this was not a theory of literature that was being developed, it was a methodology of analysis—a basic methodology usable by any competent reader of literary texts. What seemed particularly promising to me was that the methodology encouraged readers to develop their own autonomous readings. It showed how to do so in a convincing and rigorous way that could be communicated to others. In short, this was a way of helping people to talk coherently about literature.

I should like to express my thanks for the inspiration I gained from these early discussions with friends and colleagues, particularly Agnès Disson (who first showed me how things might work in practice), Patrick Rebollar, and Guillaume Marbot, as well as fellow participants in colloques at Cerisy-la-Salle, and members of the Graal reading group at the University of Tokyo.

My interest in what I encountered led me to explore the work of Gérard Genette, as well as other critics who cover similar territory, such as Paul Ricoeur,

Philippe Hamon, Jean-Michel Adam, André Petitjean, Sylvie Durrer, and Claude Duchet. I was much helped by some writers with a pedagogic focus, particularly Yves Reuter and Dominique Maingueneau. I should like to express here my appreciation for this body of writings, and my general indebtedness to it.

It was exciting to find that the methodology gave a new clarity and cogency to my own readings of English novels. I came also to see with pleasure that others in the field of English or comparative literature had been over this path already, often starting from different directions; it will be obvious from references in the book how much I have profited from the writings of Dorrit Cohn, Meir Sternberg, and Michael Riffaterre. I am, moreover, conscious of many debts to specialist works in the field of narratology and linguistics, by Mieke Bal, Ann Banfield, Seymour Chatman, Monika Fludernik, Raymond W. Gibbs Jr., and Shlomith Rimmon-Kenan, as well as to the impressive work on narrative and film theory by David Bordwell.

It has been encouraging to find so many colleagues in Japan receptive to the ideas this book contains. I should like to thank Kazuhisa Takahashi and Takaki Hiraishi, who have both given me warm and constant support. Kazumi Watanabe was an expert colleague while I was writing the book, and managed to find me every obscure text I thought I needed. Masanori Toyota and Yoshifumi Saito argued about language with me, set me right on important matters, and kindly invited me to address the Japanese branch of the Poetics and Linguistics Association. Yoshiki Nishimura steered me around issues that I find difficult in linguistics. And I am very grateful to Mariko Yamaguchi, who gave me last-minute guidance over the philosophical problem of fictional names.

Valerie Sanders, Graham Law, Jon Spence, and Stephen Clark all kindly read parts of the manuscript and gave me their comments on it. Their reactions to the early drafts were invaluable, and I am profoundly grateful for their encouragement and criticisms. Members of my graduate seminar at Tokyo University also read parts of the book as it was being written, and gave me helpful advice. I should like to thank in particular Akiko Kawasaki, Reiko Nakagami, Akemi Yoshida, Yukiko Morita, Taichi Koyama, Yuko Ashitagawa, and Li Jiang for tactful hints and corrections.

I have long-standing debts in my study of the novel to the late Patricia Thomson, to Janet Burroway, and to Sybil Oldfield (who first drew my attention to the bad reading habits of Mrs. Linnet in "Janet's Repentance"). These three excellent teachers made the study of English literature a pleasure and a challenge for me. I hope this book communicates some of the enthusiasm for the field that they once instilled in me.

Finally, Clair Hughes has throughout encouraged my work, commented, read, criticized, and suggested new ideas. Through her research on Henry James I have come to understand his importance in new ways, and to see more clearly his key position between the English and the French novel. I could not have written this book without her generous help, and I dedicate the book to her.

Introduction

Methodical Reading

According to the French poet Jacques Roubaud, every reading of a poem by every reader is a kind of translation. What makes up the poem in the end is the sum of all the readings. The same might be said of the novel. A novel is usually a long work that cannot be read in one stretch; each reader will select different things for attention, and will construct a different path through the text, which constitutes a reading. There is no final right reading for a work like *Pride and Prejudice* (1813) or *Ulysses* (1922), only the sum of the readings we have made so far.

Why then is it necessary to attempt a methodical reading? Why is it necessary to attempt analysis, or the breaking up of texts into parts? A simple answer is that, if our readings are going to be the basis for written work, and if our aim is to interest and convince other readers with an account of what we have read, then we need to approach texts in a methodical and systematic way.

This should not imply mechanical procedures: there will always be differences in the construction of individual texts that need to be given their due. Nonetheless, the idea behind this book is that it is helpful to have a clear idea of possible starting points. Methodical reading picks up what is relevant to elucidate, correct, and confirm our initial vague impressions of a text.[1]

Such a reading does not pretend to be completely objective or scientific. We are bound to feel the influence of our own life-histories as we read and write, to be affected by personal and emotional problems, as well as the social and historical context in which we live. We all start our readings from different contexts, and place them against slightly different sets of values and belief systems. But criticism that lays too much emphasis on the reader's own situation rapidly becomes narcissistic. As Umberto Eco says, "It is not at all forbidden to use a text for daydreaming, and we do this frequently, but daydreaming is not a public affair; it leads us to move within the narrative wood as if it were our own private garden."[2] Good readings direct and redirect our attention toward aspects of texts that can be confirmed by other readers, toward points that have not been widely noticed, or that others have mistaken.

Overcoming the Blocked Response

Most of us have faced the problem at some time of wanting to join in the debate about a work of literature, and yet finding we do not know what to say. Without a developed vocabulary for discussing literary texts, it is difficult to be precise, even to ourselves, about our responses. Repetitions of how we like a novel, or find it "realistic," quickly become banal. It can happen that we read and re-read a text without being sure what makes it distinctive, or what is worth taking note of, or worth talking about.

Fanny Elmer, in Virginia Woolf's *Jacob's Room*, has such problems. She tells herself that she has read quite a few books (by Scott and Dumas), but doesn't understand how her boyfriend can find eighteenth-century novels worthwhile.

> **For this dull stuff (Fanny thought) about people with odd names is what Jacob likes. Good people like it. Dowdy women who don't mind how they cross their legs read *Tom Jones*—a mystic book; for there is something, Fanny thought, about books which if I had been educated I could have liked—much better than ear-rings and flowers, she sighed, thinking of the . . . fancy-dress dance next week. She had nothing to wear.**
>
> (Virginia Woolf, *Jacob's Room*, 1922, chap. 10)

A methodical approach to analysis helps overcome blocked responses like Fanny's; it takes us beyond the vague incomprehension of phrases such as "dull stuff," or "mystic book." It should also prevent a drift from texts into thoughts of earrings, flowers, and fancy-dress dances. Methodological tools always have their limitations, and an elaboration of technical jargon becomes opaque and distracting, but method is useful when it helps concentrate on the particularities of the text in hand.

Although the techniques described in this book are not independent of literary theory, the book does not aim to be a work of theory as such. The overall aim is rather to introduce an approach to texts. Examples from the English novel, novella, and short story are given constantly, and the terms used are explained in relation to these examples. By this method, the student should be helped to develop an autonomous reading of a literary text—but an autonomous reading of a rigorous kind, one that can be communicated to others.

The following sections of this introduction explain some theoretical underpinnings of the book. Anyone who prefers to concentrate simply on testing how the techniques work would be advised to skip to chapter 1. It is quite possible to check the analyses contained in the book, to see if they are useful, and then return to questions about their theoretical basis later.

The Field of Study

Fictional texts, and novels in particular, are discussed here as works of literature. Recent criticism has often emphasized that literary discourse is part of a general social discourse, that its figures, rhymes, rhythms, and narrative forms can be found elsewhere and are not particular to literature. If this is broadly true, it does not follow that we are unable to distinguish a field of study in literature. The field is clearly recognizable if we start out with a primary interest in artworks.

All societies produce, in one way or another, things that can be identified as artworks (they give pleasure; they are not simply or directly functional, but can be considered as forms of play; they are regarded as repositories of insight and constructive skills that can be handed down from generation to generation; appreciation of them, and debate about them, unites us to other members of our community). *Literature* is a term we have come to use for a kind of artwork found in societies with a developed script. The novel, which was only slowly distinguished from "history" and "romance," and which remained for some time a sub- or para-literary form, has become the characteristic literary art form of modern societies.[3] Novels themselves are particular artworks, and deserve methods of study that respect their particularity.

Thus, although the language of novels is the same language as that used for spoken communication, and although there is a constant interplay between spoken and written forms in a literate society, we can take our field as one that consists of written and printed texts. Written texts are characterized (as Jacques Derrida points out) by their "iterability": they are extended in visual space, and can be read and re-read.[4] Re-reading is fundamental to analysis.

The term *novel* is usually (though not always) limited to long works of prose fiction. There is no particular attempt here to make distinctions related to length, although there are obvious differences in structure and scope among novels, novellas, and short stories. There are also similarities, since all are works of fiction.

If a novel is a work of fiction, then fictionality is something that is indicated, as Michael Riffaterre reminds us, by "many and well known" signs. (He lists such things as emblematic names for characters, unlikely detailed recordings of speech or thought, markers found in titles and prefaces, and a range of distinctive techniques of narration.)[5] There are, however, marginal and limit cases, where we are unsure whether to call a work fictional. A play between the fictional and the real has always been important in novels: in 1725 Mary Davys, when talking of "those Sort of Writings call'd *Novels*," called them "Probable Feign'd Stories."[6]

The texts discussed in this book include many that were specifically written as novels, but also others that have only later come to be called, or read as, novels. In the latter case we may always decide that the term is not appropriate on further consideration. Once we decide to read and discuss a text as a novel, however, it becomes possible to ask questions about how it works (or whether it works) as such: analysis can then begin to point out how different features of the text direct, confirm, and contribute to our reading.[7]

Narratology, Stylistics, Genre

Many of the techniques and terms used in this book derive from recent developments in narratology, stylistics, and generic criticism. The aim is not to present a synchronic theory of the text, or of communication as such; it is to show systematic ways of talking about novelistic texts.[8] Novels are discussed as art objects existing within a history, on the assumption that they draw from a certain available range of characteristics (which are, of course, combined and developed in a different way in each novel.) There are some common techniques used by novelists, just as there are some constraints that operate in relation to the form (which may be culturally imposed or may arise from linguistic or psychological function).

Novels are not seen here as texts that simply, or essentially, communicate the intentions of their authors; but neither is there an attempt to reduce them to the material products of social discourse (the latter aim leading on the whole to what Italo Calvino calls "Books Read Even Before You Open Them Since They Belong To The Category Of Books Read Before Being Written").[9] What is offered is a synthetic approach, drawing on various techniques that foreground understanding of the novelistic text as text.

Narratology

Narratology (the study and analysis of narratives), in particular as it has been developed by Gérard Genette, provides us with tools for describing the establishment, focalization, and development of narrative. Narrative is one of the basic features of organization in human communication, though different cultures have developed different ways of telling and structuring complex written narratives. In the novel, we are looking at a literary form that feeds the appetite for narrative of modern industrial societies. Genette's narratology has proved important for the study of the novel because, rather than focus on an abstract grammar of narrative, he has concentrated on describing how narrative is actually deployed in literary texts, how it is framed and shaped into book form, and how narratives interact with one another. He gives us a general way of talking about narrative and, at the same time, allows us to be responsive to the particularity of a text.

Narratology in general is possible because—although we exchange an infinite variety of communications with others—we organize some communications in such a way that they can be read *as* narratives. We have expectations that lead us to recognize patterns, which (as Manfred Jahn says) can be "selected, used and sometimes discarded."[10] Constraints on the use of narrative by novelists arise from fundamental characteristics of this mode of discourse, but also from the demands of publishers and audiences, from writers' views of their audience, and simply from a narrative being recorded in print.

Writers who wish to publish their work must negotiate and make strategies to deal with such constraints. They may feel they should respect them, or, in the avant-garde novel, they may fight against them. (And, in the case of the Oulipo group of writers, they may inflict a few more on themselves to stimulate their creative activity. Members of Oulipo like restrictions and constraints: "they see in them not limitation but *potentiality*."")[11] The shape taken by narrative within the novel must, however, be radically affected by its representation within language. For this reason, some of the techniques of stylistics also prove useful in analysis.

Stylistics

Attempts have been made to develop stylistics as a rigorous discipline, poised between linguistics and literature, but its continuing attraction, as Jean Molino has pointed out, derives rather from its origins in a "practice" that is profoundly rooted in our ordinary social lives.[12] The popular comedian who imitates a politician and the jeering schoolboy who imitates a teacher's funny walk are as convinced as the professional stylistician that there is such a thing as style and that it will be easily recognized by an audience.

Parodists and comedians who reproduce a style may perhaps act by instinct; we can hope to be a little more systematic. The most helpful stylistics, however, remains a form of practice rather than a single coherent theory, providing descriptions of how language is organized and suggesting explanations of how it works (in an affective sense) in a text.

In analyzing literature, the concept of style could take us in various directions. Stylisticians refer to a pyramid of styles: period styles lie at the base, above them lies the style of individual writers, and at the top is the style of a particular literary work.[13] In each case, when we study style, we are interested in the characteristics of the field in relation to a different context. In this book we are principally concerned with the analysis of the style of particular literary works. At this level, as Michael Riffaterre points out, style is what gives a text its unique characteristics: *"style is the text itself."*[14] Since stylistics is above all a practice rather than a theory, it is appropriate that it should rely to a large extent on the simple descriptive nomenclature of traditional grammar (noun, adjective, verb, adverb, pronoun; compound sentence, complex sentence; and so forth). This nomenclature has been criticized and problematized within some branches of modern linguistics, but it remains widely integrated into general discourse and has thus been used in this book.[15]

Cognitive linguistics, however, has transformed the way in which metaphor and metonymy are now discussed, and has offered new insight into how texts are apprehended and processed. Ideas taken from this developing field are used in the discussions of style and language in Part IV. But it remains important for our purposes that attention not be displaced onto problems that are proper to linguistics as an academic discipline. The aim of the book is to indicate widely accessible ways of talking about novelistic texts and to retain a focus on the field of literature.

The book also covers some basic rhetorical analysis of figures of style and construction.[16] Both stylistics and rhetorical analysis may function to show us what we have sensed in a general way in a text, but were not otherwise able to describe. Henry Green says, "A man's style is like the clothes he wears, an expression of his personality. . . . [But] there are fashions in underwear, for the most part unconscious in that we are not particularly aware of how we dress."[17] Obviously not everyone would agree with Green on the question of clothes, since some of us are more interested in what we wear than others, but stylistics and rhetoric do help when they reveal a writer's textual underwear. Moreover, the topics they deal with are not simply isolated facts; they have, in Helen Vendler's phrase, "ideational import."[18]

Genre

A sensitivity to the problems of genre is also important in this book, since generic considerations cannot be far away from discussion of literature as literature. Writers do not just sit down to write: they try to write something of a certain kind, or genre. Even Frédéric Moreau, the young hero of Flaubert's *Sentimental Education,* who "thought himself endowed with an extraordinary talent, the object of which he did not know," and who could not decide "whether he was to be a great painter or a great poet," tried to conform to ideas of genre (or subgenre) when he sat down to write "a novel entitled *Sylvio, the Fisherman's Son.*" Muddling generic stereotypes with personal fantasy, Frédéric decided that the setting was to be Venice, the heroine was to be the woman he had fallen in love with (under the name of Antonia,) the hero was to be himself, he was to murder several gentlemen, set fire to part of the town, and sing under Antonia's balcony. He did not complete his novel—he grew discouraged by the "echoes from other writers which he noticed"—but his procedures in conforming to genre are only a parodic version of those that all novelists go through.[19]

The novel is often referred to as a late, or recent, literary genre—coming historically after poetry and drama. An important body of criticism has emphasized that its genre is not an abstract or ideal category: the novel as a genre starts only in the modern world. It was not a *necessary* genre, always somehow there in the absolute. The genre of the novel is contingent, changed and shaped by history, by society, by the production and use of books.[20]

The novel is also an amorphous genre. If we can be fairly clear about the genre of some prototypical novels, we are nonetheless quite often faced with works that self-consciously attempt to test or shift the boundaries. Is Samuel Beckett's *The Unnamable* (1958) a novel? (It has no plot, no consistent characters, and does not attempt to describe a believable fictional world.) Is Julian Barnes's *Flaubert's Parrot* (1984) a novel, or a work of criticism? Is W. G. Sebald's *The Rings of Saturn* (1999) a travel narrative with anecdotes, or, since much of it may be fictional, can it be included somewhere on the margins of the genre?

With all the reservations that we may express about individual works, the notion of writing and publishing something that will be described as a novel (or will perhaps challenge readers to define it as such) remains important for writers. Even the subdivisions of genre (into detective novels, thrillers, science fiction, the historical novel, and so on) guide the decisions writers and readers make. One of the most promising suggestions in relation to the novel is that it consistently provokes its own redefinition.

The Limits of Formalism?

Literary criticism that begins with considerations such as those outlined above is sometimes attacked as "formalist." Any criticism that looks seriously at literature (and that hopes to go beyond the superficial terms of modern journalism) must, however, take account of basic textual features, and attempt some analysis of their organization and representation in language.[21]

Textual analysis has been attacked because it is "positivist" and uses "the rhetoric of objectivity," but there is no need for analysis to claim absolute objectivity.[22] We cannot pretend to offer a complete and fully competent reading of a text (whatever that would be), only one that takes a novel seriously as artwork, respects its particular features, and attempts to base generalizations on that particularity. Ford Madox Ford was no doubt overreacting when he insisted that good criticism "concerns itself with methods and with methods and again with methods—and with nothing else," but Ford's fierce outburst was part of an attack on the vague journalistic bellettrism of his day, and a defence of the prefaces of Henry James.[23] It is noticeable that James's prefaces to his novels still provoke discussion, and remain a valuable point of reference for criticism of the novel, while the fashionable criticism of the day (relying heavily on whimsical biography and evaluative chit-chat) has sunk into the great ocean of the unreadable and unread.

In looking at texts, we need a moment of analysis to detach ourselves from the simple confirmation of preexisting beliefs. The most convincing criticism is that which, as James Phelan says, does not "assume a priori that a particular set of cultural/thematic categories will be central to any given text but rather works from the text and its techniques, structures, and effects out towards the cultural categories."[24]

The techniques outlined in this book do not, then, despite their concern with form, in any way preclude the possibility of going on to social or cultural criticism (or for that matter to old-fashioned thematic and evaluative criticism). They simply assume that criticism becomes free-floating and worthless unless it can convince us *first* that the things discussed are generally available to competent readers of the texts in question. As Mieke Bal succinctly puts it, political and ideological criticism "cannot but be based on insights into the way texts produce those political effects."[25]

Literary History—Literature and History

It has been suggested that techniques of analysis are unnecessary in practical terms, because the priority for the modern student is not methodical reading, but literary history or social history (or perhaps "historicity").[26]

The opposition set up by this suggestion is, however, naive. There is no contest between history on one side and method or theory on the other. History has its own problems over methods and analysis, which are taken seriously by those who work within that discipline. Historians who ignore problems of methodology are prone (like the rest of us) to operate within unquestioned, preexisting conceptual categories. It is all very well to re-solve, like Pierre Menard, the scholar of Cervantes in the famous story by Borges, to "know Spanish well, recover the Catholic faith, fight against the Moors or the Turk, forget the history of Europe between the years 1602 and 1918, *be* Miguel de Cervantes."[27] Total recall of the past is neither possible nor (as Menard found) finally very interesting. The primary aim is to read literature.

Part of the fascination of studying the novel is, as Michael McKeon points out, that, as a genre established within modern history, it allows us to aim at a "method in which history and theory join together to inform each other."[28] Modern students of the novel are particularly indebted to recent histories of the publication, production, and circulation of novels; to work on the history of publishing houses, copyright of authors, patronage, and authors' ownership of their work; to research on censorship, circulating libraries, periodical editors, and literary agents.

Analysis in general does not have to propose a static form for the novel.

It is appropriate to remember that the spread of literacy in the eighteenth and nineteenth centuries (which remain classic points of reference for general discussions of the novel) had wide-reaching consequences, and helped to make the novel what it remains today—the dominant literary genre. The development of new forms of transport affected not only the distribution of novels but the time that many people had for reading them— and this is reflected in both form and subject matter.

The great enterprise of novelistic realism is constantly shadowed through the eighteenth and nineteenth centuries by nonfictional attempts at the systematic or scientific study of society, by developments in historical writing, philosophy, economics, statistics, political science, evolutionary studies, and medical science. (And the novel itself is an important source for definitions and descriptions of the new industrial society.)

Late nineteenth-century developments in psychology can be related to an increased complexity in the presentation of character in the novel. At the same time, the nineteenth-century pseudo-sciences, which attempted to classify racial characteristics or social and sexual deviance, can be seen to shape many narratives—as does the growth of imperialism. Adventure stories are central to the age of imperialism, and are augmented in the early twentieth century (at least in the art novel) by interior adventures. It has been suggested that the great modernist adventure story becomes the process of writing itself.[29] Certainly the "linguistic turn" of modern philosophy has its place in the twentieth-century novel: language (which had become subtle and self-reflexive for writers in the late nineteenth century) was no longer a transparent medium for modernists. Its problems appear in the foreground of their concerns, and are constantly forced on the attention of readers.

Having noted the significance of such historical generalizations, we must also note that they are not necessarily reflected in any one work that we may wish to study. The task we begin with, in analysis, is to read and describe particularity. Good literary analysis needs to recognize that the world in which literature is produced (which includes writers, editors, booksellers, publishers, reviewers, and critics) is not united by any single institutional structure; those in this world may take up positions that are independent of political and religious currents holding sway elsewhere. To study literature in depth is almost always to study it in terms of individuals.

Biography

In the Anglo-American world, focus on individuals often shifts toward a focus on biography, and biography is taken as the automatic adjunct to an interest in literature. The book pages of Sunday newspapers are stuffed with reviews of biographies, and bookstores sometimes give the impression of selling little else. Most of those published are not works of critical sophistication; they assume the kind of attention from their readers that George Eliot attributed to Mrs. Linnet, in "Janet's Repentance":

> **On taking up the biography of a celebrated preacher, she immediately turned to the end to see what disease he died of; and if his legs swelled, as her own occasionally did. . . . She then glanced over the letters and diary, and wherever there was a predominance of Zion, the River of Life, and notes of exclamation, she turned over to the next page; but any passage in which she saw such promising nouns as 'small-pox', 'pony', or 'boots and shoes', at once arrested her.**
>
> (George Eliot, *Scenes of Clerical Life*, (1857) 1858, pt. 3, chap. 3)

If details of other people's lives (and their sufferings from swollen legs) are interesting to read about, they are too often a distraction from textual study. It would obviously be useful to know something of a writer's relation to readers, to look at the problem of a writer's manuscripts and revisions and their representation in the published text, as well as the books a writer was reading when he or she sat down to write. But these have been the concerns of "genetic criticism" rather than biography.[30]

Biographies do not give a complete factual record of a writer's life (even if such a thing were imaginable): they construct a narrative based on a biographer's preconceptions. They treat letters and journals, which survive by chance, as though they were evidence of constant mental states. They speculate on how writers *must have felt* or *probably thought,* when the truth is that we do not know. We may enjoy the best biographies, appreciating their inventive reconstructions of personality, or their imaginative use of anecdote, but we should not pretend they are transparent writings that give us direct access to the truth about an author (let alone to truths about the texts an author has written.)[31]

After all, the novelist who sits down to write may represent a quite different side of the person from the alcoholic and wife-beater who occupies the pages of a popular biography. Proust, in his attack on Sainte-Beuve, points out that "a book is the product of a self other than that which we display in our habits, in company, in our vices."[32] Biography does not have special authority, and is not the key to a special understanding of literary texts. If we are interested in the field of literature, then, in reading literature, we need analysis to help us understand how those texts work.

Analysis

This book affirms the importance of systematic and appropriate techniques of analysis. It provides, in effect, a sequence of starting points. In Part I we look at how novels open and establish their narratives. In Part II we examine basic techniques and constraints in relation to description, character, dialogue, monologue, and free indirect discourse. In Part III we consider problems of narrative organization and the role of the narrator. Part IV is principally concerned with language, rhetoric, and repetition. The book concludes in Part V with a chapter on endings of the novel.

It will often be necessary for the purposes of analysis to focus on a particular passage and go over it in detail, trying to pick up what has been missed on a first reading. At the end of the book is a general checklist of topics and questions to bear in mind when focusing on a passage in such a way. Readers who come for the first time to the methods outlined in this book may find it useful to look at this final checklist when setting out seriously to re-read and analyze a novel. Not all the points will be relevant to any particular reading, but with a general sense of where analysis could coherently take place, every reader has a better chance of developing a communicable autonomous reading of a novel—and breaking through the barrier of the blocked response.

Part I
Openings

A writer has somehow imagined a world, and readers somehow follow the writer into it. This process is fundamental to novels—so fundamental that most readers, in most of their readings, simply take it for granted. If we want to develop our understanding of novels seriously, however, we need to have some insight into how it is done. We need to grasp how a text opens up what Henry James calls "the projected, painted, peopled, poeticized, realized world, the furnished and fitted world into which we are beguiled."[1]

1

Starting the Analysis

Analysis of a text begins with reconsideration and re-reading. We never encounter a novel as something completely unknown or unpredictable: we come to it with pre-expectations that will constantly be adjusted as we read on. A first reading of a novel is usually an attempt to go right through the work, to gather a global sense of its qualities. But after going through the text, we need to pause, to try to gain some sense of how the text is organized. In re-reading we approach the details within the text again, this time in the light of various hypotheses.

Paratext

As a first step it is worth giving attention to the material that surrounds the text: the *paratext*.[1] Paratext includes the dust-jacket, blurb, title-page, dedication, contents page, and any prefaces or appendices. There may be illustrations and epigraphs (short quotations from other texts, placed after the title-page or at the start of each chapter).

More loosely connected material may also be bound in with the text, such as advertisements for other books, or advertisements for other products (often in the nineteenth century for things like quack cures and breakfast cocoa). Or there may be interviews and publicity articles that came into circulation at the same time as the text.

It is easy to take all this material for granted, but the paratext sets up, in effect, an agreement, or contract of reading, between text and reader.[2] Information given in the paratext helps us decide what category to place a text in, and the choice of category will affect our reading and evaluation of the text.

Along with the name of the publisher and the publisher's trademark, the title-page of the first American edition of *The Awkward Age* (1899) gives us the following:

THE   AWKWARD   AGE

A Novel. By HENRY JAMES
Author of "Washington Square"
"Daisy Miller" "Picture and Text"
"Terminations" "The Private Life"

The wording makes clear that this text is to be read as a novel. By 1899 James had already published fifty-two books, including at least eighteen that could be described as novels. Only two out of the eighteen are chosen for mention, *Washington Square* and *Daisy Miller*: both underline, for American readers, James's background as a fellow American. (The English edition, published in the same year, advertises him as the author of two different novels.) The wide range of James's fiction is indicated by the mention of *Terminations* and *The Private Life*, two collections of short stories. Significantly, James is also described as the author of *Picture and Text*, a collection of essays on art. The contract that is set up with the reader is thus one in which *The Awkward Age* may be considered as the work of a "man of letters," with American roots and a high level of general culture. The paratext prepares us for an art novel, not a work of popular fiction.

The first edition of *Robinson Crusoe* (1719) announces the work as shown on the facing page.

We now regard *Robinson Crusoe* as a novel, but the word *novel* is not used here (though it had been used for some kinds of fictional narratives as early as 1566), and there is no mention of Daniel Defoe as author. Modern editions, even when they reproduce this old title-page for interest's sake, find it necessary to provide another title-page, where "The Life and Adventures of Robinson Crusoe" is given as the title of the novel, and the name of Daniel Defoe is given as that of the author.

It could be said that the original edition poses as a genuine memoir, and is thus a piece of impersonation (from a hostile viewpoint, a clever

THE

LIFE

AND

STRANGE SURPRIZING

ADVENTURES

OF

ROBINSON CRUSOE,

Of YORK. MARINER:

Who lived Eight and Twenty Years,

all alone in an un-inhabited Island on the
Coast of AMERICA, near the Mouth of
the Great River of OROONOQUE;

Having been cast on Shore by Shipwreck, where-
in all the Men perished but himself.

WITH

An Account how he was at last as strangely deliver'd by PYRATES.

Written by Himself.

LONDON:

Printed for W. TAYLOR at the *Ship* in *Pater-Noster-
Row.* MDCCXIX

---

fake). It is described as the "Life" of Robinson Crusoe, but it is not the full life story, since it was later to be followed by two other volumes of "Farther Adventures" and "Serious Reflections during the Life and Strange Surprizing Adventures." Strikingly, we are given an exact and real-sounding name (Robinson Crusoe), the name of the real city he comes from (York), and his job (mariner). Yet the information given here is not entirely consistent with the text. The title-page says that Crusoe is "deliver'd by Pyrates," while the text itself describes him as being saved by a ship that was having trouble with mutineers. Defoe later insisted that *Robinson Crusoe* was not "a sort of lying" but an "allogorick History."[3] It was to become typical of the nineteenth-century novel, however, to offer specific details and reference to real places when talking about fictional characters, and often to use a character's name in the title of the work.

Once we begin to read a fictional text, it is usually obvious that it is fiction,[4] but both text and paratext may be designed to play with confusions. The area between autobiographical novels, autobiographies, and memoirs has been a particularly attractive field for experiment. Charlotte Brontë's *Jane Eyre* (1847) calls itself an "autobiography" on its title-page, though we now classify it as a novel. Seamus Deane's *Reading in the Dark* (1996), which is generally assumed to be about his own youth, calls itself, in the blurb, a "novel" and a book "about growing up," avoiding the words *autobiography* or *memoir*.[5]

Some contemporary texts, from internal evidence, could either be novels or critical essays. The paratext usually indicates the genre, though uncertainty can be used as a strategy to attract the reader's interest. The title-page of Julian Barnes's *Flaubert's Parrot* gives no indication as to whether it is a novel or not. There is an epigraph from Flaubert's letters, which reads: "When you write the biography of a friend, you must do it as if you were taking *revenge* for him." Are we then to take this as a biography? The text is preceded by a contents page (which is not common for modern novels, though James used one in *The Awkward Age*). The page starts off:

Contents

1	Flaubert's Parrot	11
2	Chronology	23
3	Finders Keepers	38
4	The Flaubert Bestiary	49
5	Snap!	66
6	Emma Bovary's Eyes	74
7	Cross Channel	82
8	The Train-spotter's Guide to Flaubert	107

Is this to be a collection of essays on Flaubert? Or a novel? It seems odd for the "chronology" to come second on the list: some kind of puzzle is obviously involved. But the paratext as a whole does not leave us entirely free to guess; the dust-jacket has a blurb that introduces Barnes as "a novelist," and then says: "By turns moving and entertaining, witty and scholarly, *Flaubert's Parrot* is a work of technical audacity, a compelling weave of fiction and imaginatively ordered fact." We cannot be sure that Barnes wrote this himself, but he will have checked it—and it certainly now functions as paratext. The contract it establishes is one in which the novelist has pushed to the limits of the genre, and readers are encouraged to focus on his "technical audacity" in doing so.

Serial Contracts

There may not be a single contract with the reader, but a series of contracts; since some novels (particularly nineteenth-century ones) were published first in periodicals, or in parts, and later in book form.

Wilkie Collins, in his preface to the first book publication of *The Woman in White* (1861), wrote: "In presenting my book to a new class of readers, in its complete form, I have only to say that it has been carefully revised; and that the divisions of the chapters, and other minor matters of the same sort, have been altered here and there, with a view to smoothing and consolidating the story in its course through these volumes." He is making a new contract with a new group of readers (probably library users rather than readers who would buy the book). Collins's "sensation novel" had been a huge popular success when serialized in the weekly miscellany *All the Year Round,* and he now wanted readers to understand that the novel was more than reprinted popular journalism: it had been "carefully revised" and re-edited. The suggestions made by the new contract serve to justify a claim he goes on to make—that his novel is a serious experiment in narrative technique.

The decisions an author makes about different forms of publication are obviously limited by what is available or popular at the time, and by what arrangements can be struck with publishers, but they are nonetheless real decisions, which affect subject matter and organization within the novel, and may determine the circulation of the novel on publication. If we find it convenient to use modern pocket editions of novels for most study purposes, we should bear in mind that these are not likely to have followed the format in which a novel first appeared, and may mislead us about the paratext approved by the author. It will always be informative to look, as far as possible, at early editions.

Entering the Novel: The Incipit

Analysis of the text itself starts with a detailed consideration of the opening section of the narrative, known as the *incipit*.[6] In novels this is a particularly significant part, since it is here that the writer leads us into a new fictive text-world. We are given information that will orient us in following the rest of the novel. In realist novels, the space and time of the narrative will be established, so that we can make the first steps into it with confidence (even if there will soon be jumps backward and forward into different scenes). We may encounter the narrator for the first time, and may learn about the situation in which the narrative is produced.

The incipit is also important because it is an obvious point of reference as we proceed through a text. In a long novel readers are more likely to remember the incipit than many of the later details of the text. It is thus a small part of a novel that stands in a special relation to the text as a whole, and needs attention.

Opening the Narrative

The incipit of many traditional works of fiction starts off slowly and provides us with details of the setting, as though we were about to read a history:

> **On the pleasant banks of the Garonne, in the province of Gascony, stood, in the year 1584, the chateau of Monsieur St. Aubert. From its windows were seen the pastoral landscapes of Guienne and Gascony, stretching along the river, gay with luxuriant woods and vines, and plantations of olives. To the south, the view was bounded by the majestic Pyrenées. . . .**
>
> (Ann Radcliffe, *The Mysteries of Udolpho*, 1794)

This gives us geographical information about the setting ("Gascony," "Garonne," a "chateau") and precise indication of the date when the narrative is set (1584). We do not know who is telling the story, or when, but a coherent text-world is established. A narrative set in the past is to be told, and its geography will include places that may be known by name to us, even if we have not actually seen them. (As Umberto Eco has pointed out, Ann Radcliffe does not know much about the places herself: olive trees do not grow in Gascony.)[7] It is typical of novelistic descriptions to start by a door or a window: in the incipit such places represent a point from which to look at and through which to enter the text-world.

A complete contrast to this kind of incipit is found in *The New Machiavelli*, by H. G. Wells:

> Since I came to this place I have been very restless, wasting my energies in the futile beginning of ill-conceived books. One does not settle down very readily at two and forty to a new way of living, and I have found myself with the teeming interests of the life I have abandoned still buzzing like a swarm of homeless bees in my head.
>
> (H. G. Wells, *The New Machiavelli*, 1911)

Here, we start where the narrator is now, in "this place," and with the actual problems of writing down the things we are going to read. The time of the narrative told in the novel will be related somehow or other to the *now* of this incipit. The act of writing (and remembering) is foregrounded here: the development of the novel will in fact go back to the childhood of the narrator and then fill in the details of his story up to the present.[8]

Starting the Narrative: Origins or *In Medias Res*?

The incipit of a novel also brings up the question of the point at which the writer has decided to start telling the narrative. *Robinson Crusoe* begins with the main character and a brief family history:

> I was born in the Year 1632, in the city of *York* of a good Family, tho' not of that Country, my Father being a Foreigner of *Bremen*, who settled first at *Hull:* He got a good Estate by Merchandise, and leaving off his Trade lived afterward at *York*, from whence he had married my Mother, whose Relations were named *Robinson*. . . .
>
> (Daniel Defoe, *Robinson Crusoe*, 1719)

This moves off with the date of the narrator's birth, but such starting points in narratives are never absolute, there are always shadows of other possible previous narratives behind them. As Amos Oz says, "Can there exist, in principle, a proper beginning to any story at all? Isn't there always, without exception, a latent beginning-before-the-beginning? A foreword to the introduction to the prologue?"[9] In this case, we have no sooner started than we go rapidly backward—even in the first sentence—to learn about Crusoe's father, then about his mother, and his mother's family.[10]

Not all incipits attempt a gradual or logical introduction to the fictional world of the novel. Henry James was scornful of beginnings that are a "mere seated mass of information,"[11] and it is a common technique to throw the reader into the thick of the text-world as though we needed no initial signposts. Narratives may start *in medias res* (Latin for "in the middle of things"), forcing the reader to puzzle out what is going on. Information may be withheld or given gradually. Virginia Woolf's novel *Jacob's Room* begins with a woman in the middle of writing a letter; we have nothing but her name to start with:

> "So of course," wrote Betty Flanders, pressing her heels rather deeper in the sand, "there was nothing for it but to leave."
>
> Slowly welling from the point of her gold nib, pale blue ink dissolved the full stop; for there her pen stuck; her eyes fixed, and tears slowly filled them.
>
> (Virginia Woolf, *Jacob's Room*, 1922)

Why "of course"? Why are her heels in the sand? If there was "nothing for it but to leave," where is she going to leave? And when is all this happening? There seems to be an "instability of reference" in texts like this.

No incipit will, of course, be able to give us exhaustive explanations of the starting situation of a novel, and if we find the opening of *Robinson Crusoe* easier to absorb than that of *Jacob's Room,* it is largely because it conforms to familiar patterns of biographies and travel narratives. We must recall in looking at an incipit that we do not encounter texts with completely unformed ideas of what they will be: we come with expectations based on our previous experience, particularly our previous experience of reading (what Paul Ricoeur calls the "received paradigms").[12] We are already accustomed to using the information we are given as a cue for speculation. The cues in an incipit suggest different possibilities and modulate the narrative that we start to follow. Thus, we make guesses in *Jacob's Room* that Betty Flanders is by the sea, that she is writing a letter, that something has happened to make her sad. And these guesses will be revised or confirmed as we read on and learn more.

Orality: Traditional Openings

Some received paradigms are extremely familiar from children's stories and traditional tales. They take us into a fictive world and fictive, nonspecific story-time. The most famous is: "Once upon a time, there was . . ." Others include: "It was a dark and stormy night, and . . ." To open a story in this way, and to use a range of fixed, familiar expressions within the story, was one of the techniques of a predominantly oral culture, and reflected the habits of a time when written or printed texts were not widely available.

Our modern relation to oral culture is immensely complex, and may depend upon the kind of society in which we grew up. Private reading of printed texts has been the typical modern approach to the novel, but orality may still have its place (tapes of novels read aloud are, after all, widely sold and popular). Novels that are read privately may reflect within them our habits of exchanging anecdotes with one another, or memories of hearing stories told to us as children. If privacy is typical of our relation to the genre, we should recall that not all cultures, even in the industrialized world, value privacy in the same way.[13]

The most frequent representation of the oral in the modern novel is in the introduction of an informal conversational style, to give freshness and immediacy. But oral techniques of formulaic expression are still sometimes used, especially to make a point about the kind of narrative we are about to encounter. Thus, Henry Green begins his novel *Loving* (1945) unsettlingly, with "Once upon a day an old butler called Eldon lay dying in his room . . ." It is not a king who is dying, as in the fairy tales, but a "butler called Eldon." It is not a framework of legendary time but, as in modern realism, a particular *day*—even if no date has been given.

James Joyce's *Portrait of the Artist as a Young Man* begins:

Once upon a time and a very good time it was there was a moocow coming down along the road and this moocow that was coming down along the road met a nicens little boy named baby tuckoo. . . .

His father told him that story: his father looked at him through a glass: he had a hairy face.

(James Joyce, *Portrait of the Artist*, 1916)

The traditional opening phrases in the first paragraph are followed here by an introduction on a different narrative level, commenting on them: "His father told him that story." This is to be a novel that includes comment on the making of stories. We gather that storytelling itself is placed in the foreground, opening a text-world and at the same time overtly playing with tricks of narrative.

An incipit, then, may tell us some things about where and when the narrative will open, may tell us about the act of writing and may, or may not, attempt to start at the beginning of things. In one way or another it will try to give readers a reason for going on with the text. As George Eliot says, "curiosity becomes the more eager from the incompleteness of the first information": novelists have always known that we enjoy learning things indirectly.[14]

Personal Pronouns and Narrators

A look at personal pronouns in the incipit provides one of the basic steps in analysis, since they indicate the form of narration and help to clarify the differences noted above.

The following passage, for example, opens a novel of the 1790s:

> MY life has for several years been a theatre of calamity. I have been a mark for the vigilance of tyranny, and I could not escape. My fairest prospects have been blasted. My enemy has shown himself inaccessible to intreaties and untired in persecution. . . . I have not deserved this treatment.
>
> (William Godwin, *Caleb Williams*, 1794)

This text is loaded with first-person pronouns and first-person possessives (*I* and *my*). It is told by a first-person narrator who is also a character in his own story. The first-person pronouns come at the start of sentences, emphasizing their own importance. The narrator's self-concern is thus obvious, both in the narrative technique and in the sentence structure.

A passage like the next one, also from the start of a work of fiction, is quite different:

> Alice was beginning to get very tired of sitting by her sister on the bank, and of having nothing to do: once or twice she had peeped into the book her sister was reading, but it had no pictures or conversations in it, "and what is the use of a book," thought Alice, "without pictures or conversations?"
>
> So she was considering, in her own mind (as well as she could, for the hot day made her feel very sleepy and stupid), whether the pleasure of making a daisy-chain would be worth the trouble of getting up and picking the daisies, when suddenly a white rabbit with pink eyes ran close by her.
>
> (Lewis Carroll, *Alice in Wonderland*, 1865)

Here we find no narrative *I*, only *she* and *her*. The pronouns used most frequently in the narrative are third person, so we can call this third-person narrative. We could almost say there is no narrator here; there is certainly no direct intrusion of a personal narrator as a character in the novel.

There *is* a focal character: Alice. The narrator tells us about the situation in which Alice finds herself, but also about what Alice is thinking, or "considering in her own mind." In ordinary circumstances such direct knowledge of another person's mental states would be impossible, but it is an important and distinctive feature of third-person fictional narratives that they allow us to enter the minds of various characters.

Personal Pronouns

Personal pronouns can shift from individual to individual, and refer to different people: a Mr. Jones can be called "he," as can Mr. Smith, Mr. Brown, and Mr. Thomas. On the other hand, these pronouns do not refer to a *class* of objects (like "tables" and "chairs"). When we want to understand who "he" is, we cannot find out from a dictionary—it is the text itself we must rely on to discover that "he" is Mr. Jones. Such words are thus part of a system of the text, and observing them is part of understanding how a text works.

We can make a table of personal pronouns in English as follows:

	First Person	*Second Person*	*Third Person*
Singular	I	You	He, she, it
Plural	We	You	They

There is also the indefinite personal pronoun *one*.[15]

I obviously has a distinctive role. And it is slightly misleading that we refer to *we* as the plural of *I*. *We* equals *I* + *others*, and can imply an *I* + *I* (+ *I* etc.), or *I* + *you* (+ *you* etc.), or *I* + *he/she* (+ *he/she* etc.)

The use of *I* in language assumes that there is a *you*, someone addressed by the statement—and this pair *I–you* is basic to our acts of communication, but it is not a symmetrical pair. Before there is a *you*, an *I* of some kind must first be implied.

Many novels are concerned with exploring our sense of subjectivity, and therefore give *I* a special place. Their exploration will, of course, make constant reference to the world, but it will be shaped significantly by the fact that subjectivity is represented in language and is part of the system of the text. If other personal pronouns refer to various people during the course of a narrative, *I* is stable, and refers (unless in quotation marks in direct speech) only to the narrator. Its use can be said to bring the act of enunciation into the foreground. Where it has a dominant role it is often associated with words like *here, now, today,* and with verb forms that indicate where and when the discourse is taking place.[16]

Novelistic texts may, on the other hand, try to suppress the *I-you* pair, and give themselves the appearance of objectivity through the predominant use of third-person pronouns. When this happens, we have narrative and descriptions that are set in a place and time (usually in the past) that can be removed from, and seem to become independent of, a particular act of enunciation. Since novels are fictional texts, they are not restricted to the external and objectively observable, even when they give third-person narrative, and they have freedom to tell us about the subjective states of other people in a way we would not accept in scientific or historical texts. Exactly how they do this will, however, always be shaped by their use of personal pronouns.

First-Person Narrative

Novels with first-person narrators, who describe themselves as being *inside* the world of the story they are telling, are closely related to autobiography. Such novels often pretend to be memoirs, confessions, or journals. Even when they are rambling and anecdotal, their narratives are given a stable point of reference by the use of *I*. Their subjectivity can contribute to our sense of authenticity, and from systematic reference to a narrative *I* they often gain a compelling narrative power.[17]

A key example of first-person narrative in the English novel, which has been an important influence on other writers, is Charlotte Brontë's *Jane Eyre*. It begins:

> There was no possibility of taking a walk that day. We had been wandering, indeed, in the leafless shrubbery an hour in the morning; but since dinner (Mrs. Reed, when there was no company, dined early) the cold winter wind had brought with it clouds so sombre, and a rain so penetrating, that further outdoor exercise was now out of the question.
>
> I was glad of it: I never liked long walks, especially on chilly after-

noons: dreadful to me was the coming home in the raw twilight, with nipped fingers and toes, and a heart saddened by the chidings of Bessie, the nurse, and humbled by the consciousness of my physical inferiority to Eliza, John, and Georgiana Reed.

(Charlotte Brontë, Jane Eyre, 1847)

The opening paragraph of this incipit does not introduce the *I* of the text, only a *we*, whose reference is not at first clear; but there is no doubt that the narrator is included inside the world of the narrative. The complexity of the sentence and the level of vocabulary ("leafless shrubbery," "penetrating" rain) lead us to think it must be an adult narrator telling the story. When we do encounter the singular first-person pronoun in the second paragraph, we find that the narrator is recalling being sent out for walks with a "nurse," and is thus presumably remembering childhood experience. There is an I-narrator and an I-hero/heroine, with a difference in time between them. But there is not much evidence of a difference in feelings: the experience of childhood is still vivid and strongly expressed ("I was *glad* of it," it was "*dreadful* to me").

Other characters in the novel are given names on their first appearance (Bessie, Eliza, John, and Georgiana); but the I-narrator is so closely identified with the text itself that we must wait for a few paragraphs before we learn she is called Jane. And we must wait for the next chapter to confirm that her full name is Jane Eyre. This narrator in *Jane Eyre* claims to know herself, to remember herself, and to remember the smallest details about herself. Despite the fact that we cannot really recall day-by-day and minute-by-minute feelings of our early childhood, the strong unifying subjectivity here leads us to accept the fictional narrative as somehow authentic. (And it is not then surprising to find that Charlotte Brontë's work frequently attracts biographical speculation, which relates it directly to the writer's own life.)

First or Third Person?

When *Jane Eyre* was first published, W. M. Thackeray reported that he had started to read it, although he had other work to do, and once he had started, could not put it down all night. Perhaps this is simply the effect of an important work of art (or perhaps it was because of some strong echoes of Thackeray's own private life and his feeling that, like Mr. Rochester, he had a mad wife). It was an understandable response to a novel that speaks with such an urgent and convincing personal voice. Virginia Woolf, in contrast, complained that *Jane Eyre* was too much an expression of personal anguish—a constricted repetition of "I love," "I hate," "I suffer." Her complaints echo the views of Henry James, who disliked novels that, using the first person, show the "terrible *fluidity* of self-revelation."[18]

The choice between a first-person narrator telling about himself or herself and a third-person narrative is still an important basic step for a novelist. On the one hand, the first-person narrative may give deep thoughts of the narrator, and indicate that the narrator has a real existential motive for telling the story: the narrator, as F. K. Stanzel suggests, is "embodied" in the text.[19] On the other hand, first-person narrators cannot usually enter into the full "psycho-narration" of other characters' minds: they can only make external guesses, and are largely restricted to showing what they think themselves.[20] The great realist novelists of the nineteenth century used predominantly third-person narratives to create a social panorama and offer insight into the thoughts of a range of characters. Many modernist writers feel, like Woolf, that third-person narration best allows imaginative insight into people's interior lives, as well as a necessary detachment and artistic control.

We can see the possible complexity of third-person narratives, and the suggestion they allow of multiple subjectivities, in a modernist work such as Faulkner's *Light in August*:

> **But she is not listening apparently. She sits quietly on the top step, watching the road where it curves away, empty and mounting, toward Jefferson. The squatting men along the wall look at her still and placid face and they think as Armstid thought and as Varner thinks: that she is thinking of a scoundrel who deserted her in trouble and whom they believe that she will never see again, save his coattails perhaps already boardflat with running. . . .**
>
> **She is not thinking about this at all. She is thinking about the coins knotted in the bundle beneath her hands.**
>
> (William Faulkner, *Light in August*, 1932 [1985], chap. 1)

The narrative here observes the woman and the men, and effortlessly shifts into telling us their thoughts. We learn not just what the men are thinking (and have thought), but what they are thinking about the woman's thoughts. They think she is thinking about the man who has abandoned her, but they are wrong: "She is not thinking about this at all." We, as readers of third-person narrative, are able to move accurately into other minds: characters in the novel cannot.

Faulkner's narrative stands at one pole of fictional possibilities, with its flickering subtleties and complexities registering people's mental states; *Jane Eyre* stands at the other, with the directness and power of the narrator's compulsion to narrate all the complexities of her own story.

Third-Person Narrative
and the First-Person Narrator

When we talk of a third-person narrative, this does not mean that *I* will never be found in the text. A narrator may make a brief appearance from time to time, and when a narrator appears, he or she will speak of him or herself in the first person. The narrators found in third-person narratives, however, are not part of the same fictional world as the other characters: they are on a different narrative level, and are assumed to be producing the main narrative we have been reading and that we know to be fiction. (For this reason they are often seen as breaking the illusion of the main text-world when they appear, and were traditionally referred to as intrusive narrators.)[21]

Centers of Consciousness

If a writer decides on third-person narrative, there are then two important options ahead. The narrative may shift around from character to character, freely entering the minds of different people, as in the great social-realist novels of the nineteenth century. Or the writer may decide to focus on one character, and see other characters through that one character's mind.

If one character provides the chief center of consciousness in this way, the narrative comes closer to what we experience in our lives; moreover, since the third person is being used, there is no pretense at a fake memoir or autobiography. This is the technique associated with Henry James, who took one character as "reflector," or center of consciousness, in his later novels. A narrator may sometimes appear in such novels, and the thoughts of other characters may sometimes be suggested, but it is chiefly through the reflector's mind that we see the events of the narrative.

We can sum up the distinctions made above as follows:

First-Person Narrative

Narrator relates own experience
Largely restricted to view from narrator's mind

Third-Person Narrative

First-person narrator *may* intrude
Narrative able to enter any character's mind
    Type 1: narrator enters the minds of many characters
    Type 2: narrator uses one character as center of consciousness

Traditional criticism has often referred to narrators in third-person narratives as "omniscient." The idea behind this is understandable (since the narrative enters other people's minds in a way that we normally cannot), but the term is finally misleading, since the narrator does not know everything, and indeed, in the case of writers like Thackeray and Fielding, may insist that he has no intention of looking into the private actions of certain characters.

Starting the Incipit with Pronouns

Alice in Wonderland started off by giving us the name "Alice," and then used the pronoun *she*. Other novels do not immediately give us names: they move off from the first with pronouns. The incipit of John Banville's *Doctor Copernicus*, for example, reads:

> **At first it had no name. It was the thing itself, the vivid thing. It was his friend. On windy days it danced, demented, waving wild arms, or in the silence of evening drowsed and dreamed, swaying in the blue, the goldeny air. Even at night it did not go away. Wrapped in his truckle bed, he could hear it stirring darkly outside in the dark, all the long night long.**
>
> (John Banville, *Doctor Copernicus*, 1976)

Later we confirm that this *he* is Nicholas Copernicus, who will become the "Doctor Copernicus" mentioned in the paratext. Logically we might have expected that the name of the man would be given at the opening of the text, before the pronoun was used, but Banville's incipit overtly plays with the concept of naming. We are slowly given the man's full name, just as we are given the general name of "the vivid thing" (tree), and then its particular name ("the linden").

To open with personal pronouns before names is common in modern novels, and is indeed one of the indicators to readers of the fictionality of the text. Readers are placed in an odd relationship with the text (one that we find rather artificial when used in nonfiction), as though we could be expected to know who or what was being referred to from the start. According to Stanzel this is typical of those third-person narratives that focus on one character as reflector, or center of consciousness, and allow us to see the world largely in terms of that character's reactions and feelings.[22]

Second-Person Pronouns:
Direct Communication with the Reader

In novels, the key personal pronouns are usually *I, he, she,* and *they; you* is constantly implied as the addressee, but is less frequently used. There are, however, possibilities in its use, the most obvious being in direct address to the reader. Examining the use of *you* in a text helps establish the relationship a writer wishes to set up with readers.

Near the start of *Tristram Shandy,* the first-person narrator complains that his parents did not consider enough what they were doing when he was conceived:

> Had they duly weighed and considered all this, and proceeded accordingly,—I am verily persuaded I should have made a quite different figure in the world, from that, in which the reader is likely to see me.— Believe me, good folks, this is not so inconsiderable a thing as many of you may think it;—you have all, I dare say, heard of the animal spirits, as how they are transfused from father to son, &c. &c.
>
> (Laurence Sterne, *The Life and Opinions of Tristram Shandy, Gentleman,* 1759–67, vol. 1, chap. 1)

The first mention of "the reader" here is not a direct address; it is in a speculation about how the reader is "likely to see me." But with "Believe me, good folks," the narrator turns openly to his readers, addressing them as "you": "as many of *you* may think it," "*you* have all, I daresay . . ." It is not entirely convincing as a serious address (Steven Connor calls it "a sort of performance, or simulation of address"),[23] but the effect of the narrator reaching out and buttonholing readers like this is to make us stand in a self-conscious relation to the text-world.

To break open the illusions of a separate text-world with direct address to the reader may seem old-fashioned, but it remains a useful way of establishing complicity with the reader; we can find the same technique used in a modern short story by Ian McEwan, where the narrator suddenly changes gear mid-story and turns to the reader: "So let me begin by telling you that it was ironic, for reasons which will become apparent only very much later—and you must be patient—it was ironic that Raymond of all people should want to make me aware of my virginity" ("Homemade," in *First Love, Last Rites,* 1975).

You and One

The second-person pronoun can be a substitute for the indefinite personal pronoun *one*. Some native speakers of English find *one* too formal or upper-class in tone, and prefer to play with the slight ambiguity of reference in *you*.[24] The incipit of Kazuo Ishiguro's *An Artist of the Floating World* reads:

> **If on a sunny day you climb the steep path leading up from the little wooden bridge still referred to around here as 'the Bridge of Hesitation', you will not have to walk far before the roof of my house becomes visible between the tops of two gingko trees. Even if it did not occupy such a commanding position on the hill, the house would still stand out from all others nearby, so that as you come up the path, you may find yourself wondering what sort of wealthy man owns it.**
>
> (Kazuo Ishiguro, *An Artist of the Floating World,* 1986)

It is difficult to decide firmly whether this *you* is addressed directly to the reader and implies an intimate suggestion that the reader might, as an individual *you*, want to climb up the steep path and look at the house, or whether it is the indefinite *you* of a rather old-fashioned guidebook style. The ambivalence of tone is cleverly chosen, since the novel presents a Japanese narrator who is going to explain his behavior during World War II. Although he knows the narrative will not convince everyone, he is telling it in the hope of attracting the sympathetic understanding of some readers. In one way he wants to address an individual *you*, but in another way it might be safer to hide behind guidebook impersonality.

The indefinite *you* can also be didactic. *The History of Mr Polly,* by H. G. Wells, begins one of the later chapters:

> But when a man has once broken through the paper walls of everyday circumstance, those unsubstantial walls that hold so many of us securely prisoned from the cradle to the grave, he has made a discovery. If the world does not please you, *you can change it.* Determine to alter it at any price, and you can change it altogether
>
> (H. G. Wells, *The History of Mr Polly,* 1910, chap. 9)

As in the Ishiguro passage, the *you* goes along with a conditional *if;* but Wells's *you* is a finger pointing directly and unhesitatingly at his imagined audience. The didactic tone, intensified by italics (*"you can change it"*), is an indication of how Wells gives priority to the communication of ideas and rejects what he called the "preposterous emptiness of technical effort" found in more obviously literary novels, by writers like Henry James.[25] Wells would claim that his was a "natural" style, not an art style, but nonetheless (like every other style in fiction) it uses technical effects—in this case to embody his didacticism. Other writers are just as keen to communicate their ideas directly to the reader, but do this more commonly through statements of general truths about the world, which gain the reader's assent to their ideas unawares.[26]

Attempts have been made by writers to use *you* as the dominant pronoun throughout a novel: the best known example is in French, Michel Butor's *La Modification* (1957), but there are also attempts in English, like Edna O'Brien's *A Pagan Place* (1971). The effect is not quite so odd as we might expect, readers become accustomed to the *you,* simply adjust to its use, and read it as a substitute for the narrative *I.*

Narrative *We*

Personal pronouns thus are fundamental to the system of a novel and basic material for analysis. A final example is provided in the incipit of Charles Dickens's *A Tale of Two Cities:*

> IT was the best of times, it was the worst of times, it was the age of wisdom, it was the age of foolishness, it was the epoch of belief, it was the epoch of incredulity, it was the season of Light, it was the season of Darkness, it was the spring of hope, it was the winter of despair, we had everything before us, we had nothing before us, we were all going

> direct to Heaven, we were all going direct the other way—in short, the
> period was so far like the present period, that some of its noisiest au-
> thorities insisted on its being received, for good or for evil, in the su-
> perlative degree of comparison only.
>
> (Charles Dickens, *A Tale of Two Cities*, 1859)

This is an extraordinarily long sentence, a full paragraph, which uses rhetorical effects of repetition and variation to create a lyrical effect. Buried in
the middle of the rhetoric is an important *we*, which gives the impression
that the narrator is speaking for a whole generation: "we had everything
before us." The *we* refers to the narrator and characters in the novel, it
does not include the readers—and it stands not just for a small group, but
for the British and French nations. *A Tale of Two Cities* is a historical novel,
and Dickens is imagining a time before he was born. The phrase "the
present period" indicates an important narrative distance: what follows is
not a historical document *written* in the past, it is written in the 1850s.
Nonetheless the *we* suggests that the narrator himself somehow belonged
to the world that had "everything before" it, experienced by people in the
1790s. Most of the narrative will use third-person pronouns, but this introductory *we* briefly implies the authenticity of first-person narrative,
before Dickens moves into a large-scale fictional panorama.

Proper Names

The incipit of a novel will almost always include some proper names: often
those of the major characters in the narrative and the places where it is set.
These names may look like direct reference to the world (as when real
place names are chosen or reference is made to real people), but since
fiction is a form of play or thought-experiment, there is no consistent link
between the name and the thing or person referred to. If we think of a
novel as being like a map of a territory, then the usual relationship of map
to territory has been suspended, and the fictional map may allow new
contours to emerge.[27]

The question of how we use fictional names and discuss fictional characters will be considered in more detail later (see chapter 4); as far as the
analysis of the incipit is concerned, our chief interest is in how fictional
names are always *motivated* in one way or another—that is, they are not
arbitrary, and explanations seem possible. In comic and didactic fiction,
names often indicate physical or moral attributes. No reader can have much

doubt about the implication of the names "Mr. Badman" and "Mr. Wiseman" in John Bunyan's *The Life and Death of Mr. Badman* (1680). Dictionary definitions of the words used in names, however, do not usually give us a full explanation, since most names can be read as part of coded systems interpreted with reference to things outside the text.

Sounds and Meanings

In the modern novel, the choice of names may rely on onomatopoeic effects, on the sounds of the words when articulated, or on the meanings of words associated with the name. Evelyn Waugh's *Decline and Fall* starts:

> Mr Sniggs, the Junior Dean, and Mr Postlethwaite, the Domestic Bursar, sat alone in Mr Sniggs' room overlooking the garden quad at Scone College. From the rooms of Sir Alastair Digby-Vane-Trumpington, two staircases away, came a confused roaring and breaking of glass. They alone of the senior members of Scone were at home that evening, for it was the night of the annual dinner of the Bollinger Club.
>
> (Evelyn Waugh, *Decline and Fall*, 1928)

"Sniggs" and "Postlethwaite" are presumably chosen here because, when articulated, they sound ugly or awkward, and are therefore comic.[28] These characters are obviously not aristocratic, unlike Sir Alastair Digby-Vane-Trumpington. Social class difference is indicated by the use of a title and a first name, while the others are both plain mister. Hyphenated names like Sir Alastair's are often taken to be upper-class in English (in the past they usually showed that the person had some maternal ancestor from an important family and did not want to give up an impressive-sounding family name). "Sir Alastair" is thus aristocratic: but Waugh's satire is directed both against the middle class and the empty-headed aristocracy, so this character is made ridiculous by having *three* hyphenated names. The name "Vane" makes him sound like a weather-vane, shifting with every change in the wind—a common image for the kind of politically ambitious aristocrat who gives up his traditional loyalties out of greed for public office. (The American edition changes the spelling to "Vaine," which adds the suggestion of personal vanity.) The name "Trumpington" is a real place name, but suggests trumpeting, or boastfulness, as well as the noise of "confused roaring" at the dinner party.

Iconic and Symbolic Names

The significance we read into proper names can work at different textual levels. Sir Willoughby Patterne in George Meredith's *The Egoist* (1879) is a man who sees himself as the model, or pattern, of a gentleman: readers quickly gather, however, that the name is ironic, since he is a "pattern" largely in the sense of being stiff and fixed in his ideas. The name is also motivated in an entirely different way, because Sir Willoughby's story can be compared to the design shown on "willow pattern" china, and this design has thematic relevance to the novel. Names like Willoughby Patterne can thus be seen as iconic (directly representing something about the character) and at the same time symbolic (part of a system of symbols drawn from elsewhere and used in the text).

In contemporary realist fiction, names continue to work in this way. When Anita Brookner calls the main character of *A Private View* (1994) "George Bland," the name is not inherently unreal or unlikely; but "George" indicates symbolically that the character is very English, and part of an English world. "Bland," on the other hand, is iconic, because it is the adjective most people would use to describe this character, though it is ironically chosen: his inner life is shown as not being bland at all.

Minimal Names

Names, then, are never neutral: if they have no obvious meaning, we need simply to look in other directions to ask what has motivated the choice. The absence of a name (as for the monster in Mary Shelley's *Frankenstein* [1818]), or the use of one name only (as for Heathcliff in *Wuthering Heights* [1847]), or the use of a nickname (like "Punch" for the hero of Kipling's "Baa Baa, Black Sheep" [1888]) represents a significant choice on the part of a writer.

Most of Samuel Beckett's male characters have names that begin with M (Murphy, Molloy, Malone, Mahood). We might see this as a private obsession on Beckett's part, or perhaps he is reacting against the artificiality of choosing names for characters—using M for men and W for women. (We might also note that even when he writes novels in French, he chooses names that make his characters sound Irish.)

Some realist writers have tried to escape all suggestion of choice, to give the impression that they are using real names, and have chosen them with a pin from the telephone directory. Even such arbitrary procedures, however, represent decisions, and tell us something about the system of the text in question.

Place Names

The choice of place names in a fictional text often has direct bearing on problems of realism, since place names are likely to be either recognizable or recognizably fictitious. To use a name like "Manchester" (referring to the industrial city in England) involves a novelist at once in certain risks. While we may be well aware that what we are reading is a novel (and therefore fictitious play), readers may still raise questions over accuracy, and the name may alienate those who associate Manchester only with its history of industrialization. Elizabeth Gaskell's *Mary Barton* (1848) is subtitled "A Tale of Manchester Life," and the incipit begins: "THERE are some fields near Manchester, well known to the inhabitants as 'Green Heys Fields', through which runs a public footpath to a little village about two miles distant." "Manchester" is thus firmly stated—this is the center of the novel—but the usual associations of the name are called into question, and considerably softened, by placing it "near" fields, a footpath, and a country village. When Dickens writes about a northern industrial town, at more or less the same time, in *Hard Times* (1854), he invents a fictional name, "Coketown." The name is not pleasant to articulate, bears little relation to traditional practices of naming places, and indicates that "coke" (representing industrial pollution) dominates the life of the town. Obviously Dickens is not interested in the kind of sympathetic reconsideration of industrial landscape that attracts Gaskell, though he does give the town a life and energy of its own as the novel progresses.

As with personal names, place names may be coded in more than one way. George Eliot's "Middlemarch" is a town in the *middle* of England. This town is the setting for a novel that is subtly historical, and the town is caught in the *middle* of the *march* of history. At the same time, the name (though fictional) does not sound impossible—there are places in Britain such as Middlesbrough, areas such as the Welsh Marches, and towns with *march* or *marsh* in the name.

Franco Moretti has pointed out that Jane Austen's novels mix "geographical sites and imaginary locations"; real names are used for towns, fictional names for country houses and villages.[29] The shift between the two systems of naming does not seem to disturb readers, and indeed this pattern of usage has come to seem almost inevitable in the English novel. The interplay between invented and real place names is another marker of fictionality, and indicates to readers that they are reading a novel.

Thomas Hardy's place names in his "Wessex novels" are invented, yet they constitute a complete coded system that can be mapped out and related to a real area. (A map of "Hardy's Wessex" is found in the paratext of the Wessex edition, and Hardy gradually revised the names in his early texts to fit the map.) The names used by Hardy sound convincing as names, and are sometimes so close to the original that one wonders why he bothered to change them at all (for example, "Abbot's Cernel" for Cerne Abbas). Modern editions also provide a glossary explaining which places these names refer to. Sometimes Hardy's invented names contain rather obvious symbolic meanings (for example, "Christminster" for Oxford). They represent, however, a typical naming-effect in fictional works, since they seem to indicate a real world and at the same time stake out an elaborate fictional landscape over which the writer can claim proprietorial rights. Hardy's Christminster both is, and is not, Oxford: the choice of name allows him fictional play.

Accuracy or consistency of reference (though it may interest some readers) is never the most significant question when it comes to naming in fictional texts. The logic of fiction, with its ability to suspend the actualities of the world we experience, to create a discourse of thought-experiments, is powerful enough to extend to the mention of real names in fictional texts. Most readers will put up with a little vagueness, or even contradiction, as they read through a fictional text. But this does not mean that we can neglect to ask how names function. From place names, as from personal names and personal pronouns, we are able to gather important evidence about how exactly the text-world of the novel is being set up before us.

2
Space and Time

A common feature of modern Western art forms is that they try to fix what they show in a particular space and time. A novel will establish a text-world in which events can be related to one another, and the people and things it concerns will be placed in some kind of setting. We can expect that this will start in the incipit, and it is appropriate to try to work out exactly how it is performed.

Since we are often given place names and real times, it may seem that a novel pins down its text-world by reference to the actual world. If we read the place names "London" or "Chicago," or the date "1960," we feel we know where we are. But as we have seen already in relation to names, the kind of verifiable reference we associate with nonfiction has been suspended in a novel.[1] Suspended references only give an impression that we can anchor and orient a narrative: they work along with internal elements of the text. Novels construct their own coherent world of time and space for their narratives from a systematic use of personal pronouns, verb tenses, adverbs, and demonstratives (*this, that, these, those*). These grammatical features are known to linguists as *deictics*.

Two Basic Forms of Narration

Time and space will be determined first of all by the form of narration that is taking place. As we have seen in chapter 1, some works of fiction locate the act of writing, or telling, in a particular context and push the narrative off from there. The following incipit uses this method:

Monday Morning

Having, out of friendship for the family, upon whose estate, praised be Heaven! I and mine have lived rent-free time out of mind, voluntarily undertaken to publish the MEMOIRS of the RACKRENT FAMILY, I think it my duty to say a few words, in the first place, concerning myself.— My real name is Thady Quirk, though in the family I have always been known by no other than "*honest Thady*" afterwards, in the time of sir Murtagh, deceased, I remember to hear them calling me "*old Thady*"; and now I'm come to "poor Thady"; for I wear a long great coat winter and summer, which is very handy, as I never put my arms into the sleeves. . . .

(Maria Edgeworth, *Castle Rackrent*, 1800)

This text gives us a first-person narrator: the act of narrating is in the foreground, with a day and time specified, and it is put into the present tense with verbs like "I think," "is," "I remember." We are told that the narrator *has lived* on the Rackrent estate since time out of mind, and it seems likely that is where the narration is being made.

We can contrast this with the second common and basic form of narration. The incipit of *Tess of the d'Urbervilles* reads:

On an evening in the latter part of May a middle-aged man was walking homeward from Shaston to the village of Marlott, in the adjoining Vale of Blakemore or Blackmoor. The pair of legs that carried him were rickety, and there was a bias in his gait which inclined him somewhat to the left of a straight line. He occasionally gave a smart nod, as if in confirmation of some opinion, though he was not thinking of anything in particular. An empty egg-basket was slung upon his arm, the nap of his hat was ruffled, a patch being quite worn away at its brim where his thumb came in taking it off.

(Thomas Hardy, *Tess of the d'Urbervilles*, 1891)

There is plenty of reference to places here ("Shaston," "Marlott," the "Vale of Blakemore"), but the position of the narrator is not mentioned, and the time and place in which the narration is being made seem to be of no consequence. What counts is the scene *within* the narrative, and the personal pronouns that are used relate only to the person within it. In narratives of this kind, verbs in the past tense usually dominate ("was walking," "gave," "was slung"), and the temporal markers used tend to be more specific.

Discours and Récit

The difference outlined here is described in French as a difference between *discours* (as in the passage from Maria Edgeworth, where the focus is on the act of enunciation) and *récit* (as in the passage from Thomas Hardy, where the focus is on the narrative as a fictional written form, as though it were telling itself).[2]

Forms of *récit* that employ a range of past tenses, like the quoted passage from Hardy, are most common in the classic novel of the nineteenth century. Some contemporary novelists, while using *récit*, prefer the present as their main tense, on the assumption that this gives readers a sense of more immediate involvement with the narrative. The combination of *récit* and present tense is, however, not easy to sustain over a long narrative, and there is usually a good deal of slipping back into a more familiar sequence of past tenses as the novel proceeds.[3]

We need to bear in mind this important distinction between *discours* and *récit* when we start working on a novel, though it must be pointed out that we do not usually see pure examples of either form maintained throughout. Fictional narratives often begin with a strong sense of the scene of narration (the figure of the storyteller making an appearance) and then move into accounts of events told in the past tense, where the narrator does not appear. A *récit* may also suddenly be interrupted by a narrator talking about him or herself. Later parts of novels tend to use more *récit*, as it provides a conventional and straightforward way of getting through a narrative to its end.

We could perhaps suggest that there is always some implication of a narrator's act lurking around a narrative: every *récit* is, either overtly or by implication, embedded in some kind of narrator's *discours*. And although *récit* seems often to tell itself, it may suggest, through its language or ideas, an identity of some kind of overall narrator.[4] But in looking at the incipit of a particular novel, our first question should be which kind of narration is *now* being used; we can then go on to note whether, as the novel develops, the two forms of narration are placed in opposition to one another, or blended. With certain novelists (Joseph Conrad is a celebrated example) play between the two forms may be an important part of narrative technique and may have a deep influence on the way we read the significance of the novel.[5]

Spatial Form

Novelistic space is often indefinite and contains areas of indeterminacy. In the classic novel, even when we have reached the *récit*, we may first have to go through what Henry Fielding called "an account of as many of our hero's ancestors as can be gathered out of the rubbish of antiquity" (*Jonathan Wild* 1743, chap. 2). Moreover, when they get to describing the setting, novelists cannot cover everything: they select and emphasize important details. We use the cues provided to construct and modify our images of space and setting.

The spaces of a novel, however, are important to most readers and often easier to recall than the series of events or progress that makes up the plot. We retain some sense (however imprecise) of Dickens's London, or Crusoe's island, or Wuthering Heights. Because we can recall the spaces of these novels after we have put the book down, they contribute to our feeling that a text has some kind of overall form or organization. One important way of holding a text in mind is by attributing to it a kind of "spatial form" based on its evocation of particular places.[6] Noticing how the spaces of the text are constructed in the incipit not only helps our understanding of how the text functions, it also leads to a more convincing sense of how a novel has the kind of organization that we associate with a work of art.

Space and Focalizing

Our sense of space, however vague, implies a point from which things are seen. As Henry James says, at every window of the "house of fiction" there stands "a figure with a pair of eyes."[7] Criticism in English has often discussed the construction of space as one of "point of view." But the point from which we see things in a novel is often not a static one—it moves. And seeing may go along with other senses, such as hearing and smelling. The terms *focalizing* and *focalizor* give more indication of the active processes involved, and will be used in preference in this book.[8]

We can imagine the focalizing in a novel as if done by a sensitive eye or a camera lens: the focalizing point of the narrative gives coherence to what is described. The focalizing point, however, is not necessarily the same as that at which a narrator stands. (A narrator can, for example, produce sentences like "He saw the house." Here the focalizing is being done by "He," but the sentence is narrated by someone else who is not doing the seeing.) We must be careful to distinguish between *who speaks* and *who sees*: they are often not the same. In working out who sees, we can restrict ourselves closely to the text, but in working out who speaks, we often have to draw on exterior frames of reference.

The focalizing point may be provided by one of the characters or by a narrator, or it may shift around. We may need to consider a group of sentences to work out where this point is; it is not always possible if we look at one sentence in isolation. Dickens starts a chapter in *Barnaby Rudge*:

> **Chroniclers are privileged to enter where they list, to come and go through keyholes, to ride upon the wind, to overcome, in their soarings up and down, all obstacles of distance, time, and place. Thrice blessed be this last consideration, since it enables us to follow the disdainful Miggs even into the sanctity of her chamber, and to hold her in sweet companionship through the dreary watches of the night!**
>
> (Charles Dickens, *Barnaby Rudge*, 1841, chap. 9)

The focalizor here calls himself the "chronicler." He is a narrator who uses "us" to indicate that he is dragging his readers along with him. He insists on his freedom to go wherever he wants, but the freedom turns out to be a freedom to enter the chamber of a character, Miss Miggs. And once the narrative has placed us in that chamber, the focalizor will then change to Miss Miggs herself.

A focalizing point may remain static for awhile, or it may move inside a scene. We might compare the visualizing of a scene to the perspective techniques used in painting or to the presentation of scenes in the modern theater, but we must recall that the scenes in novels are constructed out of cues provided by language, and that they include the dynamic possibility of a focalizor moving through the scene described, something that is not possible in a painting or in the theater.

Spaces of the Incipit

The space staked out in the incipit, then, may be precise or extremely vague; it may be pictured in perspective, or we may move through it. Novelists often use the focalizor in the incipit to proceed from a "bird's-eye" view, making plain the geographical features of a country first, then a town, then a house and a room. But they may also move directly into a scene inside a house, to establish relations between characters in a setting, and then move outward. To analyze how the text operates, we need to trace such movements.

We also need to ask what kind of movement is involved. Is an interior described, for example, by a glance around the walls of a room? Or by movement down a room to a central character? Are things described because of their position in the room? Or because of their importance in the narrative? In what detail are things described? And what logic demands their inclusion? Can we find (as is very often the case) a play on sound effects made by listing the names of things in a room that sound the same?[9]

The incipit of James Joyce's story "A Painful Case," in *Dubliners*, runs:

> **Mr James Duffy lived in Chapelizod because he wished to live as far as possible from the city of which he was a citizen and because he found all the other suburbs of Dublin mean, modern and pretentious. He lived in an old sombre house and from his windows he could look into the disused distillery or upwards along the shallow river on which Dublin is built. The lofty walls of his uncarpeted room were free from pictures. He had himself bought every article of furniture in the room: a black iron bedstead, an iron washstand, four cane chairs, a clothes-rack, a coal-scuttle, a fender and irons and a square table on which lay a double desk. A bookcase had been made in an alcove by means of shelves of white wood. The bed was clothed with white bed-clothes and a black and scarlet rug covered the floor. A little hand-mirror hung above the washstand and during the day a white-shaded lamp stood as the sole ornament of the mantelpiece. The books on the white wooden shelves were arranged from below upwards according to bulk.**
>
> (James Joyce, "A Painful Case," *Dubliners*, 1914)

This kind of opening is typical of much realist fiction. It gives us Mr. Duffy as theme, and places him in Chapelizod (a real place name), then in relation to "the city" and "suburbs of Dublin." Next it makes a move into the "sombre house," with a mention of windows and a brief look outward at the Dublin riverside setting. The first two sentences start with the same pattern (X lived in Y), placing Mr. Duffy first in a geographical location, and then in the house. Afterward the focalizing turns inward, into Mr. Duffy's "uncarpeted room." It mentions a lot of things in the room, but unlike much late twentieth-century fiction, gives no brand names.

This passage from Joyce is definitely *récit*; the narrator does not appear as a figure in the text. But if we ask ourselves who speaks and who sees, we find that it is the narrator (not Mr. Duffy), and that the narrator acts as focalizor, moving through the room, tracing out the scene for us.

Although we are not given exact indications of where the furniture is placed, we can note that the description goes first round the walls and floor, then to the furniture, which is listed from the bedstead to the desk. Our attention is drawn to the bookcase, to the bed, to a mirror, and then again to the books. (Books are obviously a significant cue in a story that is interested in exploring the movement of Mr. Duffy's thoughts.) The room might be taken by a casual reader as banal—just an ordinary room—and the description as neutral or objective. But as we begin to analyze it, and consider it in relation to the development of the story, we see that all the details picked out by the description indicate the particular drab and narrow psychology of Mr. Duffy. The room is *un*carpeted; the table is *square*; the mirror is a *little* hand-mirror (presumably this indicates that Mr. Duffy has to look at himself to shave, but is censorious about vanity and would not buy a large mirror). The "iron" bedstead, the "cane" chairs, and the clothes "rack" all echo the severity of Mr. Duffy's self-discipline, his hostility to luxury or sensuality, which is to be described as the story proceeds.

The play on colors in this passage is also particularly striking. "Black" comes up twice in relation to the bedstead and the rug. (It is also suggested by mention of the iron washstand, the coal-scuttle, the fender and irons.) "White" comes up four times: the shelves are "of white wood," the bed is covered with "white bed-clothes," the lamp is "white-shaded," the books are on "white wooden shelves." The only other color is "scarlet"(often associated with sin), but even this is in combination with black. Grim austerity and repression are thus painted into the scene, without ever being overtly mentioned by Joyce.

Descriptions in realist fiction quite often contain things that seem to have no particular role in the narrative, but are there simply because, in their superfluity, they represent real life. This is what Roland Barthes refers to as the "reality effect."[10] But we should not be cavalier about the inclusion of things, suggesting they are there simply because "they would be." There are always controlling features at work in the act of writing fiction, and motivations of different kinds—a focalizing point to be maintained, a limit to the number of things that can be listed, a concern with the rhythm of the prose.

Not all writers deliberate over what they are doing in descriptions, or consciously play with stylistic effects (popular fiction tends to reproduce stereotyped descriptions to allow for quick reading). But the things described, the words used to describe them, and the movement of the focalizor represent conscious and unconscious choices. From the start of novelistic realism, writers like Defoe have used descriptive detail as a way of persuading readers into their ideas. Joyce learned many lessons from his study of French realist novelists like Flaubert and Zola, who seriously considered techniques of description, and showed how to produce a result that is richly textured in meaning, at the same time as it is convincingly realist.

The Narrator and the Opening Space

George Eliot, also aiming at a realist effect but writing within a more distinctly English tradition, starts off *Adam Bede* as follows:

> With a single drop of ink for a mirror, the Egyptian sorcerer undertakes to reveal to any chance comer far-reaching visions of the past. This is what I undertake to do for you, reader. With this drop of ink at the end of my pen I will show you the roomy workshop of Mr Jonathan Burge, carpenter and builder in the village of Hayslope, as it appeared on the eighteenth of June, in the year of our Lord 1799.
>
> The afternoon sun was warm on the five workmen there, busy upon doors and window-frames and wainscoting. A scent of pine-wood from a tent-like pile of planks outside the open door mingled itself with the scent of the elder-bushes which were spreading their summer snow close to the open window opposite; the slanting sunbeams shone through the transparent shavings that flew before the steady plane, and lit up the fine grain of the oak panelling which stood propped against the wall. On a heap of those soft shavings a rough grey shepherd-dog had made himself a pleasant bed, and was lying with his nose between his fore-paws, occasionally wrinkling his brows to cast a glance at the tallest of the five workmen, who was carving a shield in the centre of a wooden mantelpiece.
>
> (George Eliot, *Adam Bede*, 1859)

This incipit starts with *discours* that contains an overt contract made by the "I" narrator. The narrator, using present and future tenses, undertakes to show the reader a narrative about a specific place, identified with a specific person at a specific time. The two paragraphs shift us from this *discours* to the promised *récit*, supposedly produced with ink on the end of the narrator's pen. The *récit* thus has its own separate space, set in the past, when "the sun *was* warm."

The space chosen by the authorial narrator is in a workshop. It is a deliberate departure from the leisured world of upper-class society, which had provided the novelistic scene for what George Eliot dismissed as "Silly Novels by Lady Novelists." A geographical context of an English village is indicated ("Hayslope" is obviously a highly motivated place name, suggesting both soft hills and the joys of haymaking). The focalizor then moves us *into* the workshop, following the path of the afternoon sun. Again there is emphasis on doors and window frames, so that we have the sense of looking into a kind of framed painting, a "Dutch interior," with a peaceful scene of rural life. The interior is established through evocation of a series of pleasing sensations: we learn of the warmth of the sun, the "scent" of the pine-wood, the "scent" of the elder-bushes. The dog is resting on a "soft" and "pleasant" bed. The space described is made to sound familiar by deictic elements that refer to things as though we already knew them: "the workmen *there*," "*those* soft shavings." The sunbeams light up the wood against the wall, and the focalizor moves us to a pile of woodshavings, then to the dog (symbolic of the traditional virtue of fidelity), which is looking up at the "tallest of the five workmen," who is obviously going to be the focus of the scene and an important figure in the novel. The slow movement toward this man gives us a sense of the harmony of man, animal, and nature, in a world of skilled manual work, and thus also establishes some of the novel's key ethical values.

Henry Green, in the incipit of *Living*, is overtly modernist and experimental, but he also establishes first the space of his narrative:

Bridesley, Birmingham.

Two o'clock. Thousands came back from dinner along streets.

"What we want is go, push," said works manager to son of Mr Dupret. "What I say to them is—let's get on with it, let's get the stuff out."

Thousands came back to factories they worked in from their dinners.

"I'm always at them but they know me. They know I'm a father and mother to them. If they're in trouble they've but to come to me. And they turn out beautiful work, beautiful work. I'd do anything for 'em and they know it."

Noise of lathes working began again in this factory. Hundreds went along road outside, men and girls. Some turned in to Dupret factory.

Some had stayed in the iron foundry shop in this factory for dinner. They sat round brazier in a circle.

(Henry Green, *Living*, 1929)

Green starts off by dropping many of the usual formalities of style. He simply gives the time, "Two o'clock," without a full sentence. And he drops definite articles: "along [the?] street," "[the?] works manager to [the?] son." But he does start off with a place—and like many novelists, gives us alliteration in the names Bridesley and Birmingham. (Birmingham provides a real reference, Bridesley a fictional one.) There is no information about a narrator, or narrating situation, and the narrative focus is first in the streets of Bridesley, where the thousands are coming back from dinner. The fact that they come "back" indicates that the focus is to shift from the street to the factory. This is not a small workshop, as in George Eliot's novel, and Green repeats in the next piece of description that "thousands" of workers are coming back to the factories. His workers are members of a mass working class, not rural workmen like George Eliot's, in the afternoon sun.

We are not told what kind of streets these people come along. The space of the novel is created by people—who change from "thousands," down to "hundreds," then to "some." We are also immediately given voices in direct speech. Once inside Dupret factory, the focalizor takes us into the "iron foundry shop" and then to a group of men around a brazier.

Green has cut down on useless encyclopedic information or reference to the real world, but deictic elements (such as "*they*," the workers, in "*this* factory") are used to suggest that we must already know what he is talking about. This incipit rejects nineteenth-century conventions of description, and yet it encourages a certain intimacy for the self-consciously modern reader. Writing like this is, in effect, a reaction against the leisurely transition from *discours* to *récit* that George Eliot uses.

The only thing that is "beautiful" in Green's novelistic space is the machine work of the men. Instead of the movement of a wood plane in a shaft of light, we have simply a "noise of lathes," which begins again as the people move into the factories. To read this text fully is to understand how Green has rejected the conventions of nineteenth-century realism, moved into a later form of social realism, and also experimented with his own distinctive version of modernist style.

Development of Space:
The Geography of a Novel

The space of a text-world is set up in the incipit and will then be developed through the rest of a novel. Development will be made through descriptions (see chapter 3), as well as through further geographical reference in the narrative.

As a novel proceeds, and as we follow the spaces it describes, we may need to consider its space not just in terms of focalization, but also in wider terms, as a geography, or geographical system, of the novel. The map implied by the text may be suspended in its reference to the real world, but it is still a map of some kind, and will have its own coherence. Does the development of the novel, for example, follow the compass in some particular direction? Go north or south? (In Irish literature, movements east, to England or Europe, and west, to the Irish countryside and the open sea, are often particularly significant.) Is the novel focused on towns or the country? Are its spaces by the sea or inland? Does the narrative drift, as so many English novels do, toward London? Does it go abroad?

The problem of movement between places (crossing cities, for example) often plays an important role in narrative. Characters struggle with forms of transport or with life in new areas. Novels in general move across boundaries, between fictional and nonfictional spaces: they transgress usual limits, and their transgressions of space (or, we might say, their moves into "liminal space") are often tied to a transgression of social rules.

There is usually a hierarchy of places in a novel. Franco Moretti points out that in Jane Austen's novels, which represent a "small England" in geographical terms, accidents and adventures happen by the coast or in big cities, while plots are resolved and problems are settled in the countryside.[11]

Some novelists choose to set novels in artificial or arbitrarily chosen scenes, such as country houses—in order to eliminate questions about the wider social context— and concentrate on the playing out of relations between characters. (We find this in country-house novels by Ivy Compton Burnett or Iris Murdoch, or in many detective novels.) Some novelists, like James Joyce in *Ulysses,* are obsessive about the planning and plotting of moves through geographical spaces: others regard geography as a distraction from more important concerns. We cannot prejudge what a novelist should do with space, only take note of what is done.

Finally, since the suspended reference of the novel entails that its spaces are not tied to reality, but draw on images we already possess, we should recognize that novels can be involved in the formation of new images, which can then, in their turn, come to affect our idea of the real. Dickens, for example, draws on contemporary images of London, but can be said to create a new way of describing the city. The London of his novels was not the whole picture, and not necessarily a real picture, but it was one that reformulated the image of the actual city for many readers and that still interacts with images of the city today.

Establishing Time

It is difficult to imagine a whole novel where the narrative creates no sense of space. Yet as Gérard Genette points out, whatever the length of the text, "it is almost impossible for me not to locate [a] story in time with respect to my narrating act."[12] Time is fundamental to narrative, since narratives are concerned with shifts or transformations. Narrative in the form of plot moves us forward and backward in time, as it proceeds through redefinitions of causes and consequences.[13]

One of the key functions of the incipit is to establish a framework of time in which the narrative can take place. This will be done by temporal references that can be placed in relation to one another by adverbs and verb tenses *(temporal deictics)*.

Personal Time and Chronological Time

The focus in creating time in the novel may be (as in many modernist works) a personal sense of time—time as experienced. Or, in traditional realism, it may be on external chronological time—the time of a general history.

Writers of popular fiction often feel it necessary to start in an overtly referential way, with an external time that seems to indicate authenticity. Bram Stoker's *Dracula* starts:

> *3 May. Bistritz.*—Left Munich at 8.35 p.m. on 1st May, arriving at Vienna early next morning; should have arrived at 6.46, but train was an hour late. Buda-Pesth seems a wonderful place, from the glimpse which I got of it from the train and little I could walk through the streets. I feared to go very far from the station, as we had arrived late and would start as near the correct time as possible. The impression I had was that we were leaving the West and entering the East; the most Western of splendid bridges over the Danube, which is here of noble width and depth, took us among the traditions of Turkish rule.
>
> (Bram Stoker, *Dracula*, 1897)

Why should we need detailed information of this kind in a novel? There is something slightly ridiculous about the precision of "8.35 p.m." and

"6.46," especially at the start of a fantasy that is going to be about blood-sucking vampires, doomed maidens, and adventures in Transylvanian castles. But the specificity allows the reader to enjoy the feeling that the story is *almost* convincing. Stoker gives the month, the day, and the time (not the year.) And, appropriately for an incipit, we are to imagine a "start" of the narrative journey. This opening paragraph of the novel is written as a journal entry, so we can find some present tenses ("seems," "is"). They are set up against past tenses (*"left* Munich," *"feared* to go") indicating actions in the recent past.[14] There are also modal auxiliaries (*"should* have arrived," *"could* walk," *"would* start") that express feelings about verbal actions in the past. And there is, finally, a suggestion of a deep past: "the *traditions* of Turkish rule." Complex patterns of time, as well as anxieties about time, are thus contained within Stoker's narrative from its start.

Analepsis and Prolepsis

Setting up a substantial narrative in time will almost always involve movements backward and forward. We are accustomed to the use of flashbacks in films; in a similar way, novels use *analepsis* (looping backward of the narrative into the past) or *prolepsis* (looping forward into the future.)

These moves can be made at a macro-level (as when Elizabeth Bowen calls the three sections of *The House in Paris* [1935] "The Present," "The Past," and "The Present"). Or they can take place on a micro-level, working even within sentences.

The incipit of Kazuo Ishiguro's *The Remains of the Day* gives us a butler in a big country house (Darlington Hall) thinking about an expedition he is going to make in his employer's car ("Mr Farraday's Ford"). The paratext announces that this is a prologue to the main narrative, set in "July 1956."

It seems increasingly likely that I really will undertake the expedition that has been preoccupying my imagination now for some days. An expedition, I should say, which I will undertake alone, in the comfort of Mr Farraday's Ford; an expedition which, as I foresee it, will take me through much of the finest countryside of England to the West Country, and may keep me away from Darlington Hall for as much as five or six days. The idea of such a journey came about, I should point out, from a most kind suggestion put to me by Mr Farraday himself one afternoon almost a fortnight ago, when I had been dusting the portraits in the library. In fact, as I recall, I was up on the step-ladder dusting the portrait of Viscount Wetherby when my employer had entered carrying a few volumes which he presumably wished returned to the shelves. On seeing my person, he took the opportunity to inform me that he had just that moment finalized plans to return to the United States for a period of five weeks between August and September. Having made this announcement, my employer put his volumes down on a table, seated himself on the *chaise-longue*, and stretched out his legs. It was then, gazing up at me, that he said:

"You realize, Stevens, I don't expect you to be locked up here in this house all the time I'm away."

(Kazuo Ishiguro, *The Remains of the Day*, 1989)

We start off here with *discours* and a narrator who is the focalizer, but the information he gives us is complex and not easy to sort out. Phrases like "as much as five or six days," "a fortnight ago," and "a period of five weeks between August and September" serve to mark out a highly personal time, related to the narrator's thoughts about the expedition he will undertake.

In the first sentence we have mention of the future: "I really *will* undertake." Since the expedition will be one of the major topics of the *récit* that develops in the novel, the reference point of the narrative in time will have to keep shifting forward to the end of each day, allowing the narrator to look backward and recount his journey so far.

Movement backward and forward in action and retrospection is thus going to be extremely important in the novel, and the process starts off from the incipit, in details of the language. The future tense in "will undertake" quickly shifts into a past tense ("that *has been* preoccupying my imagination"). We go next to a modal auxiliary, "I *should* say," which expresses politeness—the rather ponderous politeness of the butler—and we move then to a present tense, "I *foresee*" (though "foresee" has a future implication.) The narrative loops back into past events, describing how the idea of the expedition "*came* about," and then, before that, how the butler-narrator "*had been* dusting." Next we loop forward to the present with phrases like "as I *recall*," but it is a present that implies the past.

The effect of such a complex play with tenses may be slightly confusing on first reading, but as we look at it in detail, a coherent pattern emerges of a personal map in time. The map is highly personal to the narrator, yet he recounts the details with the kind of serious attention we might feel was appropriate for a public history. The difficult relation suggested here between what is appropriate for personal and for public events will become one of the major problems of the novel: it will set the narrator's private hesitations over love against his public actions, and his personal loyalty to his old employer against his employer's public involvement with appeasement before World War II. We must pick up a large part of the meaning of the novel from unmentioned gaps in public time: the butler does not discuss the years of World War II. He ignores the most important public event of July 1956, the Suez Crisis—which signaled the closing down of the British empire. The delicate and precise negotiations of the incipit start off the novel's problems over time. They open a text-world in which careful consideration of details may hide the most appalling self-deception.

Wyndham Lewis ended his long diatribe against the "time-mind" of modern literature, in his book on *Time and Western Man* (1927), by insisting that "Space seems to us by far the greater reality of the two, and Time meaningless without it."[15] He may be right that space is as necessary as time, or at least that one is meaningless without the other. But fictional narratives are recollections that invert and destabilize the usual order of time. Unless we consider their play with time, we are not going to be able to give them a full and convincing analysis.

Part II

Description, Character, Dialogue, and Monologue

Where do we go after the opening? Novels are typically long works, and it is not feasible to attempt an exhaustive analysis of every part, even if we could agree (which seems unlikely) on what an "exhaustive analysis" would include. As we have seen, the opening section of a novel provides an important primary focus for developing a reading. Once past the opening sections, however, we may wonder where next to direct our attention, and how to attempt forms of closer examination that cover later parts of the text.

Descriptions are often easy to separate off from other parts of a novel—and for that reason are skipped by many readers. But they quite obviously contribute in an extremely important way to the setting up of imaginary worlds, and we need to develop strategies for reading them with attention. Chapter 3 discusses the basic processes of description, as well as showing how some forms of description have been favored in particular historical periods.

Questions about character seem inescapable in discussion of novels. Whether in reading groups, Internet discussion circles, university seminars, journalistic reviews, or in historicized and politicized academic criticism, there is a constant drift toward talk about character. Attempts are made from time to time in theoretical approaches to counter the tendency, to move discussion in other directions, but readers move it back again.

Rather than abandoning the topic of character, then, it is appropriate to make sure that we know what we are doing, and that such discussions retain a sense of their relation to the text. Readers and writers often talk as though the characters in novels were flesh-and-blood people. "It was with many misgivings," Trollope says in his autobiography, "that I killed my old friend Mrs Proudie [a character who appears in several of his novels]."[1] Statements of this kind create problems as we try to establish a coherent reading. But does it matter if it is the established habit of readers and writers to talk about characters in this way, as though they were real people? Chapter 4 asks what options are available to us and how novels actually go about presenting their characters to readers.

Chapters 5 through 7 consider the representation of speech in dialogue and monologue, as well as the important topic of free indirect discourse. Passages containing speech in novels allow us to imagine scenes of life and to picture people talking: they encourage us to think that we can understand or sympathize with the emotions of the characters involved. Contemporary fiction has often emphasized dialogue above everything else, making it the basis of narrative and the basis of its claims to realism. This is not surprising, since the enjoyment of dialogue and monologue is one of the fundamental pleasures of reading novels; but in a convincing account of a novel and how it works we need to go beyond simply saying that dialogue sounds real or unreal. We need to ask what forms speech takes on the page, how it is represented for us.

The elements discussed in Part II are not always equally important in any particular text—and indeed description or dialogue may be largely dropped from a novel, or character may be reduced to a minimum. Typically, however, they are present in some form. By analyzing them, we begin to see how the fictional world is being fleshed out, and we confirm or revise the first readings we made of the text.

3
Description

Most novels contain passages of description. Quick or careless readers may be tempted to skip such passages, often because they seem to lack suspense or simply to be ornamental. But, as Philippe Hamon has pointed out, they can offer a different kind of pleasure to the reader and demand a different competence in reading. A methodical reading of a text must take good note of them.[1]

It is not always possible to make a cut-and-dried distinction between what is description and what is narrative at the level of a sentence or phrase. One might say that description is constantly implied in the novel, since at the most basic level of vocabulary some words are felt to be more descriptive than others (for example, "he *walked* to London" is more descriptive than just "he *went* to London"). We are concerned in this chapter, however, with analysis at the textual level, and with description as a mode of organization of text. As far as novelistic texts are concerned, in certain passages the narrative pauses, or is given a subsidiary role, and description becomes dominant. In the classic novel such passages are used to introduce a new setting or new character. In the modern novel such passages are often shorter and are more likely to be surrounded by or intermingled with narrative, but they are nonetheless usually present.

We might say that prototypical description in novels is of landscape (urban or rural), people, or things. The gothic novel of the eighteenth century started a fashion for extensive descriptions of the exterior and interior of castles or large houses—and this continued in modified form into the twentieth century. (A variation in nineteenth-century realist novels is the minute description of the interior of slum dwellings.) The city street and the workplace are typical places for realism to describe.[2]

Descriptions are not always of static scenes: we also find descriptions of processes—such as the arrival of a train.

Pure description tends toward listing or taxonomy and thus lacks drama and suspense.[3] It is easy to dismiss it as page-filling or, as G. H. Lewes called it, the "common and easy resource of novelists."[4] Certainly, there is no single way of judging what constitutes an adequate description. And there is no logically necessary closure to a description: more could always be added if the writer wished, or if the reader's patience could be relied upon.

Description may be provided in a novel directly by an authorial narrator, but is also typically associated with characters in certain roles: for example, travelers, walkers, voyagers in vehicles like trains or cars, voyeurs, or spies. Characters such as guides, witnesses, experts, friendly local inhabitants, and teachers are often used to introduce descriptions. For quick readers (that is, hasty and careless readers), the appearance of such characters and situations works as a kind of marker, signaling that they can skip on to the next bit of narrative without too much loss.

Definitions and Characteristics

Mieke Bal defines a description as "a textual fragment in which features are attributed to objects."[5] We do not have to be told the name of the object that is being described, we may even have to guess—but there will be an implicit denomination of some thing, and our sense of that thing then holds the developed description together. After the denomination, features are attributed to the thing in an expansion, or series of expansions.

Literary descriptions may seem to be something that simply happens in a text, focused on the object that is to be described and without order or design, but in fact various operations are inevitably involved when a writer undertakes a description. There must be some form of *découpage* (that is, the thing described is cut off from its surroundings or distinguished from them by contrast); there must be some selection involved (not everything in the thing or scene can be described); and there will be some order in the description.[6]

We have seen already in relation to the incipit that it is worth trying to follow the movement of the focalizor in a text. Often, however, in a description this is more complex than a simple cameralike movement over what is to be described. Descriptions tend to move backward and forward referring to different classes of objects: we may start with a large-scale class of object (like a house) and then move to a smaller scale (the roof, the walls, the chimneys), then to a room, and then to things in a room.[7] The geographical sweep of the focus plays against these shifts from one scale to another.

Descriptive passages are often an excuse for rhetorical style. They allow writers to show an extension of vocabulary and exploration of language. Perhaps because it seems like a pause in narrative flow, description leads writers to the recollection of other texts, to allusions, names, and definitions. It often contains attempts at poetic prose, through the use of repetition, rhythmical effects, and elegant variation.[8]

Naturalist writers of the nineteenth century imposed on themselves the constraint that descriptions should be motivated by the narrative: they should seem necessary for a complete understanding of the main narrative and its context. Such descriptions may, however, also aim at transparence— that is, they do not draw attention to themselves as literary—even though reference to the real world has been suspended in the fictional text. It is an odd feature of our relation to novels that some readers go around checking whether places in novels really exist, and whether they are "exactly as described." Fiction, however, is not committed to this kind of verifiability.

Types of Description: Ornamental or Hyperbolic

Descriptions of landscape in early works of fiction are often motivated by a desire to ornament the text; they tend towards hyperbole and the hyperbolic.[9]

> The hill whereon this palace stood was just as big as to hold the house, three sides of the hill made into delicate gardens and orchards; the further side was a fine and stately wood. This sumptuous house was square, set all upon pillars of black marble, the ground paved with the same, every one of those pillars presenting the lively image (as perfectly as carving could demonstrate) of brave and mighty men and sweet and delicate ladies. . . .
>
> Coming towards it, they imagined it some magical work, for so daintily it appeared in curiosity as it seemed as if it hung in the air, the tree, fountains and all sweet delicacies being discerned through it.
>
> (Mary Wroth, *Urania*, 1621, bk. 1)

We are given some precise details in this description, but they are expanded through eulogy of the "delicate," "fine and stately," "sumptuous"
place. Not just the house and gardens, but everything associated with
them is described in terms of admiration: the black marble pillars show
perfect carvings of "brave and mighty" men and "sweet and delicate"
ladies. Sumptuous detail is revealed on closer view as dainty and curious,
"sweet delicacies."

Samuel Johnson's "Description" of the happy valley in *Rasselas* is also
hyperbolic and full of elaborate detail; it is noticeable here that the details
are not made specific with names or individual particularities:

> From the mountains on every side, rivulets descended that filled all
> the valley with verdure and fertility, and formed a lake in the middle
> inhabited by fish of every species, and frequented by every fowl whom
> nature has taught to dip the wing in water. This lake discharged its
> superfluities by a stream which entered a dark cleft of the mountain on
> the northern side, and fell with dreadful noise from precipice to preci-
> pice till it was heard no more.
>
> The sides of the mountains were covered with trees, the banks of the
> brooks were diversified with flowers; every blast shook spices from the
> rocks, and every month dropped fruits upon the ground.
>
> (Samuel Johnson, *The History of Rasselas,
> Prince of Abissinia*, 1759, chap. 1)

The valley described here is a "happy valley" and (although its limitations
become obvious to Rasselas) it purports to contain *everything* suitable for
happiness. Reference to an actual valley is of no interest to Johnson. Things
are included as members of their general class: we do not know the kind of
flowers, only that the banks of the rivers were "diversified" with them.
The hyperbolic aspect of the description is particularly noticeable through
repetitions of "all" and "every." Johnson also includes extreme or sublime
aspects of nature: the "dark cleft" of the mountain and the "dreadful noise"
of the waterfall. These details add interest and color to the description,
and are still hyperbolic in their exaggeration of dark magnificence.

Philippe Hamon has explained the prevalence of hyperbolic style in
descriptive writing from the fact that in classical and medieval literature,
description was used for formal expressions of praise concerning certain
places, times, people, and things.[10] A description was a public expression
of thanks, a "gift-in-return." The conventions of such a style and the asso-

ciation of description with formal praise survive to a remarkable degree, even in descriptive passages of the positivistic nineteenth century.

These conventions also shape the frequent use in modern descriptions of antihyperbole, or *litotes*—a stress on understatement, negation, and disappointment. Modern descriptions often foreground exactly the lack of expected beauties in a landscape. Thus, in Ian McEwan's novel *Amsterdam* (1998) we find a play between litotes and hyperbole. The novel has its central scene in England's Lake District, associated with the landscape descriptions of Wordsworth and Coleridge. In *Amsterdam*, however, the landscape is "grey," a "colossal emptiness," "one long frown set in stone." It rains; the mountainous scene is disappointingly not "a wilderness"; there are too many tourists, too many schoolchildren. All the same, the text moves constantly toward such sentences as "Now the mountains were beautiful."

Description and Painting

In the gothic novel of the eighteenth century we find growing emphasis on the particular (along with ornament and hyperbole).

> It was evening when they descended the lower alps, that bind Rousillon, and form a majestic barrier round that charming country, leaving it open only on the east to the Mediterranean. The gay tints of cultivation once more beautified the landscape; for the lowlands were coloured with the richest hues, which a luxuriant climate, and an industrious people can awaken into life. Groves of orange and lemon perfumed the air, their ripe fruit glowing among the foliage; while, sloping to the plains, extensive vineyards spread their treasures. Beyond these, woods and pastures, and mingled towns and hamlets stretched towards the sea, on whose bright surface gleamed many a distant sail; while, over the whole scene, was diffused the purple glow of evening. This landscape with the surrounding alps did, indeed, present a perfect picture of the lovely and the sublime, of "beauty sleeping in the lap of horror."
>
> (Ann Radcliffe, *The Mysteries of Udolpho*, 1794, vol. 1, chap. 5)

The description here is presented to the reader as a landscape scene, a "perfect picture," and is visualized by Ann Radcliffe as it would be shown in a landscape painting. The name "Rousillon" is a reference to the real world (Roussillon), and allows us to locate the description in the Pyrenees:

we are to imagine descending the mountains, looking east to the Mediterranean. (Here *alps* is used simply in the sense of high mountains and has nothing to with Switzerland.) If the description is hyperbolic, in that it employs terms like "majestic," "beautified," "richest," and "luxuriant," it is also in some respects informative, telling readers about a landscape they may not have seen for themselves.

Our reading of this description is helped by its being so obviously structured with perspective, while the *découpage* and selection of details recall an oil painting. The focalizor looks down the mountains over the lowlands and out to sea and evening sky: the repetition of "while" ensures that the focalization, which goes off on various descriptive expansions, and between different classes of objects, preserves a single picture of the whole scene. It is in effect a written description of a Claude Lorrain landscape, with detailed foreground, wooded middle distance, and luminous background of sea and sky. The mention of color is particularly striking. It is first generalized: "the lowlands coloured with the richest hues." Later it is specific, but in such a way as to contribute to the sense of a landscape painting with harmonized palette: "over the whole scene, was diffused the purple glow of evening."

The passage ends with a quotation that has been described as "one of the most evocative phrases" in the novel. Citations of classic poetry give descriptions of this kind an air of literary authority, and Ann Radcliffe likes to quote from Ossian, Milton, or Shakespeare when describing a scene. The problem with this quotation is that most editors of the text have been unable to find where it comes from. It has finally been identified, however, by Rictor Norton, as coming from Charles Avison, the organist of a church in Newcastle upon Tyne, who was reported by William Gilpin to have cried out at the sight of Derwentwater in the Lake District: "*Here is beauty indeed—Beauty in the Lap of Horrour!*" Ann Radcliffe has borrowed and adapted the phrase, then applied it to the Mediterranean. Interestingly enough her travel journals record that, unlike Charles Avison, Ann Radcliffe herself was rather disappointed with Derwentwater.[11]

Types of Description: Expressive

In the course of the eighteenth century originality and imagination become a focus of interest in literature, and methods of description thus change. Edmund Burke emphasized that although verbal descriptions are vaguer than paintings, they can "raise a stronger *emotion*" and convey the "*affections* of the mind."[12] English novelists begin to use natural descriptions in which the countryside is presented as a reflection of the state of mind of the person observing it. This can be either the narrator or a character in the novel. We find descriptions that are directly connected to the mental state of one observer, or sometimes multiple descriptions of a natural scene, where each description reveals a different state of mind.

> I was one night sitting at the great drawing-room window, lost in the melancholy reveries of night, and in admiration of the moonlighted scene. I was the only occupant of the room; and the lights near the fire, at its farther end, hardly reached to the window at which I sat.
>
> The shorn grass sloped gently downward from the windows till it met the broad level on which stood, in clumps, or solitarily scattered, some of the noblest timber in England. Hoar in the moonbeams stood those graceful trees casting their moveless shadows upon the grass, and in the background crowning the undulations of the distance, in masses, were piled those woods among which lay the solitary tomb where the remains of my beloved mother rested.
>
> The air was still. The silvery vapour hung serenely on the far horizon, and the frosty stars blinked brightly. Everyone knows the effect of such a scene on a mind already saddened.
>
> (J. S. Le Fanu, *Uncle Silas*, [1865] 1899, chap. 3)

Le Fanu speaks here of the "melancholy reveries of night" and of the effect of the "scene" on a mind "already saddened." It is presented as a scene, but this time in an almost theatrical way, separated from the lights of the fire in the room, and visualized out beyond the windows. The things seen through the window, and described, are exactly those that reflect the narrator's mind. Expressive descriptions of this kind are full of symbolic objects. The landscape is aristocratic, with "noblest" timber, "graceful" trees, and shadows "crowning" the undulations. In the aristocratic landscape there is also a sense of solitariness: the trees are "solitarily" scattered, and there is a "solitary" tomb. The moonlight, frosty stars, and silvery vapor all contribute to the atmosphere of mysterious sadness. Talk of the "moveless shadows" of the trees makes them sound dead and still, like statues guarding a tomb. The last sentence ends with the tomb of the narrator's mother, but to get to that tomb we have to go first through an account of moonbeams, trees, undulations (of mist?), and piles of woods. These are, as the narrator goes on to say, "funereal but glorious woods."

Thomas Hardy is famous for descriptions of the countryside that seem to many readers to evoke precisely the real landscape of the west of England. His specialist knowledge of architecture does sometimes lead to technical and detailed descriptions in relation to buildings, but for landscape he often uses expressive description. Thus, in *Tess of the d'Urbervilles*, the scene where Tess hears Angel Clare playing his "second-hand harp" is in a garden:

> **The outskirt of the garden in which Tess found herself had been left uncultivated for some years, and was now damp and rank with juicy grass which sent up mists of pollen at a touch; and with tall blooming weeds emitting offensive smells—weeds whose red and yellow and purple hues formed a polychrome as dazzling as that of cultivated flowers. She went stealthily as a cat through this profusion of growth, gathering cuckoo-spittle on her skirts, cracking snails that were underfoot, staining her hands with thistle-milk and slug-slime, and rubbing off upon her naked arms sticky blights which, though snow-white on the apple-tree trunks, made madder stains on her skin; thus she drew quite near to Clare, still unobserved of him.**
>
> (Thomas Hardy, *Tess of the d'Urbervilles*, 1891, phase 3, chap. 19)

The description here is first of the garden, then of the process of Tess's walk through it. Almost everything described is related to the sexual themes of the novel. The expressive technique is seen in the employment of terms like "damp," "rank," and "juicy." The garden's scents are "offensive smells." Its colors are a "polychrome" dazzle. The expansions of descriptions are registered directly in sensual terms, though the passage does not indicate how much this is the conscious reaction of Tess, how much is unconsciously experienced, or how much is the response of the authorial narrator. Tess is both a "fascinated bird," to be trapped by the stickiness, and a stealthy cat, moving determinedly through the profuse growth. But there can be little doubt of the significance of the "cuckoo-spittle" on her skirt, the "thistle-milk" and "slug-slime," her "naked arms," and the "madder stains on her skin" (changed to "blood-red stains" in some later editions.) The garden represents the wild "blooming" of "uncultivated" flowers and expresses a fascinated disgust at the thought of uncontrolled female sexuality.

Types of Description: Representative

The development of the modern English novel in the eighteenth century also marks the start of a certain kind of realist, or representative, description. Such descriptions give the impression of an accurate or factual account of a real scene; to do this, they fix the account to a particularized place and situation. The encyclopedic function of description is particularly noticeable here.

Representative technique is fully developed in the mid-nineteenth century—for example, in the "industrial novels" of Elizabeth Gaskell. Here we read about the interior of a working-class home in Manchester:

> The room was tolerably large, and possessed many conveniences. On the right of the door, as you entered, was a longish window, with a broad ledge. On each side of this, hung blue-and-white check curtains, which were now drawn, to shut in the friends met to enjoy themselves. Two geraniums, unpruned and leafy, which stood on the sill, formed a further defence from out-door pryers. In the corner between the window and the fire-side was a cupboard, apparently full of plates and dishes, cups and saucers, and some more nondescript articles, for which one would have fancied their possessors could find no use—such as triangular pieces of glass to save carving knives and forks from dirtying table-cloths. However, it was evident Mrs Barton was proud of her crockery and glass, for she left her cupboard door open, with a glance round of satisfaction and pleasure.
>
> (Elizabeth Gaskell, *Mary Barton*, 1848, chap. 2)

Descriptions of this kind both give us information and teach us how to respond to the scene. Gaskell describes the room as "you" might enter it. The focalizor moves around to the right of the door, past the window, then on to examine a corner cupboard, whose contents are enumerated. The description is unusually precise in its perspective on the room: novelists do not often specify whether things are to the right or the left in this way.

Elizabeth Gaskell gives such detail because she does not expect her middle-class readers to feel this is the kind of room they might be familiar with, or live in. "One" would have "fancied" that there was no use for the triangular pieces of glass, since "one" is middle-class and has no experience of what would count as a luxurious commodity in working-class culture. Great emphasis is laid on the fact that it is an ordered interior, with simple objects ("plates and dishes," not fine china), and primary colors ("blue-and-white" curtains, and a suggestion of red and green in the leafy geraniums). Mrs. Barton keeps it very clean and takes pride in her own poor possessions. This emphasis reflects certain underlying ideas that are not overtly stated: Gaskell, as a minister's wife living in Manchester, wishes to reassure her readers in the non-industrial parts of England that members of the new industrial working class are not frightening or strange: if given the opportunity, they can be as clean as middle-class families. She also wants to suggest that since there is an autonomous culture reflected in such interiors, the working class may not be so dangerously eager to grab the riches and privileges of the middle class as has been feared. Such ideas are not foregrounded: it is assumed that description can do its own work of persuading readers.

The style used by Gaskell may seem unforced or natural because of its use of unornamented details, but it is not obvious to everyone that this is appropriate for a novel, and it is indeed far from the style of many of her contemporaries. When Dickens describes a visit to "the brickmaker's house" in *Bleak House* (1852–53), for example, he is not at all interested in listing things as such: his focus is squarely on emotional reactions. He gives us expressive descriptions of the "wretched" hovels and "miserable gardens" around, then moves to the "damp offensive room" the people in it ("all stained with clay and mud, and looking very dissipated"), and switches from description to dramatic speeches about life there (chap. 8).

Representative description develops in the nineteenth century because of a particular set of ideas about what fiction can do to introduce information to readers. The techniques are of key importance in the naturalistic novel at the end of the nineteenth century, where the influence in English of French models is particularly noticeable. Gustave Flaubert, Émile Zola and Guy de Maupassant teach English writers to cut down on the moralizing that had been so typical of the English novel and to attempt what James Joyce called a "scrupulous meanness" of style.[13]

If representative description lays emphasis on information that supposedly refers to a real world and cuts down on ornamental flourishes of style, it does not, however, abandon rhetorical devices that might be considered useful in conveying, or making precise, the information it contains. George Moore in *A Mummer's Wife* describes the progress of a mixed group of people around a china factory in the English Potteries district, in Staffordshire:

In the printing-room they listened to the guide, who apparently considered it important that clergymen, actor, and dressmaker should understand the different processes the earthenware had to pass through before it was placed on toilet or breakfast table. Smoking flannels hung on lines all around, and like laundresses at their tubs, four or five women washed the printed paper from the plates. A man in a paper cap bent over a stove, and as if dissatisfied with the guide's explanations of his work, broke out into a wearisome flow of technical details. At the other end of this vast workroom there was a line of young girls who cut the printed matter out of sheets of paper, the scissors running in and out of flowers, tendrils, and little birds without ever injuring one. The clergymen watched the process, delighted. . . .

They passed through a brick alley with a staircase leading to a platform built like a ship's deck, and went on through a series of rooms till they came to a place almost as hot as a Turkish bath, filled with unbaked plates and dishes. The smell of wet clay drying in steam diffused from underneath was very unpleasant, and caused one of the ministers to cough violently, whereupon the guide explained that the plate-makers' departments were considered the most unhealthy of any in the works. . . .

(George Moore, *A Mummer's Wife*, 1885 [1922], chap. 4)

The use of a "guide" here to communicate information is typical, and it remains typical today of genres that emphasize their content of information, like science fiction or the "realistic chronicle" that Philip Roth puts in the middle of *American Pastoral* (1997). Roth gives a guided tour of a glove factory and an extended explanation of glove-making techniques.

Moore tells us about the china factory, but does not exclude irony. The guide is found to be inadequate at times, the man in a paper cap boring and pedantic, and the clergymen perhaps naive or perhaps leering over the young working girls. While the novel calls into question the guide's "wearisome flow of technical details," it gives its own expanded and lyrical version of the real work of "the young girls who cut the printed matter out of sheets of paper, the scissors running in and out of flowers, tendrils, and little birds without ever injuring one."

Moore's description advertises its transparence to the extent that it gives us an abundance of precise details (of the staircase, the platform, the series of rooms). But it is not just a picture drawn from real life, and its intertextual relation with other novels is also interesting. Flaubert's *Sentimental Edu-*

cation (1869) contained an important scene in which Frédéric Moreau follows Madame Arnoux around her husband's pottery workshops, just as Moore's heroine is being taken by her admirer around this one. Moreover Moore was self-consciously Zola-esque at this stage in his career, and wrote about the revelation it had been to him to read Zola's description of women workers in a laundry in *L'Assommoir* (1877). Memory of this famous scene very likely suggests the comparison of women workers in the pottery to "laundresses at their tubs."

It is sometimes assumed that since representative description aims primarily to communicate information, it does not rely much on comparison and metaphor; but it can be seen here that this is far from true. Moore compares the room to a laundry, then to a ship's platform, then a Turkish bath. The comparisons are exotic and indicate that Moore expects his audience to be unfamiliar with factory interiors. He implicitly assumes that they are more likely to know what Turkish baths, or ship's platforms, are like.

The purpose of the description in terms of the novel as a whole is not foregrounded, but it does have motivation. *A Mummer's Wife* suggests throughout that working-class people are trapped in a polluted, poverty-stricken environment and only struggle vainly to escape: we see here one such environment. Descriptions of this kind seem to be based on real knowledge—we may imagine the writer with his notebook observing the conditions of the pottery before writing. But we can never know how important actual observation has been. Some of the most famous examples of representative description in the English novel are not based on personal experience at all. They are worked up from newspaper articles, or interviews, or other sources (like Arnold Bennett's account of a French public execution in *The Old Wives' Tale*, which impressed early readers by its apparent authenticity, but was based on a newspaper report).[14]

If transparency may seem to be a primary aim of the realist, it can only be attempted through textual effects. Thematic concerns are echoed in descriptions, and rhetorical effects are unavoidable. Even in Conan Doyle's Sherlock Holmes stories, where the narrator insists on the importance of the factual, and on the way in which "scientific" deduction can be made from the observation of real things, we find Conan Doyle using rhetorical patterns such as repetition and alliteration: "This was a lofty chamber, lined and littered with countless bottles. Broad, low tables were scattered about, which bristled with retorts, test-tubes, and little Bunsen lamps with their flickering blue flames" (*A Study in Scarlet*, [1887] 1888).[15]

Types of Description: Productive

To modernists, the techniques of realism used in representative description came to seem a silly and tedious trick. Who needs all this superabundance of information? Virginia Woolf considered the "enormous labour" of "proving the solidity, the likeness to life" as "labour misplaced." Her aim was to "look within" at the "myriad impressions" the mind receives.[16]

The productive descriptions used by modernists are not just of things; they foreground their own production, and have as a key function unmasking the artificiality of the process of description itself. Samuel Beckett's *Watt* starts off a passage by denominating "this garden": the description then expands in a way that looks conventional, until it turns into a wildly overabundant list of irrelevant details.

> This garden was surrounded by a high barbed wire fence, greatly in need of repair, of new wire, of fresh barbs. Through this fence, where it was not overgrown by briars and giant nettles, similar gardens, similarly enclosed, each with its pavilion, were on all sides distinctly to be seen. Now converging, now diverging, these fences presented a striking irregularity of contour. No fence was party, nor any part of any fence. But their adjacence was such, at certain places, that a broad-shouldered or broad-basined man, threading these narrow straits, would have done so with greater ease, and with less jeopardy to his coat, and perhaps to his trousers, sideways than frontways. For a big-bottomed man, on the contrary, or a big-bellied man, frontal motion would be an absolute necessity, if he did not wish his stomach to be perforated, or his arse, or perhaps both, by a rusty barb, or by rusty barbs. A big-bottomed big-bosomed woman, an obese wet-nurse, for example, would be under a similar necessity. While persons at once broad-shouldered and big-bellied, or broad-basined and big-bottomed, or broad-basined and big-bellied, or broad-shouldered and big-bottomed, or big-bosomed and broad-shouldered, or big-bosomed and broad-basined, would on no account, if they were in their right senses, commit themselves to this treacherous channel, but turn about, and retrace their steps, unless they wished to be impaled, at various points at once, and perhaps bleed to death, or be eaten alive by the rats, or perish from exposure, long before their cries were heard, and still longer before the rescuers appeared, running, with the scissors, the brandy and the iodine.
>
> (Samuel Beckett, *Watt*, 1953, pt. 3)

The terms Beckett uses here are called into question as the description proceeds. The garden is enclosed by barbed wire—which does in effect provide barbs, though we do not usually distinguish between "new wire" and "fresh barbs." Repetitions start in the opening ("similar gardens," "similarly enclosed"), but then overwhelm us in enormously useless lists and permutations on the contents—which have no obvious bearing on the visualization of the garden in question. The lists themselves have their own logic (explaining that some people have to go in sideways, some frontways, and some can't manage at all). But the construction of the lists seems to be determined by repetition of words beginning with *b*, and the possible combinations of words are just as interesting as any reference to a real world. Indeed, we suddenly make a fantastic leap into a war land-scape, with people being eaten by rats and dying of exposure; and this leads to a further list, of things not irrelevant, but on another scale: scis-sors, brandy, and iodine.

We have distinguished four main types of description, which can to some extent be identified with particular periods and styles: *ornamental or hy-perbolic, expressive, representative,* and *productive.* We must not imagine that there has been a simple pattern of historical development; rather, the various forms can coexist within the same work, and often do. Productive description has been identified with modernism, but it would be possible to find examples of the technique in Sterne's *Tristram Shandy,* or even in the novels of George Eliot—just as we can find plenty of ornamental and hyperbolic descriptions in contemporary popular novels. Novelists may deliberately play in border areas between different types, as when Brett Easton Ellis juggles between representative and productive descriptions in his accounts of consumer goods in *American Psycho* (1991). From one point of view he just tells us what his characters have in their apartments, but at such length, and with such overinsistence, that the descriptive pro-cess seems to call itself into question. We cannot, then, produce a simple historical map of descriptive types, but it remains likely that some forms are privileged in certain periods rather than others.

4

Character and
Character Portraits

A focus on character, which treats fictional characters as real people, and speculates about what they would, or should, or could have done, is one of the most traditional and popular ways to approach the novel. Discussion of this kind is as typical of theorists as of antitheorists, and it is as typical of naive readings as of sophisticated analysis. It would be unrealistic to expect readers change their ways, but there is good reason to try to clarify what we are doing when we talk about characters, and to add rigor to the discussion.

The process of reading novels is, for many readers, like that of learning about real people. Percy Lubbock said in *The Craft of Fiction* that "after living for a time with people like Clarissa Harlowe or Anna Karenina or Emma Bovary we have had a lasting experience, though the novels in which they figured may fall away into dimness and uncertainty. These women, with some of the scenes and episodes of their history, remain with us as vividly as though we had known them in life."[1] We can point out, as a corrective to this approach, that fictional characters are not real, that they are constructs from a written text. As Seymour Chatman says, however, this does not fully explain how we imagine and think about them. After all, we may "recall fictional characters vividly, yet not a single word of the text in which they came alive."[2]

Fictional characters "come alive" for readers—and yet they are not real people. Fiction may seem like a description of reality, but it remains a kind of play, or thought-experiment, and the characters it contains are not flesh and blood. This must affect the kinds of things that we can sensibly say about them.

Internal and External Statements: The Story Operator

In philosophical terms, a distinction has been made between two kinds of statement that we use to refer to fictional characters.[3] On the one hand, in sentences like "Henry James tried to make Isabel Archer a typical modern young American woman," the name "Isabel Archer" refers to *dependent abstracta*—dependent, that is, on Henry James. Truths about Isabel Archer in this context are not truths about a flesh-and-blood woman, they are truths about a creation of Henry James in his novel, *Portrait of a Lady.* Characteristics of Isabel Archer are those attributed to her by James.

On the other hand, sentences that simply refer to Isabel Archer *within* the novel are different: they work under a *story operator.* When we read Isabel's name in a sentence from *Portrait of a Lady* ("Ralph had said to Isabel that he hoped she would remain at Gardencourt, and she made no immediate motion to leave the place" [vol. 2, chap. 55]), we read the sentence *as if* it referred to a flesh-and-blood woman with spatio-temporality. Critical discussion also frequently accepts the story operator, and produces comments that continue its operation, like: "Isabel says nothing to Ralph, but she knows she can't remain at Gardencourt," or "Isabel would have been thinking about her marriage and what it meant to her."

The first kind of statement, which takes the names of characters to refer to dependent abstracta, assumes that we are *external* to the fictional world. The second kind assumes that we are *internal* to the world.

External statements can be speculative (using *could,* or *would,* or *should*), but the speculations they contain are fairly limited, and of a kind that can be supported by details from the text, or by what we consider the author meant or intended to say. Internal statements, using the story operator, are generally allowed a much greater freedom, since they work under the temporary suspension of our knowledge that we are playing with fictions. They allow us to discuss characters as we would discuss real people—attributing life histories and psychologies to them. They can be confirmed not just by textual details, but by our sense of what people generally do, or what their deeper unconscious motivation might be. Using such statements, we enter the game of fiction.

The problem with internal statements is that the constraints on them are vague. It is easy to drift off into private fantasy about characters, which may not be convincing to other readers.

In extended critical discourse we often switch between the two kinds of statement, or counterpoint one way of talking against the other: we flash on and off the story operator. There is no reason why we should stop doing this—it is part of the enjoyment of discussing novels for many people—but it is important that we should realize what we are doing. Arguments about such well-worn topics as the governess in Henry James's *Turn of the Screw,* for example, and discussions of whether she *really* saw the ghosts or not, frequently become confused and unhelpful, because some readers insist that only external statements about the text and the author's intentions are acceptable, while others want to mix in internal statements about the governess and speculate on what she "would have seen" and "would have imagined" or "was unable to come to terms with in herself."

Fictional Characters and Real People

Writers of fiction frequently blur the boundaries between fictional play and nonfictional accounts of the real world—for example, mixing the names of real people with those of fictional characters. In Maria Edgeworth's *Ormond,* when Ormond goes to Paris, we read:

> The abbé Morellet's breakfast was very agreeable, and Ormond saw at his house what had been promised him, many of the literary men at Paris. Voltaire was not then in France; and Rousseau, who was always quarrelling with somebody, and generally with everybody, could not be prevailed upon to go to this breakfast. Ormond was assured that he lost nothing by not seeing him, or by not hearing his conversation, for that it was by no means equal to his writings.
>
> (Maria Edgeworth, *Ormond,* 1817, chap. 29)

Rousseau and Voltaire thus appear in the narrative, though they do not actually take part in a scene. Mention of such real people is in one sense a "corroborative technique" of realism, adding to our sense that the narrative is about real life.[4] But if it comes too close to the real world, the story operator will stop working, and we would start demanding different kinds of thing from the text. In this case, if Edgeworth had actually given a conversation between Voltaire and Ormond, it might well have distracted readers who were familiar with Voltaire's writings. Many historical novelists use a technique similar to Edgeworth's, focusing on invented fictional characters and simply giving glancing references to the great historical figures, flicking the story operator on and off in order to give a fictionalized history.

Categories of Character

To discuss fictional characters from an external point of view we can distinguish, following Vincent Jouve's classifications, four main categories:[5]

> *Types.* Characters who simply fulfill a function: the king who rules,
> the witch in the fairy story who performs spells, the publican who
> sells the hero a pint of beer.
> *Representative characters.* Characters who represent a group or class,
> such as the courtly knight or the working-class worker.
> *Individuals.* Characters who move out of stereotyped roles and show
> individuality.
> *Personalities.* Characters portrayed with interior lives, or with a sense
> of their own destiny, who can be seen as close to the complexities
> of the reader.

The kind of information we are given about characters varies between
these categories and depends to some extent on the historical development of the genre of the novel.

Premodern fiction is largely concerned with types: kings, queens, prin-
cesses, witches. It describes them in terms of generalized public knowledge—how good a king is, how beautiful a princess is. This changes, however, as consumption and the exchange of luxuries spread among the
middle classes in the eighteenth century. Detailed matters concerning
people's clothes, possessions, and individual characteristics become of
greater significance. Novelists borrow techniques from biographical and
autobiographical writing, and begin to draw in elaborate backgrounds and
genealogies.

It has always been possible for writers of fiction to develop character
portraits that imply great intensity of feeling, but the feeling is more complex as realism develops and particularity becomes of more interest to writers. Heroes and heroines of the eighteenth century are less predictable
than their predecessors. Daniel Defoe's Moll Flanders reveals herself, in
her own account, as an immoral thief, but she is not a simple character:
Defoe's novel gives her a contradictory mixture of refinement, greed,
amoral calculation, and pious reflection.

Classic novelists of the nineteenth century usually assume a certain stability in character, or at least familiar patterns of growth and change. Characters are often given a childhood, whose key events shape the development of their personality.

At the end of the nineteenth century, fictional characters reflect a general interest in psychological analysis, but also become more fragmented and then, in the work of writers like Henry James and Joseph Conrad, they become finally unknowable. Modernists reject what D. H. Lawrence called the "old stable *ego*" in novelistic character.[6] The woman in the train looks at Jacob in Virginia Woolf's *Jacob's Room* and thinks: "It is no use trying to sum people up. One must follow hints, not exactly what is said, nor yet entirely what is done" (chap. 3). Late modernism goes even further in the way of fragmentation and begins to deride any hopes of the convincing representation of character. But character is difficult to suppress entirely in the novel, since we have the habit of constructing our thought-experiments around characters, and human agents are necessary for narrative.

Thus the history of the novel moves us forward to the representation of interior states of complex personalities, but it should be emphasized that types and representatives persist as minor characters *throughout* the history of the novel, particularly in comic roles and in genre fiction.[7]

Character Portraits

When we consider character from an external point of view, we note that most novels include *character portraits,* passages that explicitly describe fictional characters.[8] A full character portrait in a novel could be said to include the development of character through dialogue, through accounts of the character's impressions and thoughts, and through narrative of actions taken by the character. But we can also separate off introductory passages devoted to describing characters in a novel, and focus on them for the purpose of analysis.

What will such passages contain? Graham Greene's narrator in *The End of the Affair*, who is a novelist, says:

> How can I make a stranger see her as she stopped in the hall at the foot of the stairs and turned to us? I have never been able to describe even my fictitious characters except by their actions. It has always seemed to me that in a novel the reader should be allowed to imagine a character in any way he chooses: I do not want to supply him with ready-made illustrations. Now I am betrayed by my own technique, for I do not want any other woman substituted for Sarah.
>
> (Graham Greene, *The End of the Affair*, 1951, bk. 1, chap. 1)

But if Greene's narrator feels that actions are most important, other novelists have concentrated on details of things, such as physical characteristics or clothes. Clothes in particular provide a convenient way of making a portrait sound probable, through detailed or topical references. They may also contribute to the overall patterning of a text and add depth to meanings implied elsewhere. Henry James, for example, severely limits his descriptions of clothes, usually to one or two dresses or hats, often with a simple contrast of black and white colors, but these few descriptions are nevertheless important as a careful reflection of the social context and the relations between characters.[9]

Material details are not always helpful. Beckett begins chapter 2 of *Murphy*:

Age	Unimportant
Head	Small and round
Eye	Green
Complexion	White
Hair	Yellow
Features	Mobile
Neck	13¾"
Upper arm	11"
Wrist	6"
Bust	34"
Waist	27"
Hips, etc.	35"

. . . **She stormed away from the callbox, accompanied delightedly by her hips, etc.**

(Samuel Beckett, *Murphy*, 1938)

This parody of official description suggests police records, sizes used in clothes shops, and the "vital statistics" of film stars given in movie magazines. It goes from the top downward, echoing Renaissance writings that use the technique of the *blazon*, praising a part or parts of the beloved's body, often itemizing them (as here) from head to toe. Beckett's description reminds us that the images we form of characters, even when we accept the story operator in fiction, are never fully independent of textuality. Body and text are playfully confused in Celia, who is "accompanied delightedly by her hips, etc."

Introducing Characters

There will always be important differences between writers as to what they choose to describe, but a character portrait might contain the following elements:

a. Exterior description of the character (physique, clothes, visible possessions)
b. Description of mentality and mental habits
c. Social placing
d. Family background and childhood history
e. Outline of career and prospects
f. General feeling of the narrator toward the character

We may take an example from *Dr Jekyll and Mr Hyde*:

> MR UTTERSON the lawyer was a man of a rugged countenance, that was never lighted by a smile; cold, scanty and embarrassed in discourse; backward in sentiment; lean, long, dusty dreary, and yet somehow lovable. At friendly meetings, and when the wine was to his taste, something eminently human beaconed from his eye; something indeed which never found its way into his talk, but which spoke not only in these silent symbols of the after-dinner face, but more often and loudly in the acts of his life. He was austere with himself; drank gin when he was alone, to mortify a taste for vintages; and though he enjoyed the theatre, had not crossed the doors of one for twenty years. But he had an approved tolerance for others; sometimes wondering, almost with envy, at the high pressure of spirits involved in their misdeeds; and in any extremity inclined to help rather than to reprove.
>
> (R. L. Stevenson, *Dr Jekyll and Mr Hyde*, 1886)

Although Mr. Utterson is described as a lawyer, so that some of the characteristics described show him as a representative of his profession, this is obviously a portrait of a character as a personality.

We learn (a) that Mr. Utterson is "lean, long"; has a "rugged countenance, that was never lighted by a smile"; but has "something eminently human" that shines "from his eye." We are not told about his clothes. He is (b) "dusty, dreary," austere with himself, though he has a taste for wine and the theater. He has an "approved" (that is, tried and tested) tolerance for others. He likes to help people, not criticize them. He is (c) a lawyer, and is prosperous and clubbable, since he mixes at "friendly meetings" where wine is drunk. We have no indication of family background or child-hood history (d), but in the next paragraph we learn that his friends come from his family circle, and that his chief companion is a distant male rela-tive, Mr. Enfield. He is a lawyer (e), and since he has not been to the theater for twenty years, we assume that he is middle-aged to elderly. The narrator finds him (f) "somehow lovable." Mr. Utterson's austerities are not particularly attractive to the narrator, since he sketches in the contra-dictions they involve, but he is not eager to criticize Mr. Utterson for coldness, or dreariness, or hypocrisy. Being lovable and tolerant are quali-ties, we gather, that may be disguised, and they are taken to be more important than cleverness, riches, or coherent moral standards. Although Mr. Utterson is not to be identified with the narrator, he is strongly indi-vidualized, and his values are certainly approved of in the description.

Virginia Woolf famously attacked realist novelists of the early twentieth century like Arnold Bennett, because they relied too much on externals in their character portraits—on physical, social, and familial details.[10] But as we see here, external details may suggest psychological states, and psycho-logical details will have to be described in terms of some factual detail; they can't simply be given as abstract accounts.

Formulaic Portraits

It is striking how little portraiture of characters is undertaken in many novels, and how formulaic it is. That need not interfere with the sense readers have of the novel containing strong or impressive characters. In Jane Austen's *Pride and Prejudice*, for example, we are introduced to the two heroes of the novel, Mr. Bingley and Mr. Darcy, when they enter a ballroom:

> Mr. Bingley was good looking and gentlemanlike; he had a pleasant countenance, and easy, unaffected manners. His sisters were fine women, with an air of decided fashion. His brother-in-law, Mr. Hurst, merely looked the gentleman; but his friend Mr. Darcy soon drew the atten-tion of the room by his fine, tall person, handsome features, noble mien; and the report which was in general circulation within five min-utes after his entrance, of his having ten thousand a year. The gentle-men pronounced him to be a fine figure of a man, the ladies declared he was much handsomer than Mr. Bingley, and he was looked at with great admiration for about half the evening, till his manners gave a

disgust which turned the tide of his popularity; for he was discovered to be proud, to be above his company, and above being pleased; and not all his large estate in Derbyshire could then save him from having a most forbidding, disagreeable countenance, and being unworthy to be compared with his friend.

(Jane Austen, *Pride and Prejudice*, 1813, vol. 1, chap. 3)

These portraits begin by suggesting representative characters (the "gentleman"), and only move on to a few details of individualization. If we go back to the list of expected elements, we find that as far as (a) is concerned, exterior descriptions are extremely generalized. Mr. Darcy has a "fine, tall person, handsome features, noble mien." Then, at the end of the passage, he is said to have a "forbidding, disagreeable countenance." The second opinion is one that is shaped by Mr. Darcy's appearing "to be proud." Jane Austen is writing before the era when there is any suggestion of an author using detailed realist techniques to record what he or she has observed in real life. The generalized terms, such as "handsome," do not point to specific bodily or facial features, but rely upon an agreed set of values, one that does not have to be confirmed by precise listing. As regards (b), all the emphasis is on social habits rather than mental ones. The points in question are the "manners" of Mr. Darcy, and whether he is "proud." Of key interest to Jane Austen is (c), the social placing—and here we note that, as so often in her work, she is hard-headed and direct. We are given details straight away in relation to money (Mr. Darcy is said to have ten thousand pounds a year) and in relation to his estates in Derbyshire.

The narrator's attitude to Mr. Darcy is not unsympathetic, but judgment is being kept in reserve. It could be the narrator who thinks that Mr. Darcy is "fine," and "tall," and "handsome"—but it could be the fellow guests at the ball. The contrary view, that he is "forbidding," is probably not the narrator's view: "he was *discovered* to be proud," and not even his fortune "could then save" him from unfavorable reports.

The description of Mr. Darcy is thus partly filtered through the reactions of people at the ball, but some of the same range of details are given when Mr. Darcy's sister is introduced much later in the novel:

Miss Darcy was tall, and on a larger scale than Elizabeth; and, though little more than sixteen, her figure was formed, and her appearance womanly and graceful. She was less handsome than her brother, but

> there was sense and good humour in her face, and her manners were perfectly unassuming and gentle.
>
> (Jane Austen, *Pride and Prejudice*, 1813, vol. 3, chap. 2)

Again there are no details of clothes, and the physical details are only that she is tall and her figure is "formed," her "appearance womanly." The question of whether she is "handsome" or not gives some indication of individuality, but her manners fit her into being a representative of her class. We are given one fairly concrete detail: she is "little more than sixteen."

Austen's method of introduction clearly follows recognizable patterns. The interest that her heroes and heroines have for many readers cannot come from full elaboration of realistic detail, nor from information about their childhood. Small but significant indications of individuality separate them from other members of their class. Much of our sense of familiarity with them will derive from access to their thoughts, which is given as the narrative develops by using free indirect discourse.[11]

Realist Portraits

Jane Austen's methods are very different from those we find in a nineteenth-century realist novel, like Gissing's *The Nether World*. Here we read about Miss Clementina Peckover:

> The speaker was a girl of sixteen, tall, rather bony, rudely handsome; the hand with which she struck was large and coarse-fibred, the muscles that impelled it vigorous. Her dress was that of a work-girl, unsubstantial, ill-fitting, but of ambitious cut; her hair was very abundant, and rose upon the back of her head in thick coils, an elegant fringe depending in front. The fire had made her face scarlet, and in the lamplight her large eyes glistened with joys.
>
> (George Gissing, *The Nether World*, 1889, chap. 1)

We meet the word *handsome* here again applied to a young woman of sixteen, but that is about all the passage has in common with *Pride and Prejudice*. The age is given precisely. The observant narrator, almost a social scientist among his clients, gives us a wealth of physical detail. He starts off with generalized expressions ("tall," "rather bony"), but then fixes precisely on the girl's hand, and even its musculature. He tells us about her "thick coils" of hair, her fringe, the shape of her head, and her eyes, and notices that her face is now scarlet.

This time we are given details of dress—though they are not strongly visual: they place the young woman in her social class (a "work-girl") and give us an idea of her pretentions and lack of aesthetic sense. The description of the dress as "unsubstantial" and "ill-fitting," though of an "ambitious cut," reveals that the narrator is not detached and objective in what he describes. He has a sense that she is poor, that she cannot afford anything substantial, but thinks she does not take care over things like the fit of her dress, and that she is, in a repellent way, ambitious. A description of this kind by Gissing manages to include both his resentment at the inequalities of society, at the fact that this girl cannot afford to dress well, and a dislike of the way Clementina actually looks. Some of the same ambivalence is indicated by his view of Clementina as "handsome" and "vigorous," but also "coarse-fibred." Her hair is "abundant" (which could be attractive), but "thick coils" sound serpentlike. Gissing's details thus indicate a concern with appearance, but a lack of certainty about his own reactions to Clementina and her environment. Although she is described as in some respects representative of her social class, her individual characteristics make her difficult to classify.

The difference in detail between portraits in Gissing and Austen is striking. It depends in part on the fact that Gissing is attempting to describe members of a class outside that of his readers. Jane Austen speaks to social equals, who know what she means by a "handsome" man. Gissing speaks to people who have not taken much notice of scenes in the slums of London, and would probably be frightened to go there. His uncertainties reflect the problems of trying to expand the social range of the novel, when its audience remains largely middle-class.

Characters as Personalities

The full portraits we find in modernist novels, like Joseph Conrad's *Lord Jim*, are often extremely long and complex. Conrad's novel starts off with three pages of overt portraiture, although the novel as a whole and its narrative are designed as a portrait-inquiry into the character of Jim. The incipit moves abruptly into description:

> HE was an inch, perhaps two, under six feet, powerfully built, and he advanced straight at you with a slight stoop of the shoulders, head

forward, and a fixed from-under stare which made you think of a charging bull. His voice was deep, loud, and his manner displayed a kind of dogged self-assertion which had nothing aggressive in it. It seemed a necessity, and it was directed apparently as much at himself as at anybody else. He was spotlessly neat, apparelled in immaculate white from shoes to hat, and in the various Eastern ports where he got his living as ship-chandler's water-clerk he was very popular.

(Joseph Conrad, *Lord Jim*, 1900)

We are given plenty of concrete physical details, but they are not simply factual, they are immediately qualified by the reactions of "you," the observer of Jim, who would see him advancing or would think of him as a "charging bull."

Character here is filtered through impressions of Jim from various points of view, so that the problem of setting it out on paper is in the foreground from the start. The details individualize Jim and yet are extraordinarily difficult to pin down into a simple pattern: he is tall ("perhaps"), yet he has a slight stoop. You think of a "charging bull" when you see his stare, yet there is "nothing aggressive." His job is given, but that is soon made complex, since we learn on the next page that he is "a seaman in exile from the sea": he is thus easily classified (as "ship-chandler's water-clerk") and yet unclassifiable. The narrator also begins to sketch in Jim's interior mental life: "his self-assertion" is directed "as much at himself as at anybody else." Knowledge of the mental life is, however, uncertain ("it *seemed* a necessity," "it was directed *apparently*") and the attempt to get closer into mental processes will be the chief driving force of the developing narrative.

It is not just the individuality of Jim that is of interest to Conrad, nor just the distinguishing features that mark him off from other members of his class: the text attempts to represent the character as a full personality. It also constantly implies that such a representation cannot be fully achieved. We learn what Jim thinks, but we are never sure what he *really* thinks. Richness of characterization thus serves strangely to underline how much is finally unsayable or (in relation to other people) finally unknown.

Distance and Detail

The amplitude of a portrait description is by no means an indication of the overall importance of the character in a novel. Indeed, since important characters are often portrayed as sharing the values of the narrator, it may be unnecessary to describe them in detail. We can contrast two very different descriptions by E. M. Forster in *Howards End*. The first is of Mrs. Wilcox, who is made to bear the weight of some of Forster's most deeply felt ideas about the countryside and human relations:

> She approached . . . trailing noiselessly over the lawn, and there was actually a wisp of hay in her hands. She seemed to belong not to the young people and their motor, but to the house, and to the tree that overshadowed it. One knew that she worshipped the past, and that the instinctive wisdom the past can alone bestow had descended upon her— that wisdom to which we give the clumsy name of aristocracy. High born she might not be. But assuredly she cared about her ancestors.
>
> (E. M. Forster, *Howards End*, 1910, chap. 3)

No physical details here, no clothes, no age, no money. Description is largely in terms of the narrator's imaginative impressions of Mrs. Wilcox: "She seemed to belong," "one knew that . . ." Her social class is placed: she is not "high born," but she is the kind of woman whom the narrator likes to think of as a (natural?) aristocrat, and "she cares" about her family background. She is a representative character—representative of a small group of sensitive people who are important to Forster—and she is seen against a timeless, nonspecific world of families, homes in the country, and nature ("the tree").

Mrs. Wilcox's portrait is quite different from that given later in the novel, of a character who is not central to Forster's values, and who has a marginal role, chiefly in setting off turns of the plot, Mrs. Bast:

> A woman entered, of whom it is simplest to say that she was not respectable. Her appearance was awesome. She seemed all strings and bell-pulls—ribbons, chains, bead necklaces that clinked and caught— and a boa of azure feathers hung round her neck, with the ends uneven. Her throat was bare, wound with a double row of pearls, her arms were bare to the elbows, and might again be detected at the shoulder, through cheap lace. Her hat, which was flowery, resembled those punnets, covered with flannel, which we sowed with mustard and cress in our childhood, and which germinated here yes, and there no. She wore it on the back of her head. As for her hair, or rather hairs, they are too compli-

cated to describe, but one system went down her back, lying in a thick pad there, while another, created for a lighter destiny, rippled around her forehead. The face—the face does not signify. It was the face of the photograph, but older, and the teeth were not so numerous as the photographer had suggested, and certainly not so white.

(E. M. Forster, *Howards End*, 1910, chap. 6)

There is a remarkable excess of detail here, it is a set-piece of portraiture, and the character is obviously again meant to be representative of a class. Some of the description mixes the realistic and fantastic. For example, Mrs. Bast has an uneven blue feather boa, and in the same sentence we learn that she *seems* "all strings and bell-pulls." At other points the narrator implicates his readers in the description: the hat resembles the punnets that "we" sowed in our childhood. Overall it is a hostile portrait, which exaggerates in order to make the woman look ridiculous, but the narrator wishes to assure readers that we are on the same side as he is, and suggests that, surely, we know what he means. The physical details concern her "bare" throat, her "bare" arms, and her bad teeth. Her hair is a repellent system of a "thick pad" and a comic fringe rippling round her forehead. We learn, rather strangely, that her face "does not signify." The narrator does then give us some description of the face (comparing it unfavorably with her photograph) but his moment of hesitation functions as part of a polite refusal to state exactly what the woman seems to him to be: "it is simplest to say that she was not respectable." He prefers to say that she is *not* respectable, rather than openly state what he implies: that she has loose morals, and has been sleeping with men for money.

The differences in detail between the two descriptions of Mrs. Wilcox and Mrs. Bast are obviously determined by the ideology of social class, and Forster's expectation of the social class of his readers. Both are representative characters, but there is a noticeable undercurrent of sexual hostility in Forster's description of Mrs. Bast. Mrs. Wilcox, trailing along, is a mother figure, not seen as a woman in a sexual role. Mrs. Bast has a sexual role, and Forster has not the smallest sympathy for it: his description registers dislike, disgust, and even fear of female sexuality.

Character Development

As a novel progresses, some portraits will be amplified, and characters may seem to have changed or developed. This, of course, is not possible for all characters. Typical characters are usually brought on by novelists to keep doing the same thing—to act as a foil for the major characters. E. M. Forster discussed this difference in his *Aspects of the Novel* (1927), distinguishing "flat" and "round" characters. He suggested that flat characters are predictable, while round characters do something that we have not entirely expected.

The question of predictability is difficult to apply in a rigorous way to texts: in the complex world of a realist novel there may be many actions that are explicable but not entirely predictable. We can easily agree, however, that there are flat characters who have, as Seymour Chatman says, "only a single trait (or one clearly dominating the others)."[12] Their use is striking in the work of Dickens. Mrs. Micawber in *David Copperfield* tells us often that she will "never desert" Mr. Micawber. This kind of repetition is one of the techniques used in theatrical farce, but it also presumably depends on the habit of serial publication of novels in the nineteenth century. Readers might well have wanted to pick up the story in the middle, or might only read one episode, and would need to have a quick idea of who is who and what characters are like.

Changes or developments in a central character in a novel may be specified by the narrator, or may be hinted at by descriptions of different behavior. The history of the English novel, particularly of fictionalized autobiography, obviously owes a great deal to Christian narratives of conversion (among which St. Augustine's *Confessions* is usually taken to be the paradigm). There are many examples of heroes and heroines, from Jane Austen to George Eliot, who learn from their mistakes and become better people. The central figures of the modern novel, in contrast, tend not to become better, but develop by revealing hidden depths or repressed urges.

Characters do not, however, always increase in depth as their portraits in novels extend: they may become more stereotypical. As Umberto Eco has pointed out, James Bond starts off as a character of some complexity in Ian Fleming's *Casino Royale* (1953), but by the end of the series "Bond ceases to be a subject for psychiatry and remains at the most a physiological object . . . a magnificent machine." Eco notes that in the early texts Bond has an interior life, he is a personality who meditates on truth and justice, but in the later ones he does not—"except in rare moments of boredom and doubt, usually in the bar of an airport."[13]

Characters of all kinds—flat, round, developed, undeveloped, typical or individualized—may still seem real to readers involved in following a story (as James Bond no doubt does to his many fans). If we allow the story operator to work, and stick to internal statements, we can enjoy letting our fantasies work freely on characters. But external statements are more convincing as literary analysis. The analytic point of view attempts to come back again and again to details of the text and how it is constructed. Without such attempts we cannot be sure that our insights will be available to other readers.

5

Dialogue

In the traditional novel, dialogue is one of the chief sites where novelists seem to show real life directly. Quick and superficial readers skip through descriptions and immerse themselves in dialogue with relief. Dialogue changes the look of the text, producing blank spaces on the page, a variation that is pleasing to the eye and relaxing to read.

For the purposes of analysis, we need to remember that novelistic dialogue is not the real thing: it is conventionalized representation. Even when we are given what is called "direct speech," it is an idealized version of the way people speak. Novelistic dialogue may be said at times to look or feel real, but in fact its obvious unreality is one of the indications that we are reading a work of fiction. The novelist has to split the sounds of speech into discrete words, using conventions of spelling and punctuation. Words are put into sentences, when much of the time we do not speak in sentences. The hesitations, stray noises, and repetitions we make in actual speech are cut down or schematically represented.

What has been considered as appropriate representation of conversation varies from age to age, and from writer to writer. The modern novel tends toward a more "oralized" style, introducing more representation of sounds along with redundancies, incomplete statements, and exchanges at cross-purpose.[1] The nineteenth-century novel used dialogue to introduce character, give information, and set up dramatic conflict. A modern novelist may want to do all these things, but is quite likely also to want to expose the limitations and banalities of ordinary life through dialogue. Flaubert was perhaps the first to define the "monstrous" task of the modern novelist: "portraying characters by dialogue, making it no less vivid, precise, or distinguished, while it remains banal."[2]

The conventions of dialogue in the theater have had a great influence on the novel. There are important differences, however: theatrical dialogue is designed to be spoken, and must be understood without looking at the page. Novelistic dialogue is always framed in some way by printed text. It is often set off from narrative, but is not autonomous.

Basic Characteristics

For there to be dialogue in the novel, two or more characters are required. The characters should take turns in speaking, and show some kind of interest in each other's speeches. (Thus Virginia Woolf's *The Waves* [1931] gives the thoughts of a group of characters one after another, but does not show them listening to one another, and so is not a novel in dialogue.) Novelistic dialogue is often shown in familiar scenarios: the love scene, the confrontation over money matters, the dinner party, the picnic, and so forth.

When we analyze dialogue, we should note exactly how it is represented in the particular novel. Are the speakers on the same level? Is one shown as having superiority over the other? Do they have the same knowledge of the subject discussed? We should ask what links individual speeches into passages of dialogue, and whether any result arises from the conversation.

Textual Representation: Direct and Indirect Speech

Dialogue uses speech that is represented in novels in the form of direct speech, indirect speech, or narrative reports of speech acts (though there are many possible mixtures and intermediate forms).[3] In direct speech, characters are purportedly speaking in their own words and, in effect, taking responsibility for them ("'I love you,' he said"). Thus, direct speech seems at first more authentic. In *Pride and Prejudice,* when Lady Catherine arrives at the Bennet house to try to prevent an engagement between her nephew and Elizabeth Bennet, we read:

> **"A report of a most alarming nature, reached me two days ago. I was told, that not only your sister was on the point of being most advantageously married, but that *you*, that Miss Elizabeth Bennet, would, in all likelihood, be soon afterwards united to my nephew, my own nephew,**

Mr. Darcy. Though I *know* it must be a scandalous falsehood; though I would not injure him so much as to suppose the truth of it possible, I instantly resolved on setting off for this place, that I might make my sentiments known to you."

"If you believed it impossible to be true," said Elizabeth, colouring with astonishment and disdain, "I wonder you took the trouble of coming so far. What could your ladyship propose by it?"

"At once to insist upon having such a report universally contradicted."

"Your coming to Longbourn, to see me and my family," said Elizabeth, coolly, "will be rather a confirmation of it; if, indeed, such a report is in existence."

"If! do you then pretend to be ignorant of it? Has it not been industriously circulated by yourselves? Do you not know that such a report is spread abroad?"

"I never heard that it was."

"And can you likewise declare, that there is no *foundation* for it?"

"I do not pretend to possess equal frankness with your ladyship. *You* may ask questions, which *I* shall not choose to answer."

(Jane Austen, *Pride and Prejudice*, 1813, vol. 3, chap. 14)

This gives most of us the sense of a real conversation, but it is of course highly theatrical, and not the way people talk at moments of real tension. Despite the atmosphere of personal, generational, and class conflict, Austen's characters have framed exact sentences with elegant inversion and sharp repartee. It is not surprising that in the recent BBC television version of *Pride and Prejudice* the exchange was spoken more or less as it stands, with the classical actress Barbara Leigh Hunt playing Lady Catherine in full theatrical comedy-of-manners style.

Indirect speech tells us what has been said in narrated form, changing verbs and pronouns accordingly ("'I love you,' he said" is changed to "he said that he loved her"). We can easily transfer direct speech into indirect, but we can't reverse the process: when given indirect speech, we do not necessarily have a clear idea of the words supposedly used in each speech. We can also make a summary, or narrative report, of speech, in which "only a minimal account of the statement is given."[4] All these forms are often blended in one novelistic scene. It is common in the nineteenth-century novel for questions to be given in direct speech (for brevity's sake) and answers in indirect speech or report.[5] When Darcy proposes to Elizabeth, we read:

Elizabeth was too much embarrassed to say a word. After a short pause, her companion added, "You are too generous to trifle with me. If your feelings are still what they were last April, tell me so at once. *My* affections and wishes are unchanged, but one word from you will silence me on this subject for ever."

Elizabeth feeling all the more than common awkwardness and anxiety of his situation, now forced herself to speak; and immediately, though not very fluently, gave him to understand, that her sentiments had undergone so material a change, since the period to which he alluded, as to make her receive with gratitude and pleasure, his present assurances. The happiness which this reply produced, was such as he had probably never felt before; and he expressed himself on the occasion as sensibly and as warmly as a man violently in love can be supposed to do. Had Elizabeth been able to encounter his eye, she might have seen how well the expression of heart-felt delight, diffused over his face, became him; but, though she could not look, she could listen, and he told her of feelings, which, in proving of what importance she was to him, made his affection every moment more valuable.

(Jane Austen, Pride and Prejudice, 1813, vol. 3, chap. 16)

The passage moves from direct speech to indirect ("gave him to understand, that her sentiments had undergone . . .") and to summary of speeches ("he told her of feelings . . ."). A dramatic exchange has been set up; then the narrator stands back to recount what follows, bringing in nonlinguistic features of the scene (for instance, that Elizabeth does not "encounter his eye," but that Darcy's face shows delight, and that it "becomes" him).

The young couple in *Pride and Prejudice* have had their problems, but in this exchange they are shown to feel and behave exactly in the appropriate way for a young upper-class couple with integrity and a capacity for affection. Darcy has the requisite combination of good sense and heartfelt delight: Elizabeth has the requisite modesty and understanding. This fitting of characters into their socially preordained roles at the end of the narrative is what counts as realistic in Austen's aesthetic. When dialogue in direct speech is used by Jane Austen, it is not because it provides the best access to the real; it is simply one of several tools that go towards creating a larger image of a real (that is, in Austen's world, fundamentally conventional and sensible) couple.

Quotation Marks and Tags

It is customary in English to enclose direct speech in quotation marks.[6] Not all novelists accept this convention. It is not used in French and is not strictly necessary in English. Thus in Joyce we find:

> He laid the brush aside and, laughing with delight, cried:
> —Will he come? The jejune jesuit.
> Ceasing, he began to shave with care.
> —Tell me, Mulligan, Stephen said quietly.
> —Yes, my love?
> How long is Haines going to stay in this tower?
> Buck Mulligan showed a shaven cheek over his right shoulder.
> —God, isn't he dreadful? he said frankly.
>
> (James Joyce, *Ulysses*, 1922 [1960], chap. 1)

A dash is substituted for the opening quotation marks. And the end of a speech is either obvious, because it is the end of the line, or it is indicated by a *tag phrase* ("Stephen said.") Tag verbs (like "cried") are also combined with sentences of "stage-directions" ("He laid the brush aside and . . .").[7]

Aspiring writers have often been advised in creative writing classes to vary tag verbs, invert them, or give them adverbs. Thus, not just "he said" again and again, but "said he" or "he shouted loudly," "he burst out forcefully," "he whispered inanely." Vladimir Nabokov's narrator in *The Real Life of Sebastian Knight* (1941 [1959]) talks of "the problem of blending direct speech with narration and description which an elegant pen solves by finding as many variations of 'he said' as may be found in the dictionary between 'acceded' and 'yelped' " (92).

Some writers find the use of tags annoying and artificial (in French there has been a debate since the eighteenth century on how to cut down on them).[8] Joyce thought the attempts of writers at varying tags something of a joke, and in the chapter just quoted from *Ulysses* we find him deliberately overdoing it. He uses, in quick succession, "called up coarsely," "said sternly," "cried briskly," "said gaily," "said quietly," "said frankly," "cried thickly," "said gloomily," and so on.

Virginia Woolf also parodies tag conventions in a party scene in *Jacob's Room*:

"Are you going away for Christmas?" said Mr Calthorp.

"If my brother gets his leave," said Miss Edwards.

"What regiment is he in?" said Mr Calthorp.

"The Twentieth Hussars," said Miss Edwards.

"Perhaps he knows my brother?" said Mr Calthorp.

"I'm afraid I did not catch your name," said Miss Edwards.

"Calthorp," said Mr Calthorp.

(Virginia Woolf, *Jacob's Room*, 1922, chap. 7)

The general problem is that dialogue seems to give access to real life, but once we note the conventions used to record it, we become aware of its artificiality. One solution is simply to cut out tags.

Stella was usually silent when George had one of his rages. On this occasion she spoke up.

"George, let me drive."

"No."

"Let me drive."

"I said no!"

"Don't drive so fast."

"Don't touch me, damn you, leave me alone!"

"I am leaving you alone."

"You never do, never, never."

"Change gear, you're straining the engine."

"It's my car, I can do what I bloody like with it."

"Don't drive so fast, you can't see."

"I can see with my own eyes. You can't see with my eyes, can you? So shut up."

"You're drunk."

(Iris Murdoch, *The Philosopher's Pupil*, 1983, Prelude)

Absence of tags here helps create a sense of crisis and bad temper, and it is not confusing, since it is quite obvious who is speaking in each case. This is from a contemporary novel, but the use of tagless dialogue is not new: we find it in nineteenth-century novels like *Jane Eyre*. Readers rely principally on the framing narrative sections to distinguish between speakers, though differences may also be indicated through the use of dialect or repetition of phrases associated with a particular character.[9]

Forms of Dialogue

Exchanges of dialogue take a variety of forms in the novel, and we can make some broad distinctions between the different kinds of exchange that are likely to be shown.[10]

Phatic Dialogue

This is dialogue apparently at its most simple. "Phatic communion" includes ritual greetings and similar social forms with high redundancy. It is a kind of verbal signaling that establishes social bonds and does not, at first sight, communicate much information.

Novelists tend to reproduce sparingly the kind of ritual greetings we use constantly in real life. When they show phatic dialogue, it is usually not because they wish to record social rituals as they actually are, but to make some special point. In *Wuthering Heights*, Lockwood meets Heathcliff:

> I announced my name.
> "Mr Heathcliff?" I said.
> A nod was the answer.
> "Mr Lockwood, your new tenant, sir. I do myself the honour of calling as soon as possible."
>
> (Emily Brontë, *Wuthering Heights*, 1847, vol. 1, chap. 1)

The garrulity of Lockwood, his excessive mannered politeness, and the surliness of Heathcliff, his disregard for conventions, are established at once. The simple exchange dramatizes a fundamental opposition of the novel, though it is placed within Lockwood's narrative.

Phatic exchanges function as borders between dialogue and narrative; they work as limiting passages and may sometimes be loaded with a substratum of implicit meaning—as when enemies or lovers say their farewells. Perhaps their most impressive use is when they give readers an impression of access to unspoken aspects of human relations, to a nonconventional, nonliterary reality.

Didactic Exchanges

The most frequent form of dialogue in most novels is the didactic exchange, in which the speakers are not presented on an equal footing, and one speaker has information the other wants to acquire, or that will be imposed upon him or her. Didactic exchanges are the staple of detective novels and thrillers:

> "Well," said Mr Gilmore, "what have you found out?
>
> "I have found out, sir," answered the man, "that both the women took tickets at our station, here for Carlisle."
>
> "You went to Carlisle, of course, when you heard that?"
>
> "I did, sir, but I am sorry to say I could find no further trace of them."
>
> "You inquired at the railway?"
>
> "Yes, sir."
>
> "And at the different inns?"
>
> "Yes, sir."
>
> "And you left the statement I wrote for you, at the police station?"
>
> "I did, sir."
>
> "Well, my friend, you have done all you could, and I have done all I could; and there the matter must rest till further notice."
>
> (Wilkie Collins, *The Woman in White*, (1859–60) 1861,
> epoch 1, chap. 15)

The dominant link between speeches, in passages like this one, is question and answer: one person asks questions, and the other answers. These exchanges usually come to some resolution when the information has been passed on, or some agreement made about it.

The servant here shows his sense of social inequality by referring to Mr. Gilmore throughout as "sir." But it is Mr. Gilmore who wants the information about the women at the station, and in this particular exchange he is having to rely on the servant. At the same time, there is little doubt that Mr. Gilmore is the one who ultimately has most information about why the women should have been at the station, or what dangers they might have faced. The inequalities registered by the text are thus not simple. What organizes this particular exchange, however, is that the servant has superiority through immediate access to information that Mr. Gilmore wants.

Nineteenth-century novelists use such exchanges to communicate, in a more dynamic form, ideas and information about society, psychology, religion, and the world in general. H. G. Wells adopts a common pattern, using an informed guide (referred to as the Time Traveller), in *The Time Machine*:

"I do not mean to ask you to accept anything without reasonable ground for it. You will soon admit as much as I need from you. You know of course that a mathematical line, a line of thickness *nil*, has no real existence. They taught you that? Neither has a mathematical plane. These things are mere abstractions."

"That is all right," said the Psychologist.

"Nor, having only length, breadth, and thickness, can a cube have a real existence."

"There I object," said Filby. "Of course a solid body may exist. All real things—"

"So most people think. But wait a moment. Can an *instantaneous* cube exist?"

(H. G. Wells, *The Time Machine*, 1895, chap. 1)

The basic structure here is that of the Time Traveller communicating his information, while the group of listeners ask questions. Linkage is partly provided by the flow of didactic assertions on the part of the Time Traveller and partly by interposed questions and answers. Wells's readers are meant to be impressed by the aura of science: he does not take much trouble to make the conversation sound real—for example, conversational contractions like "isn't" or "don't" are not used. Wells does, on the other hand, emphasize key words and indicates them with italics (*"instantaneous," "nil"*). There is no real attempt to give novelistic depth by using substantial characters. This kind of exchange has its place in a tradition that stretches back to Renaissance moralistic dialogues, to catechisms and schoolbooks—as well as works like Harriet Martineau's *Illustrations of Political Economy* in the nineteenth century. The tradition continues today in some blockbuster novels—especially the kind that tell their readers about life behind the scenes at glamorous big hotels or airports.

Polemic Exchanges

We frequently read about other people's arguments as we go through novels, enjoying the unexpected triumphs of our heroes and heroines, or regretting their failure to assert themselves. These are often the most dramatic parts of the texts. Speakers in such exchanges are, in effect, on an equal footing. (Or, as they exchange polemic, we may have a shifting sense of what counts in the argument, and therefore who is in command.) The aim of the speakers is to produce a decisive argument (that is, each one hopes to call into question some presupposition of the previous speaker). The links are usually of assertion and counter-assertion. Where there are questions, they are rhetorical. Exclamations are common. The exchange from *Pride and Prejudice*, quoted above, is of this type. Lady Catherine de Burgh seems to be the socially dominant speaker, and to have the cards stacked in her favor, because she has money and class status. She loads her speeches with rhetorical questions ("If! do you then pretend to be ignorant of it? Has it not been industriously circulated by yourselves?") But Elizabeth Bennet calls into question first the wisdom of Lady Catherine's visit, then the social superiority of Lady Catherine, by asserting her own independence and moral authority. We are rooting for Elizabeth and relish her counter-attack ("I do not pretend to possess equal frankness with your ladyship. *You* may ask questions which *I* shall not choose to answer."). Polemic exchanges of this kind do not usually end in accord.

Choral Exchanges

Choral exchanges take place between a couple (often love scenes) or between a group of similar people.[11] The speakers are on an equal footing and can contribute to the exchanges in different ways, though they share common presuppositions. Dialogue in such exchanges contains both statements and questions: speakers take turns rather than adding new information. Choral exchanges (unlike polemic exchanges) are sealed off with accord. In *Jude the Obscure*, after Jude has gotten drunk and made a fool of himself in a pub, he rushes to Sue Bridehead's cottage:

> Jude stepped close to the wall, and tapped with his finger on the pane, saying impatiently, "Sue, Sue!"
>
> She must have recognized his voice, for the light disappeared from the apartment, and in a second or two the door was unlocked and opened, and Sue appeared with a candle in her hand.
>
> "Is it Jude? Yes, it is! My dear dear cousin, what's the matter?"
>
> "O, I am—I couldn't help coming, Sue!" said he, sinking down upon the doorstep. "I am so wicked, Sue—my heart is nearly broken, and I could not bear my life as it was! So I have been drinking, and blaspheming, or next door to it, and saying holy things in disreputable quarters—repeating in idle bravado words which ought never to be uttered but reverently. O, do anything with me, Sue—kill me—I don't care! Only don't hate me and despise me like all the rest of the world!"

"You are ill, poor dear! No, I won't despise you; of course I won't! Come in and rest, and let me see what I can do for you. Now lean on me, and don't mind." With one hand holding the candle and the other supporting him, she led him indoors, and placed him in the only easy-chair the meagrely furnished house afforded, stretching his feet upon another and pulling off his boots. Jude, now getting towards his sober senses, could only say, "Dear, dear Sue!" in a voice broken by grief and contrition.

She asked him if he wanted anything to eat, but he shook his head. Then telling him to go to sleep, and that she would come down early in the morning and get him some breakfast, she bade him good-night, and ascended the stairs.

(Thomas Hardy, *Jude the Obscure*, 1895, pt. 2, chap. 7)

The passage mixes direct and indirect speech, tagged and tagless. The speeches themselves do not provide readers with new information, and Jude's recounting of his evening's drinking is hardly clear. In purely factual terms the statements exchanged are not accurate: Jude is not ill, he is drunk. Sue is not really asking for information when she says "Is it Jude?"—she is asking for confirmation. Jude's "Dear, dear Sue!" is simply a form of phatic communication.

The idea of a drunken man turning up late at night on a young woman's doorstep is not particularly romantic, but this choral dialogue is set off in the novel as a small scene. It becomes an amorous exchange in which the couple express their sympathy and deep regrets toward one another (the best that love can do in *Jude the Obscure*). Their common presuppositions mean that the characters do not have to search for information, they take turns in filling the silence with contributions to the chorus. The exchange ends with peaceful accord—though Sue goes upstairs to bed and Jude is left in the chair—and it functions in the way that a more explicit scene of sexual encounter might in a modern novel.

Dialectic Exchange

Dialectic exchange is the type that we typically find in the modern novel. The characters are in a position of comparative equality; they are puzzled or troubled by some problem and are working out their position toward it. They are not necessarily shown as polished speakers, and may be struggling to express themselves. There is less of a sense of a unified theatrical scene than in the exchanges we have been considering above. Characters make statements and ask questions, take turns in speaking, and try to move toward some kind of agreement. The exchange cannot be a simple dialectic of ideas (or the text we are reading will hardly qualify as a novel); the different contributions of the speakers will reflect the depth of the presentation of their characters within the novel. The exchange may be punctuated with silences, with deviations, with false trails, as characters go off on some pattern of thought.

Quite often, in modern novels, the characters will seem not to understand one another, or will speak in broken snatches of dialogue that do not make obvious connections. Ford Madox Ford, writing of his collaboration with Joseph Conrad, says: "One unalterable rule that we had for the rendering of conversation—for genuine conversations that are an exchange of thought, not interrogatories or statements of fact—was that no speech of one character could ever answer the speech that goes before it. This is almost invariably the case in real life where few people listen, because they are always preparing their own next speeches."[12] Links may thus seem at times to be uncertain, but for the exchange to come to an end, there is usually, at some level, a final position of tacit agreement.

At the end of James Joyce's *Portrait of the Artist as a Young Man* we find a long dialectic exchange, between Stephen and Cranly. It starts off when Stephen reveals that he has had an argument with his mother about attendance at church, and Cranly begins to ask him about it.

There is a slight deviation, as Cranly is eating a fig, and Stephen insists, "You cannot discuss this question with your mouth full of chewed fig." They wonder why they are so much affected by the religion they have been brought up in, and discuss their loyalty toward their parents. Cranly asks why, if he no longer believes in Christianity, Stephen doesn't treat religion as a charade and go to church anyway:

> You disbelieve in it. It is a form: nothing else. And you will set her mind at rest.
>
> He ceased and, as Stephen did not reply, remained silent. Then, as if giving utterance to the process of his own thought, he said:
>
> —Whatever else is unsure in this stinking dunghill of a world a mother's love is not. Your mother brings you into the world, carries you first in her body. What do we know about what she feels? But whatever she feels, it, at least, must be real. It must be. . . .

Stephen, who had been listening to the unspoken speech behind the words, said with assumed carelessness:

—Pascal, if I remember rightly, would not suffer his mother to kiss him as he feared the contact of her sex.

(James Joyce, *A Portrait of the Artist
as a Young Man*, 1916, chap. 5)

Both characters are here trying to work out their attitudes toward these problems, but the discussion is deeply based in their lives. It is typical of Stephen that he brings up a clever, erudite reference to Pascal in his reply to Cranly (as a way of avoiding the strong point Cranly has made). Stephen's disbelief in Christianity does not prevent him using the Christian tradition for his own purposes. But the point of the discussion as it emerges is not religion as such, it is the question of what Stephen has to do to become an artist. It becomes slowly clearer that what he has to do is escape: from religion, family, and even friends. Cranly asks whether it is not most important to have one person with whom one can communicate. There is a moment of uncertainty about this:

His words seemed to have struck some deep chord in his own nature. Had he spoken of himself, of himself as he was or wished to be? Stephen watched his face for some moments in silence. A cold sadness was there. He had spoken of himself, of his own loneliness which he feared.

—Of whom are you speaking? Stephen asked at length.

Cranly did not answer.

(James Joyce, *A Portrait of the Artist
as a Young Man*, 1916, chap. 5)

The exchange thus ends with a question and silence—apparently inconclusively. But it is also a moment of understanding between the two. Stephen has looked at Cranly in the silence to see what he is talking about, and realizes that Cranly's wish to keep him in Ireland is finally selfish. Cranly has nothing to say, because Stephen's question has forced him to understand this about himself. The dialectic can thus be sealed off at this point, and the novel can end with Stephen's escape, with his resolve to be a modern artist.

Frames and Settings

To understand a dialogue it is necessary for us to have some sense of when and where it is taking place. The place may be extremely vague, but it nonetheless remains imperative that there be a possible one. The novels of Ivy Compton-Burnett are often said to be largely dialogue, but if we look closely, we find that important frames are provided for us, in which dialogue is set. *Two Worlds and Their Ways,* for example, provides an incipit that throws us into the middle of a conversation, but then after fourteen lines we find:

> **Maria gave him a smile and extended a hand in his direction, or gave the smile to herself and put a hand into space. He tapped a spoon on a saucer with more acquiescence than impatience, and rested his eyes upon the scene beyond the window. His most satisfying vision was the flat, green land about his fading walls, and his only music the wind in his native trees sighing over the ground where he would lie. To be without it would be to be without a grave.**
>
> (Ivy Compton-Burnett, *Two Worlds and Their Way*, 1949, chap. 1)

No place names have been given, but we gather we are in a room in an upper-class house, where the characters are having either tea or coffee. We can even guess that it is in the east of England, since that area is associated with flat, green lands. No precise date is given, but the evocation of a leisured life, the emphasis on "native land," the stress on family property, and the gloomy concern with graves suggest that this is the late Victorian period.

One reason we are able to perform such guesswork on dialogue is that there are certain privileged spaces where novelistic exchanges take place. Philippe Hamon lists some of them: firesides; sofas where confidences can be exchanged; forms of public or communal transport; reception rooms where people are introduced or where they gossip; border zones like alleyways or pavements; neutral zones like public places; balconies and windows or doorways from which one observes; gardens and stretches of landscape where promenades take place. The list is long, but the setting is of key importance, since it will shape the dialogue. The way we speak depends on where we are. Moreover, there are certain familiar patterns or scenarios that take place in particular settings, and that novels may follow (or self-consciously deviate from).

Dialogue and Different Voices

When various speakers are represented in dialogue in a novel, we may think of various "voices" being represented along with the main narrative voice. Many novelists go to considerable trouble to distinguish various speakers by tricks of speech, and to sustain this throughout the novel. In Dickens's work, for example, this is done on a verbal level in the confusion Sam Weller of *Pickwick Papers* makes between *v* and *w* (e.g. "You're wery right, old friend" and "Tell 'em not to vait dinner for me") (chap. 38). At a phrasal level we find it in the speeches of Mr. Jingle. Disconnected phrases are joined with dashes, leaving out any except the key words necessary for comprehension:

> Head, heads—take care of your heads! . . . Terrible place—danger-ous work—other day—five children—mother—tall lady, eating sand-wiches—forgot the arch—crash—knock—children look round—mother's head off—sandwich in her hand—no mouth to put it in—head of a family off—shocking, shocking!
>
> (Charles Dickens, *Pickwick Papers*, [1836–37] 1837, chap. 2)

In one respect speech like this contributes to our sense of the real, since a particular style of speech is identified with Mr. Jingle, and his character gains in consistency. But giving a character this kind of idiosyncrasy is very close to traditional practice in theatrical comedy. It ensures that we remain external observers, rather than sympathetic followers of the character's mental process.

Dickens's techniques have influenced other writers (for example, Olive Schreiner, whose character Bonaparte Blenkins in *The Story of an African Farm* [1883] speaks just like Mr. Jingle at first, then changes to speak like Dickens's Mr. Pecksniff). Many readers obviously enjoy such comedy, and see it as the creation of literary "characters." It is not, however, a defining quality of excellence in fiction. It seems to matter very little that the characters in a Henry James novel all talk much like Henry James, with only the slightest variations for class and circumstances.

Dialect and Foreign Languages

The use of a few words of dialect in passages of dialogue may allow both the distinction of certain characters and the identification of characters with a particular place or class. Perhaps most common in the English novel has been the occasional dropped *h* (*'ave, 'ere, 'e*) to give an impression of Cockney or working-class speech.[13] Dialect is particularly associated with comic characters, and since it uses nonstandard English, it usually indicates a distance between the character and the narrator. (Thus a central character in a novel can sometimes be shown as speaking in standard English, like the narrator's, while other members of his or her family use dialect.)

Representation of regional dialect has also been strongly connected with the novel in English since Walter Scott (who used it to communicate the feel of ordinary life of characters like fishermen, peasants, and servants), and its use is at present enjoying a revival among Scottish writers. In novels we are not confronted by accurate recordings of dialect (indeed, a fully coded transcription would have to note distinctive features and their values, and would be impossible for nonspecialists to read.) Novelists change a few key words, following conventions that are often inaccurate.

Accuracy is, however, of no great consequence. As Ann Banfield explains, novels are written texts, and we read them to ourselves in voices that we supply.[14] Given some conventional hints with deviant syntax or spelling, we supply our own idea of Glasgow dialect or Cockney in our internal reading (no doubt more accurately if we happen to have lived in the relevant place). We also supply foreign accents—or even foreign languages.

In Paul Bowles's *The Sheltering Sky* an Arab speaks in a representation of nonstandard French to the character called Port. "*Qu'est-ce ti cherches là?*" Then we read:

> **The Arab waited a bit. He walked to the very edge of the slope. A dislodged tin can rolled noisily down toward the rock where Port sat.**
> "*Hé! M'sieu! Qu'est-ce ti vo?*"
> **He decided to answer. His French was good.**
> **"Who? Me? Nothing."**
> (Paul Bowles, *The Sheltering Sky*, 1949, bk. 1, chap. 4)

From then on the dialogue is largely in English. Port is the center of consciousness of the text here, so using English for his words (even when they are supposed to be in his "good" French) is a way of making the English text at ease in Port's consciousness—while the Arab is shown as distinctively foreign.

Deviant Speakers

When we analyze dialogue in a novel, we cannot assume that all speakers represented will follow straightforward patterns of agreed social interaction. Novels also present us with liars, unreliable or boastful speakers, and speakers who are unable to articulate their thoughts. Our analysis should thus consider the relation of speakers to the transactions taking place, and note changes in the course of a novel. In *Jane Eyre,* for example, we are given a full account of the mental life of the first-person narrator, but she is at first apparently unable to explain herself to others. It is part of the progress of the novel that she learns both to explain herself and to use silence at important moments. Her growing ability in communication, through dialogue with others, is in stark contrast with the "madwoman in the attic," the first Mrs. Rochester, who does not speak and cannot communicate except by violent actions.[15] Dialogue and the absence of dialogue can thus be equally significant for the analysis of a novel.

6

Monologue and
Stream of Consciousness

The modern sense of *monologue* is, according to the *Oxford English Dictionary*, a "dramatic composition for a single performer" or "a long speech or harangue delivered by one person." It is also "a literary composition of this nature." Insofar as it resembles a speech, then, a first-person novel may be seen as a kind of monologue. But we also find sections in third-person narratives where long speeches are given over to a single speaker and function as monologue. Monologue may be addressed directly to the reader, or to other characters in the novel. It is also important as a way of representing the inner life or the flow of consciousness.

For the purposes of analysis we need first to ask whether the entire work we are looking at can be seen as a monologue, or whether the monologue is quoted within a work. Are we given theatrical-style monologue, which is to be imagined as spoken aloud? Or are we given interior monologue of the self-reflective consciousness?

Quoted Monologue

Quoted monologue, of the type that is to be imagined as spoken aloud, is frequently used as a form of embedded narrative in traditional forms of the novel.[1] We often find this when a new character is introduced (someone who gives his or her life story), or when a character has been off-scene for some time and returns to tell the others what has happened.

In Maria Edgeworth's *Belinda*, the heroine goes to stay with Lady Delacour, comes to understand that something is wrong with her, and is then summoned to her room. Lady Delacour starts to tell "the history of her life and opinions in the following manner":

"I do nothing by halves, my dear—I shall not tell you my adventures, as Gil Blas told his to the archbishop of Grenada—skipping over the *useful* passages—because you are not an archbishop, and I should not have the grace to put on a sanctified face, if you were. I am no hypocrite, and have nothing worse than folly to conceal. . . . But I begin where I ought to end, with my moral, which I dare say you are not impatient to anticipate—I never read or listened to a moral at the end of a story in my life—manners for me, and morals for those that like them. My dear, you will be woefully disappointed, if in my story you expect anything like a novel. . . . Of all lives, mine has been the least romantic."

(Maria Edgeworth, *Belinda*, 1801, vol. 1, chap. 3)

This obviously draws on theatrical traditions (Lady Delacour dramatizes her life of suffering and bravery for the young listener, while readers are placed in the position of an audience in the theater). But it also suggests traditions of the storyteller, and plays with ambivalences between spoken and written modes of narration. The sentences broken with dashes (which are unlike Edgeworth's usual style) suggest oral narratives, just as mention of "the moral at the end of a story" may suggest traditional fables or children's tales. Lady Delacour, however, blends different modes, since she says she has "*read* or listened" to them. She talks of Gil Blas *telling* his story—but Gil Blas's tale has not come to her or Belinda through oral tradition: it is something she has read in the novel with that title. She denies that what follows will be an account of life "like a novel"—though most readers are going to read it as just that.[2]

Embedded monologues containing life-stories of the kind Lady Delacour tells are no longer common, but monologue in the novel can still draw on echoes of the theatrical, when the novel quotes a public speech or sermon. In Brian Moore's *The Lonely Passion of Judith Hearne*, Father Quigley's sermon is a long rant against the modern world:

"You know what I mean, you people up there," he shouted in hard flat Ulster tones. "You that's jiggling your feet and rubbing the back of your heads along the fresh paint that was put on the walls. I mean the disrespect to the Holy Tabernacle and the Blessed Body of Our Lord here in it. I mean coming in late for Holy Mass. I mean inattention, young boys giggling with young girls, I mean running out at the Last Gospel before the Mass is over, I mean dirtying up the seats with big bloothers of boots, I mean the shocking attitude of people in this parish that won't give half an hour to God of a Sunday morning but that can give the whole week to the devil without the slightest discomfort."

(Brian Moore, *The Lonely Passion of Judith Hearne*, 1955, chap. 4)

The speaker here is given effortless eloquence, in theatrical style, with no hesitations. The speech communicates the individual character of Father Quigley, using occasional nonstandard syntax ("you that's jiggling") and local dialect terms ("bloothers of boots"). But, in general, we are given well-formed sentences, even if strung together with commas, rather than full stops or semicolons. The sermon is long (just under five pages) and rambling. Father Quigley's complaints wander from conventional religious questions ("disrespect to the Holy Tabernacle"), to typical concerns of an authoritarian and interfering older generation ("giggling with young girls"), to the housekeeping pride of the priest in his parish church ("the fresh paint that was put on the walls," "dirtying up the seats"). This is quite unlike the famous sermon in Joyce's *Portrait of the Artist*, where the elegance of language and fierce logic of the religious discourse temporarily overwhelm Stephen Dedalus (though that sermon, too, is quoted monologue.) Father Quigley's sermon is banal, badly organized, and broadly comic: his vision of hellfire would not convert a modern young intellectual. The overall tone of theatricality allows Moore to interpolate descriptions similar to stage-directions: Quigley leans forward, grabbing the pulpit, appearing to be about to jump out of it, while Mr. Madden falls asleep below. Judith Hearne's reactions to modern Catholicism are important to the novel, so we are given her thoughts as commentary, in a fragmentary style that represents thought processes: "Not the old style of priest at all, doesn't mince words, does he? But the young people, well, I think he's right, goodness knows, those young girls I saw at . . ."

We can make a crude distinction between theatrical and nontheatrical monologue in novels. The theatrical is presented (as in Father Quigley's sermon) as external and spoken, while nontheatrical monologue tries to represent thought processes or the movement of consciousness. The theatrical monologue assumes an audience of listeners or readers; the internal, nontheatrical monologue works under the assumption that the character is thinking to him or herself.

Quoted Interior Monologue

Dorrit Cohn points out that it is often forgotten that the interior monologues of James Joyce's novels are *quoted* interior monologues. We are
given a discourse that has not been spoken aloud and thus has no listeners,
but that expresses a character's intimate thought. In such passages we find
the great paradox of modern narrative fiction: it "attains its greatest 'air of
reality' in the presentation of a lone figure thinking thoughts she will never
communicate to anyone."[3] Joyce's quoted monologues exist within a narrative framework, and we understand them in terms of the supporting
narrative.

At the end of *Ulysses,* Molly Bloom is lying in bed thinking about the
"old faggot," the religious Mrs. Riordan:

> telling me all her ailments she had too much old chat in her about
> politics and earthquakes and the end of the world let us have a bit of
> fun first God help the world if all the women were her sort down on
> bathingsuits and lownecks of course nobody wanted her to wear I sup-
> pose she was pious because no man would look at her twice I hope Ill
> never be like her a wonder she didnt want us to cover our faces but she
> was a welleducated woman certainly and her gabby talk about Mr
> Riordan here and Mr Riordan there I suppose he was glad to get shut
> of her. . . .

(James Joyce, *Ulysses*, 1922 [1960], p. 871–72)

We are given the impression of being close to thought processes here
because punctuation has been cut out, and because the logic of the passage seems to be a logic of association rather than one of public argument.
The cutting of punctuation is found not only in the sentence structure,
but also in contractions ("Ill," "didnt," and the omitted hyphens in
"lownecks" and "welleducated"). Some parts could easily be separated off
into sentences using standard conventions ("She had too much old chat
in her about politics, and earthquakes, and the end of the world"). Others
are fragmented ("of course nobody wanted her to wear . . ."). It is assumed to be thought at a basic level, revealing Molly Bloom's own tricks
of style: there is heavy reliance on the use of cliché ("let us have bit of fun
first," "he was glad to get shut of her") and some distinctively Irish usages
("old chat").

There are other ways of representing thought in the novel (like free
indirect discourse). Since Joyce's quoted interior monologue allows the

character to speak for herself, with no shift in personal pronouns from *I* to *she*, it is generally assumed to come very close to the real processes of thought. But this assumption is not well justified: after all, we are unsure what exactly the processes of thought consist in, and whether they are the same for everyone, or the same at all times. In Joyce's work there is no doubt that thought is directly linked to vocalization.[4] He has restricted Molly in this monologue to her bed, so that in effect the words she produces are in an independent stream detached from her body, and themselves make events. Some writers take another view entirely of consciousness or the interior (Cohn cites Robert Musil, Nathalie Sarraute, and Marcel Proust), trying to represent the movement of consciousness before it reflects on itself.[5]

Monologic Works

We have been looking so far at monologues with third-person narratives. First-person narratives may also have the characteristics of monologue. Poe's story "The Tell-Tale Heart" starts:

> TRUE!—nervous—very, very dreadfully nervous I had been and am; but why *will* you say that I am mad? The disease had sharpened my senses—not destroyed—not dulled them. Above all was the sense of hearing acute. I heard all things in the heaven and in the earth. I heard many things in hell. How, then, am I mad? Hearken! and observe how healthily—how calmly I can tell you the whole story.
>
> (Edgar Allan Poe, "The Tell-Tale Heart," 1843)

This is given as if it represented speech, addressed to "you," an unspecified audience of someone or some people who think the narrator mad. The attempt by the narrator to persuade the audience that he is not mad persists throughout the story, but the actions he describes and the increasingly hysterical tone, persuade us that he is in fact mad. Although the text is broken up by exclamation marks and dashes (even more so at the end), it does not depart far from normal syntax. The tension that exists between our concepts of sanity and madness is written into the style: the actions described by the narrator, and his account of his motives, indicate madness, but the logic of narrative order is quite coherent, and we have no problem in following what he describes.

Long monologic works drift constantly toward autobiography. Even when there is an attempt to avoid the clichés of the autobiographical form (as in the work of Beckett), there is a counter-attempt by many readers to push the works back into an autobiographical relation with the life of the author.

Memory Monologue

Cohn makes a useful distinction between autobiographical monologue and memory monologue. In autobiographical monologue it is the standard pattern of the narrative of a person's life that emerges (obviously not life and death, but the movement toward a conversion or learning experience). In memory monologue it is the act of remembering that structures the monologue, directs the attention of the narrator toward events, and decides on their importance. Beckett's Molloy writes:

> I say that now, but after all what do I know now about then, now when the icy words hail down upon me, the icy meanings, and the world dies too, foully named. All I know is what the words know, and the dead things, and that makes a handsome little sum, with a beginning, a middle and an end as in the well-built phrase and the long sonata of the dead. And truly it little matters what I say, this or that or any other thing. Saying is inventing. Wrong, very rightly wrong. You invent nothing, you think you are inventing, you think you are escaping, and all you do is stammer out your lesson, the remnants of a pensum, one day got by heart and long forgotten, life without tears, as it is wept.
>
> (Samuel Beckett, *Molloy*, [Fr. 1951] 1955, pt. 1)

The narrative foregrounds *discours*, commenting on itself and its methods as it goes along. It does not need a chronological account of events—the search through memory provides the underlying structure—but the memory itself is shaped by "what the words know,"— which in this case is doubly complex, because the novel was originally written in French. The text echoes deformed familiar phrases (such as the title of language-learning texts, "French Without Tears," the promise of language schools to teach "German as it is spoken"). And it plays on deformed familiar ideas (the demand in Aristotle's *Poetics* that plot should have a beginning, a middle, and an end, transferred here to the "well-built phrase" and "long sonata of the dead"). The monologue destabilizes itself, correcting itself as it goes along, suggesting that all writing of this kind matters little, since it is "inventing"—but then canceling that statement out ("Wrong") and condensing the contradiction within an oxymoron ("rightly wrong").

Beckett is unusually self-aware and self-critical in relation to fictional techniques, but his texts play (as do all the monologues we have been considering) on our ambivalent sense that writing of this kind represents "voice." In *The Unnamable* it is called: "My voice. The voice." It is an interior voice, speaking to itself, and Beckett's narrator complains, "I hardly hear it any more. I'm going silent." The voice seems constantly to be reducing itself to the idiocy of solipsism, a voice talking of itself to itself. Yet as soon as it threatens to become silent, with "no one to talk to, no one to talk to you, so that you have to say, It's I who am doing this to me, I who am talking about me," then, once again, it begins again to revive:

> . . . there's someone there, someone talking to you, about you, about him, then a second, then a third, then the second again, then all three together, these figures just to give you an idea, talking to you, about you, about them, all I have to do is listen, then they depart, one by one, and the voice goes on, it's not theirs, they were never there, there was never anyone but you, talking to you about you, the breath fails, it's nearly the end. . . .
>
> (Samuel Beckett, *The Unnamable*, [Fr. 1953] 1958)

The memory monologue has come to seem to many writers (such as Proust, Beckett, or Philip Roth) the most searching, most truthful form of modern fiction. But, ironically, such monologues prove endlessly uncertain in their location in a voice, on the page, in a subjectivity that (as we have seen in chapter 1) arises from and now disappears into problems of syntax. Fictional voice is never real voice, it is a construction of the text. As monologists explore the limits of fiction, they may confront their own silence, since they have abandoned the tasks of the realist novel, which in the nineteenth century surveyed the whole panorama of the social world.[6]

7

Free Indirect Discourse

In Doris Lessing's *The Good Terrorist* Alice is sitting at the kitchen table thinking about housework. We are given something like interior monologue, but which is narrated to us using the third-person *she*:

> All these things that must be done. Alice knew that she would do none of them, until she heard from Mary. She would sit here, by herself, doing nothing. Funny, she was described as unemployed, she had never had a job, and she was always busy. To sit quietly, just thinking, a treat, that. To be by oneself—nice. Guilt threatened to invade with this thought: it was disloyalty to her friends. She didn't want to be like her mother who was selfish. She used to nag and bitch to have an afternoon to herself: the children had to lump it. Privacy. That lot made such a thing about privacy; 99 per cent of the world's population wouldn't know the word. If they had ever heard it. No, it was better like this, healthy, a group of comrades. Sharing.
>
> (Doris Lessing, *The Good Terrorist*, 1985, p. 103)

Alice's thoughts are represented here ("just thinking"), but in a style that can also be used for speech, called *free indirect discourse*.[1]

The direct form for thoughts would give us: "She thought, 'I will sit here, by myself, doing nothing.'" The indirect form would give us: "She thought that she would sit there by herself doing nothing." Here we find a form that does not represent the narrator's words, and yet is not in quotation marks. Some of the passage seems to be in the words (or directly from the standpoint) of the character, but using *she* and not *I*. This is called *free indirect style*. A typical example at the sentence level is: "She would sit here, by herself, doing nothing."

What we have, then, is a useful way of representing speech or thought. It is not quite clear how much is supposed to come directly from the character and how much is the report of the narrator, but the vagueness in this respect is functional, because it allows us suggestions of proximity to the mental processes of the character. Thought or speech can be represented in this way without being regimented into well-formed sentences. The style is used to communicate the way we think certain things but don't fully articulate them to ourselves, or the way in which our speeches are something of a rag-bag of odds and ends of phrases, and yet characteristic of the speaker and able to communicate sense to someone who knows the context.

Characteristics of Free Indirect Discourse

Linguists have attempted to produce a definition, or formal description, of free indirect discourse, and associate the following with it:

1. Pronouns referring to the speaker or thinker are in the third person, as in indirect speech (in the passage quoted above: "*she* was described," "*she* had never had a job").
2. Frequent use of exclamatory words and phrases, as well as rhetorical questions. Such words alert readers to the sense that a different kind of discourse is being used. *Yes* and *oh* are common (in the quoted passage, "*nice*," "*no*").
3. Frequent use of modal auxiliary verbs—particularly the "shifted" modals, *could, would,* and *might* ("she *would* do," "she *would* sit").
4. Time and place deictics referring to the here and now of the character ("she would sit *here*," "like *this*"). They are not transferred to the past and to a distanced place *(there, that, then)* as they would be in reports of indirect speech.[2]
5. Fragmentary sentences *("Privacy." "Sharing.")*.
6. Tag phrases used at the end of sentences, such as "XXXX, he thought." Or they are in parenthesis, after we have adjusted to reading the rest of the sentence as free indirect discourse.

It is not impossible to use free indirect discourse in nonfiction reporting, but it is more characteristic of fiction—and is frequently taken as a marker of fictionality. Use of this style for representing speech and thought develops through nineteenth-century fiction (possibly it is found earlier, though it is not common). It comes to play a key role in late nineteenth-century realism (in the work of George Moore and George Gissing, for example) and is then also central for the twentieth-century psychological novel.

Jane Austen often uses free indirect discourse, as in this passage from *Emma*:

> **Emma sat down to think and be miserable.—It was a wretched business, indeed!—Such an overthrow of every thing she had been wishing for!—Such a development of every thing most unwelcome!—Such a blow for Harriet!—That was the worst of all. Every part of it brought pain and humiliation, of some sort or other; but, compared with the evil to Harriet, all was light; and she would gladly have submitted to feel yet more mistaken—more in error—more disgraced by mis-judgment, than she actually was, could the effects of her blunders have been confined to herself.**
>
> (Jane Austen, *Emma*, 1816, vol. 1, chap. 16)

Austen's fictional world is one where relationships between a limited group of people are important, and there is not much lengthy description of place. The free indirect discourse is chiefly a way of recording how characters feel about each other (here, how Emma feels about Harriet), and of giving the subtle changes in feeling that characters do not articulate in public speech. Some phrases might be the narrator's ("every part of it brought pain and humiliation"); others give Emma's thoughts in the process of forming and articulating themselves ("more mistaken . . . in error . . . disgraced by mis-judgment"). The style allows the authorial narrator to seem self-effacing, to cut down on moralistic commentary and communicate a richer sense of the inner life of a character.

Because this style has been so important in modern fiction, linguists have been fascinated by the problem of how exactly it works. It has become clear that we cannot say whether we are looking at a piece of free indirect discourse when we examine an individual sentence in isolation: we read something as free indirect because it is in an appropriate context, where some of the characteristics listed above are found.[3] (If we isolate the sentence "She didn't want to be like her mother who was selfish" from the

Lessing passage, for example, it looks like a perfectly ordinary statement about the character's mental state, yet in its context it reads as free indirect discourse.)

Perhaps the most helpful way of understanding what goes on in free indirect discourse is Manfred Jahn's suggestion that it is a question of contextual "frames."[4] When we read a phrase or sentence, we always need to read it *as* something, to place it in some kind of contextual frame that indicates what kind of thing it is. In ordinary circumstances we stick with a frame as long as we can, but we shift into a new frame if the first one no longer works. This frame shifting is not something we do consciously; rather, it is a mental operation we perform to make sense of what is in front of us, analogous to the way in which we flash in and out of interpretations of certain ambiguous pictures (like the famous drawing that can be seen as a duck or a rabbit, but not a duck-rabbit, or the vase-face illusion, the two profiles that we can see either as separate faces or as a vase). In reading free indirect discourse, we shift in and out of three levels of frame: we take some statements as the character's own words or thoughts, some as the character's inarticulate perceptions, some as the summary of the narrator.

The examples so far have been of characters thinking, but free indirect discourse is also important for speech in novels. Mr. Skimpole describes himself to Esther in Dickens's *Bleak House*:

> . . . he must confess to two of the oddest infirmities in the world: one was, that he had no idea of time; the other, that he had no idea of money. In consequence of which he never kept an appointment, never could transact any business, and never knew the value of anything! Well! So he had got on in life, and here he was! He was very fond of reading the papers, very fond of making fancy-sketches with a pencil, very fond of nature, very fond of art. All he asked of society was, to let him live. *That* wasn't much. His wants were few.
>
> (Charles Dickens, *Bleak House*, (1852-53) 1853, chap. 6)

We have characteristic features of the style here (exclamations, third-person pronouns, deictics referring to the character), though in this case it is obviously close to theatrical monologue. The most important frame for reading is one that suggests this is a character's speech. But we can also flash into a frame that sees it as the narrator's quotation, since the speech comes within the narrative of Esther (who starts off, "I gathered from the conversation, that Mr Skimpole . . .") and the pronouns accord with such a frame ("he," "his").

Another way of seeing this flashing on and off of frames is, as Mieke Bal says, that "we have a form of interference between the narrator's text and the actor's text. Signals of the personal language situation of the actor and of the (im)personal language situation of the narrator cross."[5] Free indirect discourse above all gives us a novelistic style—the illusion of entering and recording other people's minds and mental processes. It is frequently used when the narrator does not agree with the character and where it represents antiphrasis or irony in the text.

Nonreflective Discourse

Ann Banfield suggests that one of the most important things free indirect discourse can do in a novel is to give us the nonreflective consciousness of the characters.[6] She explains this through the example of our thoughts when we step aside for a puddle. Something goes through our minds when we do so: if asked we might say, "I stepped aside because I did not want to get wet," but we did not actually clearly *say* anything to ourselves at the time we did it. Free indirect discourse can enter the mind at such moments, and allow the writer to suggest the processes of consciousness without pretending that we have the exact right words at our command. As Henry James put it in "Crapy Cornelia" (1909): "He had said to himself then, or had as good as said it" (201).

Banfield emphasizes how important it is that we are dealing with a written form of language. We can put on voices and imitate people in spoken language, but the complex frame shifting and the fruitful vagueness that we find in free indirect discourse need the written page.

Voice

It is tempting to see free indirect discourse as a way of representing different "voices" in fiction: the use of phrases that we can identify directly with characters suggests to some readers that characters' voices are somehow "emerging" through the text. Writers themselves sometimes talk about representing voices,[7] and it is one of the clichés of newspaper reviewing that we "hear the true voice of the writer" or "the wonderful range of voices of different characters." We must be careful, however, in talking about voices in fiction. In the first place, we should note that such voices are always a textual construct—they are not real presences recorded by the writer. Second, we should note that what we are given from a character does not have to try to imitate reality: writers are well able to suggest the individual consciousness of different characters without any real attempt to register verbal mannerisms. Henry James gives us the thoughts of the young child Maisie in *What Maisie Knew* (1897) through free indirect discourse, though no child could be imagined actually using the kind of sentences that James produces. Skimpole, in the passage quoted above, may seem Skimpole-ish, but his rhetoric (in particular his repetition) is very much like Dickens's own narratorial style. The flashing in and out of different frames in free indirect discourse is thus a key technique that represents speech and gives readers the illusion of "voice."

Part III

Narrative and Narrators

Edith Wharton starts off *Ethan Frome* (1911): "I had the story, bit by bit, from various people, and, as generally happens in such cases, each time it was a different story." Part III of this book is concerned with how stories like that in *Ethan Frome* are put together "bit by bit" and told—in other words, with problems of narrative and narrators.

We have already encountered some simple differences in narrators, when considering the incipits of novels. In this part we begin by considering what is meant by the term *narrative,* and how we can summarize narratives in novels. Paul Ricoeur points out that "a story . . . must be more than just an enumeration of events in serial order: it must organize them into an intelligible whole."[1] We look here at how narratives are organized, and consider conventional patterns of narrative, or plots.

Such considerations lead on inevitably to questions about who narrates—about the different types of narrators used in novels. If we are interested in what novels say, after all, we need to take note of how exactly the saying is done.

8

Narrative I

In looking at works of fiction, we are looking at narratives, and we need to have some sense of what that implies. Roland Barthes famously said that narratives are "international, transhistorical, transcultural": they are "innumerable," "simply there, like life."[1] It is certainly true that we constantly exchange narratives; we understand narratives told in other times and places, and narratives can cross cultural boundaries. We assume that narratives can transfer from medium to medium—from novel to film, or theater, or opera, or comic strip—though they will take different forms in different media.

We understand our lives, our history, and the world about us (including much of science) through narratives. What, then, do we mean by "narrative"? And how does this apply to the novel?

Fundamental Patterns

Narratives provide a way of structuring our accounts of the world. They concern events. But a narrative is not just a series of events (that would be a list or description). It is a series of events put together and *understood* in a certain way.

A narrative requires a state of affairs, which changes or transforms in some way. Because of this transformation, a narrative is always involved in one way or another with time. Narratives lead toward some goal, resolution, or closure.[2]

A narrative has to be told. Usually we expect a narrator to tell a narrative to a narratee, but the same person can perform both functions: given some events, we can tell narratives to ourselves. But we do not have to know who the narrator is to follow a story. Narratives can be told in a series of anonymous pictures, or by films.

The telling of a narrative means that events are linked by some kind of intentionality—they are not randomly placed. Narratives constantly involve problems of causality. They typically assume that the agents concerned have a consistent personal identity.

Events in a narrative may appear jumbled at first. Narratees understand narrative through an active process of recognizing, anticipating, making assumptions and hypotheses. Our involvement in this process—as readers, listeners, or spectators—depends on what David Bordwell calls "a central cognitive goal," "the construction of a more or less intelligible story."[3]

We can list some fundamental elements of narrative:

- A state of affairs
- Transformation
- Closure
- Intentionality
- Coherence

How does this apply to the novel? A novel does not contain only one narrative. Rather, it contains many interlocking narratives, which expand forward and backward as we proceed, and which suggest various possible closures. When we get to the end, we may feel that the narratives are linked in one convincing act of closure, though it is often more complex.

Narrative Expansion in the Novel

We can consider how narrative works by taking an example from the incipit of a novel by Henry Green:

> A country bus drew up below the church and a young man got out.
> This he had to do carefully because he had a peg leg.
>
> The roadway was asphalted blue.
>
> It was a summer day in England. Rain clouds were amassed back of a church tower which stood on rising round. As he looked up he noted well those slits, built for defence, in the blood coloured brick. Then he ran his eye with caution over cypresses and between gravestones. He might have been watching for a trap, who had lost his leg in France for not noticing the gun beneath a rose.
>
> (Henry Green, *Back*, 1946)

The first sentence of this passage gives one small narrative that could be read as complete: there is a state of affairs (the church and country bus), a transformation (the bus drew up), and closure (the man got out).

But the sentence is not given to us in isolation—it is part of a text. The state of affairs is expanded upon (we learn of the man's "peg leg," the "blue" road, the "summer day," and so forth), and there is further transformation as the man acts (he looks up, he runs his eye over things). Although we do not know the man's name or background, we assume it is the same man whose actions are described throughout, and that he has a personal identity.

So far the narrative is concerned with a succession of events on the summer's day, but the temporal frame expands to tell us that the man "had lost" his leg in a trap in France. Since he lost it from a gunshot wound, we guess it might have been in a war. (And the novel goes on shortly to confirm: "It was a time of war.")

The narrative has thus moved backward to explain the history of the man's leg. It has also begun to suggest expectations and forward movement: he "might have been watching for a trap." He is a man who watches for traps (or seems to be doing so). Are we to expect that he has enemies? Or are we to imagine that he will suffer from some kind of nervous state brought on by his war experience?

As practiced readers of narrative, we do not need to ask these questions consciously, but when we read the passage for its narrative, we are inevitably involved in a process of trying to sort out cues and integrate the information we are given—something we may, of course, do in a slightly different way every time we encounter the text.

Summarizing Narratives

When we come to the end of the novel, we can look back and sum up the narratives we have encountered in a simpler outline, leaving out speculation and sidetracks. On the cover of the paperback edition of *Back*, for example, we find the following blurb: "It is 1945. Charley Summers, back from the war in Europe, is home to mourn the death of his lover Rose who lies buried in the village churchyard. . . . Charley is so haunted by the death of Rose, whose image was his guiding light as he lay wounded in a prison camp, that he begins to imagine that her half-sister Nancy is not just like Rose, but is Rose herself." This summarizing narrative does not tell us what happens at the end of the novel (no doubt to entice prospective buyers), but it is typical of the attempts we constantly make to give outlines of narratives, including what we think most significant. It gives the basic situation, with a transformation and an event caused by the transformation. For the purposes of analysis we will need to summarize narrative, and we should be aware that there are various options when we do so.

Fabula and Suzjet

Narratologists talk of a narrative summary of the basic events placed in their *logical and chronological* order as a *fabula*.[4] When we give a summary with the events in the *actual order as found in the text,* it is referred to as the *suzjet*.

Samuel Beckett's character Watt is a storyteller who changes the order of events in a typical fashion: "As Watt told the beginning of his story, not first, but second, so not fourth, but third, now he told its end. Two, one, four, three, that was the order in which Watt told his story" (*Watt*, [1953], pt. 4). For the purposes of clarity we often want to summarize the narratives of complex works in chronological order. Thus, if Watt gave the fabula of his story, the order would be first, second, third, and fourth. In large-scale texts there is no one perfect way of performing this reordered summary of events: all readers will make different selections depending on their aims and abilities and the terms they use. We can make an analogy with court cases: there is no definitive account of what actually happened that could include all possible relevant details, but that does not prevent participants attempting one, or a verdict being given.[5]

Kernel and Satellite

It is often suggested that the summary of a narrative text needs to include narrative *kernels* (or key events.)[6] Kernels are moments when a particular path has been taken: they advance the plot and could not be omitted without changing the logic of a particular narrative. Texts also contain *satellite* events (people getting up, opening doors, and so forth), which are not essential. A distinction between kernels and satellites is useful to bear in mind (particularly when we are considering how a narrative has been transferred from the novel to the cinema or the theater), but it is not an absolute one. Watt as a storyteller has no trouble in deciding that his story needs "first," "second," "third," and "fourth," but most of us are less confident about which events to include. In general, our sense of kernels will depend on the kind of reading we are giving the text and the kind (or length) of summary we have in mind to make.

Fabula, suzjet, kernel, and *satellite* are general terms that can be used for outlines of narrative in any of its forms (in film, for example).[7] We are particularly concerned here, however, with narrative as it is realized in literary texts, and we therefore primarily need a terminology that draws attention to narrative as it emerges in the process of reading.

Plots

When we focus on the process of reading, the most useful concept is that which has traditionally been described by the term *plot* (Aristotle's *muthos*). To describe the plot of a novel is also to give a summary, but a summary that is related to certain familiar prototypical patterns (for example, the "marriage plot," or "murder-suspense plot"). A plot is more than a series of events, it is a series that may conform to (or deviate from) one or more prototypes, but it will in important respects be shaped by them.

Plot is not just an abstraction we can derive from a text, it is something that readers are concerned with as they read. From the reader's point of view it is, as Paul Ricoeur explains, "an operation, an integrative process," which comes to fruition as the story is told. It is "what makes a single story out of multiple incidents."[8] The need to trace a plot out of events draws readers on and is something we react to as we read a novel: in this sense it is the joint work of text and reader.

There are prototypical plots, which we can recognize in many cultures and in many historical periods; there are also fashions in plots. The kind of plot used in novels bears a relation to the current historical situation, including the conditions of publication at any time. This is not to say that writers simply adopt fashionable plots—rather, there is a constant dialectic in operation, in which the use of current plots goes along with a critique or ironic distancing from them.

Romance Plots versus Life-Stories

Much early prose fiction relies on romance plots—episodes of marvelous adventure and chivalry that confirm the traditional values of courtly society.[9] Romance plots demonstrate the bravery of knights and princes and the importance of chastity for women. They show how noble character is to be associated with aristocratic lineage and will emerge even when high-born children are lost or brought up in poverty.

An important step for the modern realist novel is the development of *antiromance*. This is a prose fiction that mocks or criticizes such plots (in a tradition starting with *Don Quixote* [1605–16]); it contrasts romance with "a familiar relation of such things, as pass every day before our eyes, such as may happen to our friend, or to ourselves."[10] Even while it is mocking romance plots, however, fiction may be influenced by them and use them. Realism becomes the dominant form of the novel in English, but there is always a counter-tradition in gothic or adventure novels, which sticks to the imaginative freedom of the romance plot. And even within the realist novel, romance plots surface often. For example, it is remarkably difficult to overcome the notion that somehow "breeding will out,"— so that a fascination with the true lineage of lost children shapes (even if it is questioned in) such novels as Dickens's *Oliver Twist* (1837–38), Anthony Trollope's *Doctor Thorne* (1858), Henry James's *The Princess Casamassima* (1886), or Philip Roth's *American Pastoral* (1997).

A plot that sets itself up in opposition to the romance is the "true history" of an individual life: "We speak of the story of a life to characterize the interval between birth and death."[11] The life-story, particularly in the form of spiritual biography, has been of outstanding importance in the tradition of the English novel, from *Robinson Crusoe* to *Jane Eyre, Marius the Epicurean* (1885), or *Portrait of the Artist as a Young Man*, and it even has its resonance with a contemporary novel like J. M. Coetzee's *Disgrace* (1999). The spiritual biography need not attempt to cover a full life, but often follows the pattern of "rebellion-punishment-repentance-deliverance."[12] Such stories may be obviously fictional, yet claim to tell essential truth: "I would . . . [I] could tell you more of these stories: True stories, that are neither *Lye* nor *Romance*" (John Bunyan, *The Life and Death of Mr Badman* [1680]).

Providential Plots

Robinson Crusoe, on his island, thinks about his repentance and deliverance:

> Before, as I walk'd about, either on my Hunting, or for viewing the Country; the Anguish of my Soul at my Condition, would break out upon me on a sudden, and my very Heart would die within me, to think of the Woods, the Mountains, the Desarts I was in; and how I was a Prisoner, lock'd up with the Eternal Bars and Bolts of the Ocean, in an uninhabited wilderness, without Redemption. . . .
>
> But now I began to exercise my self with new Thoughts; I daily read the Word of God, and apply'd all the Comforts of it to my present State: One Morning being very sad, I open'd the Bible upon these Words,

I will never, never leave thee, nor forsake thee; immediately it occur'd, That these Words were to me, Why else should they be directed in such a Manner, just at the Moment when I was mourning over my Condition, as one forsaken of God and Man?

(Daniel Defoe, *Robinson Crusoe*, 1719)

Robinson Crusoe gives us a life-story (based rather on the unity of the soul than on a coherent personal identity in the modern sense), but as we see in this passage, it also suggests a providential plot: Crusoe opens the Bible to find words that have been directed to him by God. He suffers, but can bear his suffering, because events have been ordained by providence for his final redemption.

Providential plots in the English novel allow many happy last chapters, when characters can look back and think that all their struggles were worthwhile (though there are also important counter-examples, like the last chapter of Thackeray's *Vanity Fair* [1847–48], when characters realize that providence wasn't on their side, and the struggle wasn't worth it after all). The process of the plot as it develops in providential narratives is not necessarily predictable: in the dynamic tension set up by text and reader there may be continuing uncertainties. We can't be sure of redemption until the very end. Moreover, novels do not simply offer one version of the way providence works. God may be seen as a divine weaver, planning and moving the events of the world at each stage, whose plans are incomprehensible unto the day of our salvation; but in another view God is a "divine watchmaker," who has created the world to function according to benign laws, and then sits back to let us get on with it.[13] Freedom and individual responsibility are always in a complex dialectic with the workings of providence.

The Marriage Plot

Perhaps the most familiar plot in the modern novel is the 'marriage plot': young people meet, suffer complications, and finally marry. This is famously the pattern of Jane Austen's novels, deriving many of its situations from dramatic comedy. Dramatic comedy traditionally shows the integration of young people into society through marriage, an ideal unification of private emotions and social roles, which gives promise of the renewal of life in future generations.

As we read *Pride and Prejudice,* we follow minor threads of narrative and their complications, but when we come to the end, Jane Bennet finally marries Bingley, Elizabeth Bennet finally marries Darcy. Jane Austen's marriage plots end happily for responsible young women in the property-owning classes. This does not mean that they follow a single pattern throughout: in the process of reading we encounter characters who are faced with very different possibilities. Fictional play and thought-experiment are obviously involved in what Jane Austen herself described as *working on* a small group of characters: conventional closure does not in itself determine the steps of the novel's plot.[14]

At the end of an Austen novel, however, the good girls *do* marry; at the end of a modern novel, such as those by Anita Brookner, they often do not. As we move forward in a Brookner novel, the plot leads us constantly toward Austen-like situations: marriage is what the heroines desire, and we are led to desire it for them. But looking back from the viewpoint of the ending, we can quite well see that marriage, after all, would have been an impossible risk and an unpleasant compromise.

Tragic Plots

Tragedy may also provide a plot for the novel, with the death of a hero or heroine as closure. As in tragic drama, we can find variations on the simple pattern: tragedies that are redemptive, like Samuel Richardson's *Clarissa* (1748–49), as well as those that are a cry of anguish against the contradictions of the modern social condition (like Hardy's *Jude the Obscure* [1896]), or against the unfairness of gender relations (like Elizabeth Bowen's *To the North* [1932]).

Money Plots

Plots that concern money are typical of the nineteenth-century novel: the desire to be noble becomes confused with and contrasted with the desire to be rich. Dickens famously shows that money is a kind of social poison destroying people's lives, and the capitalist system becomes a distribution of muck, based on criminality. Money plots are thus shaped by the features of capitalist society, but they are not so different from residual patterns of romance plots, since they so often deal with adventurous speculations, with inheritance or the miraculous discovery of lost heirs, and with ensuring that the morally upright characters end up happy, rich, and in positions of social superiority. Despite their attacks on capitalism, the last chapters of Dickens's novels generally allow the good people to make the best marriages, have enough money, and live happily ever after. George Gissing is unusual in that his novels quite often simply refuse to allocate the money and success where we want it (though they still encourage the reader to *desire* the money for favoured characters).

The Adultery Plot

Women's adultery provides another plot that can be traced back to romance, but that gains renewed force and energy in the novel of bourgeois life: a woman transgresses her marriage vows and must end with death, ruin, or exile.[15] (Husbands do not have to suffer quite the same fate: they are allowed to sow a few wild oats.) The ancient story (that, after all, of Clytemnestra, or Phaedra, or Guinevere) is reworked into modernity by novels like *Madame Bovary* (1857), *Anna Karenina* (1873–77), and Theodor Fontane's *Effie Briest* (1895). A popular English version is found in M. E. Braddon's *The Doctor's Wife* (1864), commonly said to be a "rewriting of *Madame Bovary.*" Braddon's heroine has a boring husband, falls in love with another man in the usual way, but doesn't actually commit adultery; her husband conveniently dies, and she ends up "useful, serene, almost happy, but very constant to the memory of sorrow . . . altogether different from the foolish wife who neglected all a wife's duties" (vol. 3, chap. 12). Readers have on the whole found Flaubert's version of the plot more profound.

Suspense and Curiosity Plots

Suspense and curiosity plots are typical of what Kathleen Tillotson calls the "novel-with-a-secret": "a secret of whose effects the reader is made aware just so far as to excite his continued curiosity, and which when finally disclosed should both surprise and gratify his expectations."[16] Suspense leads us on, but retards events in order to entice us forward. Curiosity, in contrast, leads us to want more information, usually about the causes of things in the past. Suspense is thus prototypically identified with the thriller, curiosity with the detective story.

Suspense and adventure are not new: they are found in romance and in the gothic novel. In the 1860s, however, the suspense plot moves into novels of contemporary life, and novelists refine their skills in working up the reader's curiosity—in effect, learning how to write narratives backward. Trollope said of Wilkie Collins that "before writing, [he] plans everything on, down to the minutest detail, from the beginning to the end; but then, plots it all back again, to see that there is no piece of necessary dove-tailing which does not dove-tail with absolute accuracy. The construction is most minute and most wonderful."[17]

The "sensation novel" of the 1860s generally employs secrets linked with crime: "fraud, bigamy, robbery and murder being the favourites."[18] This leads on to the modern detective and crime story. In such novels the working out of the details of plot becomes more important than an attempt to give depth of character, but we should be careful about separating such novels too firmly from classic realism. Although George Eliot spoke contemptuously of the "vulgar coercion of conventional plot,"[19] she (like both Dickens and Hardy) was influenced by the popularity of the sensation style, and included a suspense plot in, for example, *Felix Holt* (1866).

Interlocking Plots

The great realist novels of the nineteenth century often weave several prototypical plots into a rich social portrait—as in the four interlocking plots of George Eliot's *Middlemarch* (which contains versions of the money plot, the suspense and curiosity plot, the adultery plot, and the marriage plot).[20]

As Harry E. Shaw points out, it is a great mistake to identify the meaning or implication of texts with a conventional summary of their plots. Marriage, for example, can end many novels, but it can mean very different things in different texts. The implications of a plot develop only as it is textualized. Moreover, there is always more than one way to weave one's way through a heterogeneous text like a novel. The function of plot in the realist novel is to "energize our encounters," to "lend force to our imaginings." Realist plots, Shaw rightly says, are, for readers, "a matter of developing affect," or changing emotional response, not of "objective structural patterning."[21]

Modernist Epiphanies and Moments of Vision

If the nineteenth century is a period for the development of new and complex plots, it is also the period when the necessity for plots comes to seem "coercive" and to contradict the aims of realism. By the twentieth century this feeling of artificiality leads some modernists to reject obviously progressive plot patterns and focus simply on a chunk of time in ordinary lives—like the single day covered in Virginia Woolf's *Mrs Dalloway* (1925) or the morning in Saul Bellow's *Seize the Day* (1956).

If such novels simply listed events in their chunk of time, they would be descriptions, not narratives: but this is not the case. They remain teleological, oriented toward particular outcomes. Instead of marriage, money, and death, they move toward moments of intense experience and visionary understanding ("epiphanies" in James Joyce's terminology).[22]

In modernist epiphanies the focalizor pauses on an apparently simple and trivial event, allowing readers to project large-scale narratives onto it. A pause on such moments makes readers see the central or creative role of the consciousness, pulling the randomness of the universe briefly into shape. Thus, after the dinner party in Virginia Woolf's *To the Lighthouse*, Mr. and Mrs. Ramsay are alone together: he has been reading, she is standing by the window knitting a stocking. The depth of the Ramsays' married relationship has been emphasized in the novel, and here husband and wife both sense what is passing through the other's mind. Mr. Ramsay admires his wife, but wishes she would for once tell him that she loved him:

> But she could not do it; she could not say it. Then, knowing that he was watching her, instead of saying anything she turned, holding her stocking and looked at him. And as she looked at him she began to smile, for though she had not said a word, he knew, of course he knew, that she loved him. He could not deny it. And smiling she looked out of the window and said (thinking to herself, Nothing on earth can equal this happiness)—
>
> "Yes, you were right. It's going to be wet to-morrow." She had not said it, but he knew it. And she looked at him smiling. For she had triumphed again.
>
> (Virginia Woolf, *To the Lighthouse*, 1927, pt. I, chap. 19)

In terms of traditional plots, the event here is almost nonexistent: she smiles, looks though the window, and says something that has no connection to what they have been thinking. But in terms of events within consciousness there is a deep significance, since they have both communicated their feelings of married love.

At the same time, another narrative pattern found in the novel has suggested that Mrs. Ramsay, who appears to place herself in a secondary position to her husband, has in fact a deeper, stronger, female will. In this scene she has still refused to articulate her feelings, and has "triumphed again."

With regard both to the love the couple feel, and her strong will, the state of affairs has been transformed; we have been given a closure (though this will lead on to a *peripeteia*, or sudden change of direction in the plot, when Mrs. Ramsay dies unexpectedly in the next section of the novel).

The moment of epiphany is not just something we recognize, it is something we *understand*. The events of this moment are an affirmation of unity within the marriage, as well as an indication of the uncompromising triumph of Mrs. Ramsay. We could say that an apparently trivial event, which sounded like a narrative satellite, has become a narrative kernel. We could also say that a new change has been rung on the traditional marriage plot.[23]

9
Narrative II

If we accept that one of the chief ways in which readers consider the treatment of narrative in fiction will be through accounts of plot and the variants they encounter on the prototypes of plot, we have still to clarify what happens at a local level in the text. What options are available in organizing the narratives that will be read as contributing to the plot? And how are these narratives likely to be structured?

Hierarchy of Narratives

Within the text of a novel we often discover that there is a *hierarchy of narratives*. It is common to find narratives embedded in other narratives. The simplest form is where a *récit* is embedded in *discours*: the narrator starts by foregrounding the act of writing, the present situation, then proceeds to give us an *embedded narrative*, a *récit* set in the past.

Embeddings may also be a kind of digression, when the storyteller briefly abandons the main thread of narrative, usually to include a personal history told in the first person. This was conventional in the Spanish picaresque tradition, and was imported into the English novel in the eighteenth century. In Henry Fielding's *Tom Jones* (1749) two of the characters come across an old man who is known as "The Man of the Hill," and Tom Jones asks him to tell his life-story. The narrator says: "The gentleman then, without any farther preface, began as you may read in the next chapter" (bk. 8, chap. 1). And off we go on a digression for four chapters. The Man of the Hill's story can be related thematically to the main narrative, but nonetheless is a break in the narrative, and such embeddings came to seem old-fashioned and artificial to nineteenth-century novelists. Trollope thought that episodes of this kind "distract the attention of the reader and always do so disagreeably."[1]

Frame Narratives

A more obviously significant use of embedded narrative is found in novels that open with a first narrator, who then gives us a narrative as told by another narrator, which constitutes the main intrigue of the novel. Sometimes the narrator introduces letters or journals; sometimes he or she is described as listening to a long account given by the second narrator. Emily Brontë's *Wuthering Heights* (1847) starts with the city-dweller Lockwood, who makes a visit to the farm of Wuthering Heights. Lockwood wants to hear what the story of the place is, so listens to the narrative of the housekeeper, Nelly Dean, about the inhabitants, and this narrative includes the story most often considered central to the novel, of Heathcliff and Cathy. Lockwood's opening narrative can be imagined as a kind of picture-frame around the Heathcliff narrative, and is thus called a *frame narrative*.

The process by which one narrative is embedded in another has been compared to those carved ivory boxes where we can look through one box to see another (and perhaps even further boxes) inside, and such novels are thus often said to have a Chinese-box narrative structure.

In the case of *Wuthering Heights*, one of the most striking things about the Chinese-box structure is the care of the planning. Critics have established that Emily Brontë must have worked out a complex (and almost maliciously confusing) scheme of family relations through several generations. The intricate patterns of repetition, as Dorothy Van Ghent pointed out in her classic essay on the novel, stand in opposition to the immoderate excesses of the central characters.[2] The framework of embedded narratives is not a digression here, but integral to our readings of the novel.

To talk in this way of texts as "embedded" or "framed" is to project spatial metaphors onto them, and to do so is misleading if it suggests we can actually hold the whole text in a single focus, as we do in looking at a picture. Some kind of metaphorical projection, however, is necessary in order for any discussion to take place, and spatial metaphors retain an important clarifying and mnemonic function in discussion of texts.

Order, Duration, and Frequency

When we try to analyze how a narrative is conducted in particular sections of a novel, we can use the convenient categories formulated by Gérard Genette: order, duration, and frequency.[3]

Order

Narratives often come to us in disordered sequence, but we sort them out as we proceed and gain a sense of coherence and intelligibility (if we are able to consider them as narratives). The events described may be continuous or discontinuous. If continuous, they may be described in the order in which they are supposed to take place; but more frequently they will be given in such an order as to subvert our expectations. As the tyro novelist says in Trollope's *The Three Clerks* (1857), "You must always begin with an incident now, and then hark back for your explanation and description; that's what the editor says is the great secret of the present day" (chap. 19). Discontinuity can be produced either by an interruption, which forces the narrative to stop and continue later, or by suggestions of anticipation and the creation of suspense.

If we are often presented with disorder, the reordering and adjustment of events is something we perform almost automatically as readers, as part of the general struggle to understand. We use, as Paul Ricoeur says, "narrative intelligence," which is closer to practical wisdom and moral judgment than to reason or science.[4]

Reordering itself can become a major topic of a narrative. In Conan Doyle's fictions, for example, new information is provided piecemeal, in such a way as to stimulate and then satisfy our curiosity. A clarification of the order of events is necessary to understand what has happened and, according to Sherlock Holmes, depends on being able to "reason analytically." Holmes says to his friend Watson:

> Now let me endeavour to show you the different steps in my reasoning. To begin at the beginning. I approached the house, as you know, on foot, and with my mind entirely free from all impressions. I naturally began by examining the roadway, and there, as I have already explained to you, I saw clearly the marks of a cab, which, I ascertained by inquiry, must have been there during the night.
>
> (Arthur Conan Doyle, *A Study in Scarlet*, (1887) 1888, chap. 7)

The "showing" of the steps of reasoning provides one narrative here; the narrator begins "at the beginning" and goes on from there. Another narrative is provided by events on the night of the murder in London, when Holmes first examined the roadway and saw "the marks of a cab": we might say this second narrative is embedded in the first. The narrative of the actual murder (a third sequence of events, which took place before the visit of Holmes) will also be embedded in the description as we go along. And if we read the full text of *A Study in Scarlet*, there is a further embedded narrative in a long analepse (so long as to displace the primary narrative) that loops back to the history of the "Great Alkali Plain" in the United States, and tells us about Utah and the Mormons. This Utah narrative explains the motive of the murderer, and therefore gives a large-scale explanatory narrative to project onto events in London. It is typical of the detective genre that the process of sorting out is the test of whether it has been a good detective story or not. (The question of whether the details along the way are plausible is only of secondary interest.)

Duration

The telling time of a narrative is not the same as the time a narrative covers. It is true that some narratives move swiftly and some seem to slow down to what we imagine as the pace of writing or authorial speech. In *discours* we may even have the illusion that the story is bringing us there, as it is all happening, but that is an effect produced by tricks of style. Fielding's *Shamela*, which parodies the epistolary novel, portrays Shamela writing as things take place:

> Mrs. Jervis and I are just in bed, and the door unlocked; if my master should come—Odsbobs! I hear him just coming in at the door. You see I write in the present tense, as Parson Williams says. Well, he is in bed between us, we both shamming a sleep; he steals his hand into my bosom, which I, as if in my sleep, press close to me with mine, and then pretend to awake.—I no sooner see him, but I scream out to Mrs. Jervis, she feigns likewise but just to come to herself; we both begin, she to becall, and I to bescratch very liberally.
>
> (Henry Fielding, *Shamela*, 1741, letter 6)

The joke here relies on Shamela using the epistolary style, with verbs in an impossible present tense.[5] She couldn't actually be writing this while her master is in bed with her, and while she is pretending to be asleep. What we read, however, is not entirely nonsensical, because in ordinary conversation we often tell narratives using the present tense ("And then he does this, and then I say this to him, and then he tells me . . ."). Shamela's account highlights the disjunction of writing time and described time.

There are also some *meta-narratives,* in which writers discuss the problems of writing (and what we are actually reading). Jacques Roubaud begins his *Great Fire of London*:

> **This morning of 11 June 1985 (it's five o'clock), while writing this on the scant space left free by the papers on my desktop, I hear passing, in the Rue des Francs-Bourgeois, two floors below on my left, a delivery van . . . while I was listening to the sound of voices and crates, the previous moment has just invisibly ebbed, intense with anguish and hesitation over starting to write this piece in lines that will be black, composed in minute, close-packed letters, without deletions, regrets, reflection, imagination, impatience, promising nothing but their ensured existence line after line on the page of the notebook in which I am writing them.**
>
> (Jacques Roubaud, *The Great Fire of London*, [1989]
> trans. D. Di Bernandi, (1991))

This is *discours,* and the writing process is conjured up for us, but it is also a kind of elaborate game, done as if to persuade us that Roubaud's own writing does not involve the usual forms of artifice. In fact, it has had to be processed in various ways before it is published (and, in this case, translated), and then it may be read in different ways and at a different speed by every reader. There are so many imponderables involved in the transitions between writing and reading (such as speed of thinking, speed of articulating, speed of getting pen to paper, speed of reading), that we must acknowledge radical and incalculable differences between writing time, story time, and reading time.

Changes in Narrative Pace

What we can see more clearly is that there are bound to be changes in pace in narrative in a long text. Again Genette gives us a helpful framework. He suggests that there are two extremes: *ellipsis,* when the narrative jumps over time and leaves things out, and *pause,* when the narrative in effect stops, to dwell slowly on something like a description or comment by the narrator. Between these two extremes we have the categories of *summary* (when the narrative moves swiftly over a period of time) and *scene* (when a scene is presented through dialogue and thus seems to us much as in real life). These changes can be placed in order as:

- ellipsis
- summary
- scene
- pause

Ellipsis

It is inevitable that there will be some ellipses in the narrative of a novel.[6] An ellipsis is a gap in the narrative and, as Meir Sternberg says of literary texts in general, they "may be conceived of as a dynamic system of gaps."[7]

Sternberg points out that a text may contain temporary or permanent gaps. When we read M. E. Braddon's *Lady Audley's Secret*, we may wonder what Lady Audley has been doing in her youth: we finally find out. We would like to know who Tom Jones's mother is, and we duly find out. But there is a permanent gap in Thackeray's *Vanity Fair*, for example, so that we never know whether Becky Sharp really murdered Jos Sedley. Similarly, we never learn whose footprint it was that Robinson Crusoe saw on the sand on his island.

No text can be absolutely exhaustive in the details it provides—and we are used to filling in gaps automatically. As cognitive linguists remind us, we constantly make inferences in using language, filling in scripts and event sequences.[8] When a character in a novel walks into a restaurant and buys lunch for a friend, we don't have to be told that they both sit down at a table, or that the waiter comes and shows them the menu.

The filling in of gaps is sometimes automatic, sometimes conscious (as when we puzzle our way through a detective story), and sometimes impossible or confusing. We can take the example of two narrative sequences about a visit to a restaurant:

1. John went into a restaurant. He asked the waitress for coq au vin. He paid the bill and left.
2. John went into a restaurant. He saw a waitress. He got up and went home.[9]

The first narrative sequence makes a comprehensible story, while the second is confusing. F. Ungerer and H.-J. Schmid suggest that the first fits "our internalized script" of a meal in a restaurant, while the second doesn't. Apparently, even in the first case, it is not necessary to mention actually eating the meal.

In terms of literary analysis, we can confidently expect that the system of a novel will contain gaps, and that they will not necessarily be obvious on a first reading. In re-reading the text, it becomes part of our fuller experience to note gaps, not just to try and fill them in, but to observe what is being done with them.

Novelists sometimes draw attention to them. Chapter 10 of *Jane Eyre* begins with a rather awkward maneuver:

> **Hitherto I have recorded in detail the events of my insignificant exist-ence: to the first ten years of my life, I have given almost as many chapters. But this is not to be a regular autobiography: I am only bound to invoke memory where I know her responses will possess some de-gree of interest; therefore I now pass a space of eight years almost in silence: a few lines only are necessary to keep up the links of connec-tion.**
>
> (Charlotte Brontë, *Jane Eyre*, 1847)

The flow of narrative events is obviously not preserved here. As so often with *Jane Eyre*, however, it could be said the slight awkwardness is a way of adding to the effect of authenticity that makes the novel so powerful.

Summary

An alternation between summary and scene is fundamental to the novel. Scenes are often more exciting, and we are drawn to them as readers, but summary is functionally important and may be just as rewarding for analysis.

The ending of Flaubert's *Sentimental Education* provides a classic example of effective summary. Most of the novel has moved at an agonizingly slow pace through all the details of a love affair that never comes to anything, filling in the context of young people's lives in all the complexity of Parisian society, at a moment when history is stalled and confused. In the last two chapters, the novel suddenly changes pace: it takes off, and goes through the rest of Frédéric's life with extraordinary speed:

He travelled.

He came to know the melancholy of the steamboat, the cold awakening in the tent, the tedium of landscapes and ruins, the bitterness of interrupted friendships.

He returned.

He went into society and he had other loves. But the ever-present memory of the first made them insipid; and besides, the violence of desire, the very flower of feeling, had gone. His intellectual ambitions had also dwindled. Years went by; and he endured the idleness of the mind and the inertia of his heart.

(Gustave Flaubert, *Sentimental Education*, 1869,
trans. R. Baldick, pt. 3, chap. 6)

The passage echoes the start of the novel, since the first apparition of Madame Arnoux, which led to Frédéric's love for her, was on a steamboat, but the change of pace against the rest of the novel, and the changes within the passage, are remarkable. Short flat sentences cover huge stretches of time: "He travelled"; "He returned." Longer ones do not summarize events so much as emotions, to suggest the tedium of Frédéric's useless journeys, and the fading intensity of his desires. We have learned that what matters to Frédéric may seem totally inconsequential to outsiders. Now it seems that nothing much matters to Frédéric: there is a devastating flatness in "He went into society and he had other loves." These last chapters give us the sense of a spiraling vortex of negativity, the coming of old age, the "idleness of the mind," and the eventual "inertia" of the heart. Summary here is not just reporting on events, it is an active part of thematic development.

Summary: Adventure, and Romance

In novels of adventure, summary needs to be not just brisk but actually exciting. Robert Louis Stevenson, deliberately situating his writing in opposition to realism, draws on the freedoms of the romance plot to focus on extraordinary events. His summary is necessary to pull readers into an unfamiliar fictional world. In *The Master of Ballantrae* the two first chapters are overtly called "Summary of Events." The problem Stevenson has set himself is that of twisting together narratives of the lives of two brothers (the Master of Ballantrae and his brother Henry) who have parallel and opposite careers after fighting on different sides in the Jacobite Rebellion of 1745. Their stories are told largely through the account of an old servant of the house of Ballantrae, who describes how the brothers fought a duel, in which the Master was wounded and then taken on board ship to France:

> It was near six months before we even knew for certain that the man survived; and it was years before I learned from one of Crail's men, turned publican on his ill-gotten gain, some particulars which smack to me of truth. It seems the traders found the Master struggled on one elbow, and now staring round him, and now gazing at the candle, or at his hand, which was all bloodied, like a man stupid. Upon their coming, he would seem to have found his mind, bade them carry him aboard, and hold their tongues; and on the captain asking how he had come in such a pickle, replied with a burst of passionate swearing and incontinently fainted. They held some debate, but they were momently looking for a wind, they were highly paid to smuggle him to France, and did not care to delay. Besides which, he was well enough liked by these abominable wretches: they supposed him under capital sentence, knew not in what mischief he might have got his wound, and judged it a piece of good-nature to remove him out of the way of danger. So he was taken aboard, recovered on the passage over, and was set ashore a convalescent at the Havre de Grace.
>
> (R. L. Stevenson, *The Master of Ballantrae*, 1889, chap. 5)

The impersonation of the long-winded narrator provides part of the interest here, but the passage also shows extremely clever manipulations of time. Mentions of "six months" and "years" at the start make us aware that this summary is going to cover a substantial period; then Stevenson moves us back in an analepse to the duel scene, and picks out the image of the Master lying "bloodied" on the ground, "now," "gazing at the candle." The scene is developed and the motives of the men described, then suddenly we are jumped, in one sentence, onto the ship, the journey to France and recovery from the wound in France. We thus move with great speed from image to image. H. G. Wells wrote about Stevenson's novel that he could not forget the "succession of pictures" of "flaring candles" in *The Master of Ballantrae*.[10] The candle here presumably gave one such picture.

Summary: Social Depth

Thackeray's *Vanity Fair* shows summary moving in a different way to cover various levels of public and private history. Thackeray has several narrative threads running at the same time, and the aim is to give a cross-section of fashionable English society against the background of European history.

[I]n the month of March, Anno Domini 1815, Napoleon landed at Cannes, and Louis XVIII fled, and all Europe was in alarm, and the funds fell, and old John Sedley was ruined.

We are not going to follow the worthy old stockbroker through those last pangs and agonies of ruin through which he passed before his commercial demise befel. They declared him at the Stock Exchange; he was absent from his house of business: his bills were protested: his act of bankruptcy formal. The house and furniture of Russell Square were seized and sold up, and he and his family were thrust away, as we have seen, to hide their heads where they might.

John Sedley had not the heart to review the domestic establishment who have appeared now and anon in our pages, and of whom he was now forced by his poverty to take leave. The wages of those worthy people were discharged with that punctuality which men frequently show who only owe in great sums—they were sorry to leave good places—but they did not break their hearts at parting from their adored master and mistress. Amelia's maid was profuse in condolences, but went off quite resigned to better herself in a genteeler quarter of the town.

(W. M. Thackeray, *Vanity Fair*, (1847–48), no. 5, chap. 18)

In the first sentence we move rapidly through great disasters of European history to the individual ruin of John Sedley. We might expect the ruin to be described in detail, but the narrator is not going to do so: what he gives is rapid summary, moving from public sphere (the Stock Exchange) to private sphere (John Sedley and his servants). Thackeray refuses to be sentimental in the conventional Victorian way: John Sedley has been a good employer, he has punctiliously paid his servants even when ruined. The servants are moderately sorry, but they do not "break their hearts": they are pleased to get some money from him and go off to jobs in a "genteeler quarter" of the town. It could not be claimed that *Vanity Fair* gives a complete cross-section of society, but this rapid shift from hearing about "all Europe" to the question of John Sedley's servants moving to a genteeler quarter of town gives an impression of social depth and historical scope that we have come to identify with classic nineteenth-century realism.

Scene

Seymour Chatman appositely says that "scene is the encorporation of the dramatic principle into narrative."[11] The difference from drama is that scene is framed by narrative in the novel, and that rapid changes of setting can be made within a novelistic scene. It is not always easy to say exactly where the limits or boundaries of a scene are. In one sense, a scene is just an extended passage of dialogue, but in most novels dialogue is both framed and interrupted by narrative or description.

In the late nineteenth century emphasis on scenes became an important way of cutting out moralizing narrators and their comments. Henry James, in writing *The Awkward Age* (1899), wanted to stop "going behind" the scene to the "storyteller's great property-shop of aids to illusion," to avoid "explanations and amplifications." He decided to use the form of "the successive Acts of a Play" and aimed at "really constructive dialogue, dialogue organic and dramatic, speaking for itself, representing and embodying substance and form."[12]

Scenes need not be single units in a novel, they can be blended together and interwoven, juxtaposed with other scenes, in what George Moore calls "fugal treatment."[13] In Moore's *A Drama in Muslin*, for example, there is a complex double scene that not only contributes to the marriage plot but also describes developments in the social situation in Ireland, a major topic of the novel.

Moore's scene is set in and around an Irish "Big House." Inside the house, Mrs. Barton tells Captain Hibbert that she will not allow him to make an offer of marriage for her daughter, because she wants a richer husband. Mr. Barton is outside on the lawn, negotiating rents with his tenant farmers. The whole complexity of the Irish social situation is represented by this disjunction between inside and outside.

We start off with Mrs. Barton, who wraps up her speeches in compliments: "There is, of course, no one whom I should prefer to *le beau capitaine*—there is no one to whom I would confide Olive more willingly." The pace slows as information is added about the Captain's looks: "The eyebrows were contracted, the straight white nose seemed to grow straighter, and he twirled his moustache angrily." The Captain and Mrs. Barton confront each other, and Mrs. Barton says:

"We are living on the brink of a precipice. We do not know what is, and what is not, our own. The Land League is ruining us, and the Government will not put it down; this year the tenants may pay at twenty per cent. reduction, but next year they may refuse to pay at all. Look out there; you see they are making their own terms with Mr. Barton."

"I should be delighted to give you thirty per cent. if I could afford it," said Mr. Barton, as soon as the question of reduction, that had been lost in schemes for draining, and discussion concerning bad seasons, had been re-established, "but you must remember that I have to pay charges, and my creditors won't wait any more than yours will."

(George Moore, *A Drama in Muslin*, 1886, chap. 7)

The switch between the inside and outside of the house is sudden and even disorienting. Mrs. Barton says, "Look out there" (that is, on the lawn), and we jump to Mr. Barton's speech: "I should be delighted to give you thirty per cent." Only after the scene on the lawn has opened does the narrative feed in a quick analeptic summary, to let us know what has been going on outside while Mrs. Barton has been talking. The farmers in the garden refuse to accept Mr. Barton's offer, and begin to move off, while Mrs. Barton watches. The confrontation between inside and outside is briefly internalized in her consciousness; she wants to listen to what her husband is saying, and is not concentrating on Captain Hibbert:

She could see that some new and important point was being argued; and it was with a wrench she detached her thoughts from the pantomime that was being enacted within her view, and, turning to Captain Hibbert, said:

"You see, you see what is happening; we are, that is to say, we may be, ruined at any moment."

(George Moore, *A Drama in Muslin*, 1886, chap. 7)

How long are we to suppose these reflections on her part have taken? There is no particular indication of the extent of the pause. From the statement "She could see that some new and important point was being argued" we gather that she has not heard all the conversation going on outside—so our rough assumption is that the conversations inside and outside are going on at the same time. Through Moore's technique we are, in effect, able to imagine two scenes of private life and public life continuing together, linked by the financial concerns and family interests of Mr. and Mrs. Barton.

To the modern reader this kind of effect may seem comparable to techniques of cutting that have become familiar in film narrative. The fact that the novel can change pace so rapidly, can shift backward and forward, and can suggest simultaneity, as Moore does, however, means even more narrative complexity than can be achieved on film.

Pause

A pause in the progress of the narrative is a chance for the novelist to introduce some description, or a reflection on themes of the novel, or a comment on general topics. From a superficial point of view we might say that pauses are what many readers skip—they want to get on with the narrative. There is a long-standing association with tedious page-filling. Publishers in the nineteenth century demanded that novels run to three volumes, and pages of general reflection were a useful way of filling space. "All fashionable historians stop to make reflections," says a character in Maria Edgeworth's *Belinda* (1801), "supposing that no one else can have the sense to make any" (chap. 3). Henry James complained that "the English novel has come in general to mean a ponderous, shapeless, diffuse piece of machinery, 'padded' to within an inch of its life."[14]

But pauses are not always padding. As Meir Sternberg points out, retardation is a highly significant part of the technique of narration. Narratives become more interesting, more capable of stimulating suspense, as they frustrate our desire to get to the end. The Russian formalist Viktor Shklovsky talked of the "staircase construction" of narrative—a staircase that has also been described as "less like an elevator than a spiral staircase which, littered with toys, dog leashes, and open umbrellas, impedes our progress."[15]

The role of retardation in narrative is easily recognized when we consider how film narrative works, but there are interesting differences between the role of retardation in film and in the novel. The viewers of a film cannot skip, they are forced to sit through retardatory material. Moreover, they cannot usually review material, so they must be able to keep the main narrative in mind even when retardatory material is being used.

Sternberg points out that retardatory structure "relates directly to the temporal nature and potentialities of literary art." It need not just be description or authorial commentary, it can also take the form of a shift to an analogical scene, or "syntactic or stylistic tortuousness" that slows things down.[16] Retardation is an important technique, but it is also one in which authors must make fine judgments and indicate their assessment of their audience. There is, after all, a stage at which many readers will consider that the pause is too long, and the process has become tedious. It may reflect the authority of a writer that he or she feels able to intervene with comments. It may also reflect a certain courage, and the desire to challenge the limitations of art, when a writer like Beckett uses his style to produce endless delays—retardations that threaten the emergence of any narrative at all. "Raise your point for the love of God," says Mr. Fitzwein in the endless committee meeting that Arthur recounts in the middle of Beckett's *Watt*, "and let me get home to my wife. He added, And children. The point I was in the act of raising, said Mr. O'Meldon, when I was so rudely interrupted, was this, that if in the left-hand column, or column of roots . . ." and so forth, for three more pages until Arthur "seemed to tire" of his story, and as for Watt, "it tired him, in the end, and he was glad when Arthur left off, and went away" ([1953], pt. 3). Most readers will have lost track of the point long before: retardation itself has become the chief subject matter here.

In the classic realist novel, however, it is the pause for interjected commentary that is most noticeable, and it may be an important adjunct to narrative, indicating to the reader how the narrative fits into a general picture of the world.

Meta-narrative

A pause in the narrative may provide an opportunity for the narrator to comment on the fictionality of the text itself, and on the techniques that are being used. Laurence Sterne defends his own methods in the middle of *Tristram Shandy*:

> **Digressions, incontestably, are the sun-shine;—they are the life, the soul of reading;—take them out of this book for instance,—you might as well take the book along with them;—one cold eternal winter would reign in every page of it; restore them to the writer;—he steps forth like a bridegroom,—bids All hail; brings in variety, and forbids the appetite to fail.**
>
> (Laurence Sterne, *Tristram Shandy*, 1759-67, vol. 1, chap. 22)

Pauses of this kind are an affront to realism: they discourage the assumption that a novel can be a transparent record of real life. But Sterne is, broadly speaking, right: in any long narrative, readers need shifts of scale, perspective, and pace: pauses and digressions are the "life of reading." What is particularly striking here is how (in the phrase of Russian formalist criticism) Sterne "lays bare the device." He establishes a special relationship between reader and text that is typical of the artwork—and that constitutes a form of defamiliarization.[17]

Frequency

If narratives tell us about sequences of events or actions, then a question must arise about how many times these sequences have taken place. The narrative recounts something. Are we reading about single events? Or is the narrative iterative (that is, telling us once about events that have happened many times)? Is the sequence of events recalled or repeated during the course of the novel? In other words, what is the frequency of the narrative sequences?

In talking of frequency, we are concerned with repetition in texts. Gérard Genette reminds us that repetition itself is a "mental construction." Our decision to say that something is repeated is made when we choose to ignore many factors, and consider a series of events "only in terms of their resemblance."[18]

By focusing on frequency in our analysis, we observe how a text deepens, extends, and makes complex its picture of the world. Realism, in particular, uses iterative narration to make events seem customary and ordinary, and then creates opposition to the customary with dramatic developments. Iterative narration (to suggest time passing) becomes the frame for a dramatic scene. Thus, in *Great Expectations*, Pip recounts that:

> I NOW fell into a regular routine of apprenticeship-life, which was varied beyond the limits of the village and the marshes, by no more remarkable circumstance than the arrival of my birthday and my paying another visit to Miss Havisham. I found Miss Sarah Pocket still on duty at the gate, I found Miss Havisham just as I had left her, and she spoke of Estella in the very same way, if not in the very same words. The interview lasted but a few minutes, and she gave me a guinea when I was going, and told me to come again on my next birthday. I may mention at once that this became an annual custom.

> (Charles Dickens, *Great Expectations*,
> (1860–61) 1861, vol. 1, chap. 17)

This is from the start of a chapter, and it establishes the "routine" of Pip's life, so that we can move gradually from his childhood to adolescence. It includes events, but the events mentioned are repeated ones: his birthday, the regular visits to Miss Havisham, and the annual custom of receiving a guinea. The repeated phrases ("I found Miss Sarah Pocket," "I found Miss Havisham," "in the very same way," "in the very same words") underline the repetitiveness of events. From another point of view, Pip's life would not have seemed repetitive (no two birthdays are really alike, and his visits to Miss Havisham could have been seen as a break in his work routine), but the process of mental construction selects and foregrounds routine in this part of his life.

Time—both years and minutes—is reduced to repetitive sequence for Pip, and connected in the following paragraph to his feelings about Miss Havisham's house, where he feels time has actually stopped. There is an opposition, however, between Pip himself and this world of repetition in which he lives: the narrative shifts slowly to singular events, as "imperceptibly" Pip becomes conscious of observing change in a young woman, Biddy. Slow changes are mentioned in her appearance, and then we read: "she had not been with us more than a year . . . when I observed to myself one evening that she had curiously thoughtful and attentive eyes." Once "one evening" is specified, we have reached a particularized moment, and can move into a dramatic scene which will push the narrative rapidly forward.

The shifts in frequency in *Great Expectations* may seem simply natural to most readers; they draw on conventional contrasts between boredom and excitement that we all use constantly in recounting events. But in a long narrative of this kind, such shifts also represent decisions made by the writer. Choices have to be made about where to stop, where to pause or recapitulate. Dickens's skill as a novelist may be seen from the seeming naturalness of the shifts and how they suggest the contrast between passing and stopped time, which is one of the central themes of his novel.

Frequency: Modernist Experiment

Frequency is naturalized in *Great Expectations*, and we follow the novel without effort, as though its organization were how it "really happened." Modernists feel the need to reveal to us that all is not so simple. Gertrude Stein, for example, in *Ida*, refuses to accept conventional patterns of repetition:

So Ida settled down in Washington. This is what happened every day.

Ida woke up. After a while she got up. Then she stood up. Then she ate something. After that she sat down.

That was Ida.

And Ida began her life in Washington. In a little while there were more of them there who sat down and stood up and leaned. Then they came in and went out. This made it useful to them and to Ida.

(Gertrude Stein, *Ida*, 1941, pt. 4)

We expect certain repeated events in novels: we often hear of characters waking up, and getting up—but we do not usually hear about them standing up regularly (though no doubt they do), or leaning, and we may wonder why Ida should sit down *after* eating (perhaps "sat down" is a shorthand way of saying "took a rest"). The narrative satellites seem to be obscuring any possible narrative kernels. "That was Ida," we are told, after the superficially simple but confusing list of events. We can hardly think it sums up Ida: and sure enough, the text promptly begins all over again with her "life in Washington."

Repetition in most texts would establish what "it" and "them" might refer to, but Stein tantalizes us by leaving the denominations out. Frequency has become an area of play and experiment. We have a series of events (or perhaps nonevents) that we struggle unsuccessfully to fit into appropriate narrative contexts. It all seems like a narrative, and may be a life-story, but it is extraordinarily difficult to integrate into a plot.

10

Narrators

Some aspects of the narrator's role have already come up in discussion of the incipit (see chapter 1). Proceeding with analysis of a novel, we need to distinguish between different kinds of narrator that are likely to emerge, the ways in which they can be developed, and their involvement with narrative.

We may start this analysis by asking a fundamental question: Is the narrator included as a character in the main narrative? Or is the narrator an authorial narrator, at a different narrative level from the main fictional narrative?

Protagonist Narrators

If the narrator is included as a character in the narrative he or she is telling, we should consider how large a role this character plays in the developing novel. Is the narrator the central figure, or *protagonist*? Are we reading a fictional autobiography?[1]

The incipit of J. D. Salinger's *The Catcher in the Rye* uses first-person pronouns and a protagonist narrator in the foreground:

> If you really want to hear about it, the first thing you'll probably want to know is where I was born, and what my lousy childhood was like, and how my parents were occupied and all before they had me, and all that David Copperfield kind of crap, but I don't feel like going into it. In the first place, that stuff bores me, and in the second place, my parents would have about two haemorrhages apiece if I told anything

pretty personal about them. They're quite touchy about anything like that, especially my father. They're *nice* and all—I'm not saying that— but they're also touchy as hell. Besides, I'm not going to tell you my whole goddam autobiography or anything.

(J. D. Salinger, The Catcher in the Rye, 1951)

This narrator denies that he is going to tell his "goddam autobiography" (later he says that he will just "tell you about this madman stuff that hap- pened to me around last Christmas"), but there is no doubt that what develops in the novel is a narrative about recent episodes in his own life, with the overall shape of an autobiography.

Although we are not given a conventional character self-portrait, we quickly pick up hints of the narrator's individual characteristics. We gather that he comes from a fairly literate background, since he has read *David Copperfield*, but that he is in rebellion against this kind of literacy, since he thinks the novel "crap." He rejects, or perhaps does not know how to produce, a formal literary style, and uses loosely structured sentences, in- cluding colloquial redundancies ("kind of," "and all," "or anything"). What he tells us here already reveals that he is young, still in awe of his parents, and yet trying to show a rather unconvincing independence from polite adult conventions by using slang ("crap," "touchy as hell").

Our sense of this narrator's character thus emerges rapidly, and we may imagine that he shares certain features with J. D. Salinger (in his youth), though it seems unlikely that author and narrator can be identified di- rectly. We can believe readily enough that a protagonist/narrator of this kind might feel a need to tell his story: but telling a story is one thing, and having the confidence and self-discipline necessary to construct a novel (let alone the skill to pace and organize the narrative) is quite another. There is something *faux naif* about the self-presentation of the young boy narrator, and we can have little doubt that he is an impersonation and a fully dramatized narrator.[2]

Distance

A further question that naturally arises is: What distance is there between the dramatized narrator and the narrative he tells?[3]

In works like *Jane Eyre* and *David Copperfield* there is an adult narrator telling us about details of childhood; in *The Catcher in the Rye* we have a young narrator telling us about his recent past. In none of these cases does the ability to recall past events in extended detail conform to the way memory actually works, but the dramatization comes closer to what might be imagined as recorded oral autobiography in *The Catcher in the Rye*.

The problem of distance also leads us to consider whether the narrator is trying to present us with his or her feelings as they actually were in the past. Or is the narrator now elaborating on *present* feelings about what took place? For some novelists of first-person narratives—Marcel Proust, for example, or George Gissing in *The Private Papers of Henry Ryecroft* (1903)—the whole point of recalling the past is to use it as a source for present reflection. Proust can't resist interrupting his account of Marcel kissing Albertine with some reflections on the recent art of photography. In the case of Salinger's novel, the narration and the events described are close in time, and the point seems rather to present the crisis of youth in the most vivid fashion possible.

Unreliable Narrators

Dramatized narrators draw on our associations of a narrative *I* with authenticity, but they remain impersonations. One of the most interesting forms of experiment in the modern novel has been to take account of this, and to use *unreliable narrators*—that is, narrators who give a first-person version of a story that seems to convince themselves, although the text is constructed overall in such a way that we gather they are not telling the truth. As Wayne Booth says, "the narrator is mistaken, or he believes himself to have qualities which the author denies him."[4]

The narrator of Henry James's *The Aspern Papers* (1888), for example, tells us "I felt . . . a mystic companionship, a moral fraternity with all those who in the past had been in the service of art." We learn that he is searching for the "truth" about the dead poet, Jeffrey Aspern; yet, with all his talk of truth and morals, he seems to have forgotten that, in order to gain information about Aspern, he has embarked on a series of lies to other people. He is the narrator of his story, and we are only given his account of what has happened: from what he tells us, however, we are able to read back a network of ambivalent self-deception. We come to agree with one of the characters, who calls him a "publishing scoundrel," though he continues to insist on his own moral integrity to the end.

Participants and Observers: The Rule of Consistency

Dramatized narrators are not always there simply to tell their own stories: first-person narrators as storytellers may recount events in which they have been only minor participants or observers. In Willa Cather's *My Mortal Enemy*, for example, we learn the narrator's name, and something of her life-history, but the focus in the novella is not on her, it is on the problematic life of a woman called Myra Henshawe, a friend who has thrown away a fortune for love. The narrator visits Myra Henshawe (now old and sick) and overhears her talking to herself, while her husband Oswald is in the room:

> From my chair by the open window I could see her bed. She had been motionless for more than an hour, lying on her back, her eyes closed. I thought she was asleep. The city outside was as still as the room in which we sat. The sick woman began to talk to herself, scarcely above a whisper, but with perfect distinctness; a voice that was hardly more than a soft, passionate breath. I seemed to hear a soul talking.
>
> "I could bear to suffer . . . so many have suffered. But why must it be like this? I have not deserved it. I have been true in friendship; I have faithfully nursed others in sickness. . . . Why must I die like this, alone with my mortal enemy?"
>
> Oswald was sitting on the sofa, his face shaded by his hand. I looked at him in affright, but he did not move or shudder. I felt my hands grow cold and my forehead grow moist with dread.
>
> (Willa Cather, *My Mortal Enemy*, 1926, pt. 4, chap. 6)

As we have seen in chapter 1, the usual rule of consistency for first-person narrators is that they cannot enter the minds of other characters. Willa Cather preserves the rule, but only by the fictional device of letting her narrator overhear a private monologue that makes her think she hears "a soul talking." Cather does this in order to open up to us a triangular relationship between the communicative but enigmatic Myra, the silent husband, and the observing, rather frightened, narrator.

A large part of the interest of Cather's novella depends on how we come close to Myra Henshawe's mind through the narrator's observation of her, but (since we are limited to first-person narration) cannot enter it fully. Although the narrator hears a "soul talking," she still does not know *exactly* what Myra Henshawe means by "mortal enemy," nor how seriously that phrase can be applied to Oswald. Oswald himself is mysterious: in effect he speaks through his silence. The traditional mode of the storyteller, using first-person narrative to recount observed experience, is thus adapted to expose a modern sense of the unknowable in human relationships.

The rule of consistency in first-person narratives can in fact be transgressed, or circumnavigated, in several ways. Philip Roth in *American Pastoral* (1997) has a first-person narrator who is a writer, telling us about his life. He goes to a class reunion, dances with one of his old classmates to the tune called "Dream," and says: "I dreamed . . . I dreamed a realistic chronicle. I began gazing into [the Swede's] life" (89). Before long we have moved off into the Swede's mind, and into a third-person narrative that then occupies the rest of the novel. As with so many occasions when novelists test the limits of the genre, we are confronted with some form of logical incoherence, but it is justified in new ways, in effect making a comment on the necessary limitations of realist narrative.[5]

Dramatized Narrators at a Different Level

In the examples considered so far in this chapter, the narrator is on the same level as the main narrative, but in the classic realist novel we have third-person narrative where an authorial narrator appears on a different narrative level, as the agent inventing, constructing, or writing the (obviously fictional) story.[6] These narrators may also be dramatized, and may present themselves to us as fictional characters (like Scheherazade in *The Arabian Nights*) who have their own story, which is different from the narratives they tell.

A famous example of a dramatized narrator on a different level from the main narrative is Thackeray's *Vanity Fair*. This narrator does not have a full life-story, but is certainly dramatized and presents himself to us in a short preface called "Before the Curtain," as "Manager of the Performance" who "sits before the curtain on the boards, and looks into the Fair." He refers to the characters as "puppets," and during the course of the novel interrupts the narrative with cynical comments.

We are reading third-person narrative about the financial problems of the Crawley family, for example, when Thackeray's narrator intrudes:

> **What a dignity it gives an old lady, that balance at the banker's!**
> **How tenderly we look at her faults, if she is a relative (and may every**
> **reader have a score of such), what a kind, good-natured old creature we**
> **find her! . . . Is it so, or is it not so? I appeal to the middle classes. Ah,**
> **gracious powers! I wish you would send me an old aunt—a maiden**

aunt—an aunt with a lozenge on her carriage, and a front of light cof-
fee-coloured hair—how my children should work workbags for her,
and my Julia and I would make her comfortable!—sweet vision! Foolish—foolish dream!

(W. M. Thackeray, *Vanity Fair*, (1847–48) 1848, no. 3, chap. 9)

The speaker here obviously has characteristics we are tempted to identify
with Thackeray himself (like worldliness and cynicism), but a simple identification will not work. He is an invention of the text: he does not have
Thackeray's life-history behind him. (For a start, Thackeray's wife's name
was Isabella not "Julia.") We can say that he has been dramatized as a
character—or alternatively we can regard him as a kind of dramatic mask.

Commentary between Narrative Levels

Narrators may make comments from one narrative level to another.[7] Narrators in nineteenth-century classic realism often use a narrative pause to
comment with a directly instructional or didactic import, and in the case
of an author like Balzac or George Eliot, they may go well beyond the
instructional, to assume the posture of a philosopher, as though establishing general laws of human behavior.

George Eliot's narrator in *Middlemarch* (who is dramatized as an author constructing the text) stops the narrative flow to address readers directly about Dorothea Brooke and her marriage to Mr. Casaubon:

One morning, some weeks after her arrival at Lowick, Dorothea—but
why always Dorothea? Was her point of view the only possible one with
regard to this marriage? I protest against all our interest, all our effort
at understanding being given to the young skins that look blooming in
spite of trouble; for these too will get faded, and will know the older
and more eating griefs which we are helping to neglect. . . . Mr Casaubon
had an intense consciousness within him, and was spiritually a-hun-
gered like the rest of us. He had done nothing exceptional in marry-
ing—nothing but what society sanctions, and considers an occasion for
wreaths and bouquets.

(George Eliot, *Middlemarch*, (1871–72) 1872, bk. 3, chap. 29)

This is a confident narrator who speaks to readers as, in some degree,
equals ("*our* interest," "*our* effort") and yet feels that they are liable to fix

their attention on pretty and sentimental topics ("young skins that look blooming") unless drawn by her guidance to sympathetic attention of the "intense consciousness" of the older Mr. Casaubon. She shares the inclinations of readers perhaps (since she talks of "our" interest), but it is implied that we need her nonetheless, to manipulate us back from frivolity to a more serious path.[8]

Narrator or Author?

George Eliot's narrator is very definitely authorial (represented as both novelist and thinker), and there is obvious common ground with the individual we usually refer to as George Eliot (though "George Eliot" was a pen-name for Marian Evans). Is there any point, then, in trying to make a distinction between narrator and author? Might we not just as well say that the narrator here is George Eliot herself, and leave it at that?

As Dorrit Cohn points out, it is not intrinsically wrong to identify a narrator of this kind with the author; it is one possible perspective based on a "genetic" approach to the text—an approach that emphasizes the *origins* of the text, rather than the way in which it is read.[9] In conversation about texts like *Middlemarch,* we tend almost automatically to elide author and narrator, maintaining that "George Eliot says . . .," or "George Eliot thinks . . ." But our conversational habits are not necessarily an infallible guide for analysis, and this can become reductive, leading rapidly from the text to speculations about the personality of the author. If commentary by the narrator may stem from real-life opinions, it *may* also be part of an impersonation, and it cannot possibly represent the full, lived-through personality of the author, since it is fixed by the text at a particular time in a particular place. At its most impressive, such commentary has its effect as part of the system of the text, and as a reflection of the primary narrative level.[10]

Commentary forms only a small part of a novelistic text. What about those parts where a narrator is not overtly dramatized? What about texts that do not specify a narrator? Do we have to imagine a narrative agent?

There is considerable disagreement among theorists of narrative on this point. Gérard Genette insists that there is no escape from narrators: the novelist's choice must always be "to have the story told by one of its characters, or to have it told by a narrator outside of the story."[11] When we read a third-person narrative, "the slightest general observation, the slightest adjective that is little more than descriptive, the most discreet comparison, the most modest 'perhaps,' the most inoffensive of logical articulations introduces into its web a type of speech [*un type de parole*] that is alien to it, refractory as it were."[12] Ann Banfield, however, maintains that written narrative is not like spoken language; we do not have to imagine someone speaking it: it has a special "classless status." It can be separated from "the person of its author and . . . subjective coloration."[13] If there is no narrator overtly present, then we do not have to invent one. Denis Donoghue suggests that the assumption of a narrative voice is not necessary for modern readers, since we are used to texts without narrators (like newspaper editorials), and "fracture and ambiguity" can be aspects of printed text.[14]

We are unlikely to escape entirely from the idea of a personal narrator, since reading narrative as narrative involves associating it with intentionality, and it is difficult to think that this intentionality derives from nowhere. Moreover, we have in general strong habits of personification, which we constantly use in our conceptual processes. We imagine computers with 'personalities of their own' and motor cars which seem 'unfriendly' or 'bloodyminded' when they don't start in the morning. We do not stop talking about personalities behind things, even when we know quite well that there is no factual basis for such talk. When confronted by texts (as Genette suggests), we see idiosyncrasies of style, and style does usually suggest a distinctive subjectivity (or subjectivities working together) to produce the text.

The "Nobody" Narrator

One way of discussing the narrator behind the full text in third-person narratives has been developed by Elizabeth Deeds Ermarth, who suggests that in the nineteenth-century realist novel there is a "Nobody" narrator. The narrator is a "collective result, a specifier of consensus, and as such it is not really intelligible as an individual."[15] If we ask *who* speaks throughout most of a realist text, it is not the author, not the characters, not a dramatized narrator, but a collective consciousness that can conceive of a "society" in the modern sense: "an extended invisible community of consciousness in time, a community that extends to the reader."

According to Ermarth the "Nobody" narrator is not omniscient like God (there are many things that the narrative consciousness cannot see or know), but it suggests a kind of consciousness that is social, consensual, or communal. And it is this that makes possible the great social-realist novels of the nineteenth century (for example, George Eliot's *Middlemarch*, Thackeray's *Vanity Fair*, Dickens's *Our Mutual Friend*, Trollope's *The Way We Live Now*, or Elizabeth Gaskell's *Mary Barton*).

Ermarth's argument does not imply that all nineteenth-century novels are alike in the way they view society: there are considerable differences. Moreover, some narrators "inch towards personification" or dramatization, while others do not.[16] The significant point is that the third-person fictional realist narrative is not produced out of nowhere, it is produced by a kind of narrator made possible in a particular historical context, because of a general development of the social sciences and of modern concepts of history.

Ermarth sees this form of narration and the view of society it implies as typical of the mid-century realist novel. By the end of the nineteenth century writers have lost confidence in such a consensual view; society has come to seem fragmented and ungraspable in new ways, and the individual consciousness more deeply problematic. Modernism takes over from this loss of confidence, focusing on the lack of community and the *unknowability* of other minds.

As an example of how this approach can be used in analysis, we might take the incipit of a story written late in the nineteenth century by George Gissing:

> **Here and there in the more populous London suburbs you will find small houses built with a view to the accommodation of two families beneath the same roof. Considering the class of people for whom this advantage was contrived, the originator of the idea showed a singular faith in human nature. It does, however, occasionally happen that two distinct households prove themselves capable of living in such proximity for a certain time without overt breach of the peace—nay, with a measure of satisfaction on both sides. This was the case with the Rippingilles and the Budges. Rippingille, salesman at a large boot warehouse, and Budge, a coal-merchant's clerk, were young men of sober disposition, not incapable of modest mirth, content with their lot in life, and rarely looking more than a month or two ahead.**
>
> (George Gissing, "One Way of Happiness," 1898)

The narrator here is not located in a specific time and place, and imagines the possibility of sharing an experience of the world with readers ("you will find . . . "): to that extent there is certainly a "Nobody" narrator. But he is obviously skeptical about a benevolent "human nature" and has a strong sense of class distinctions. There is a distinctive style throughout the passage—a choice of pompous and formal phrases ("more populous," " a singular faith," "in such proximity," "not incapable of modest mirth") that creates an interesting dissonance with the subject matter (working-class or lower middle-class life in London). As the story develops, the characters are shown to have vitality and a capacity for rough, combative enjoyments, but the position of the narrator in relation to them becomes less and less certain.

Thus, the consensual view of society that produces the "Nobody" narrator is here under stress, or in the process of breaking down. We could read the story in purely "genetic" terms, and say that the dissonance reflects Gissing's own attitudes and problems, but such a reading will always be speculative. The attempt to understand the narrative process is more directly related to a reading of the text.

The Decline of Narrators

As the consensus surrounding the "Nobody" narrator becomes problematic at the end of the nineteenth century, overt intrusions by a didactic dramatized narrator and direct addresses to the reader come to seem old-fashioned. On the whole, direct address is rejected by modern novelists. Henry James called intrusions of this kind a "want of discretion" on the part of the writer: "Such a betrayal of a sacred office seems to me, I confess, a terrible crime."[17] Ford Madox Ford says that "the object of the novelist is to keep the reader entirely oblivious of the fact that the author exists—even of the fact that he is reading a book."[18]

Instead of the "Nobody" narrator, novelists can use devices such as the following:

Reflectors. As we have seen already in chapter 1, Henry James uses
the technique of concentrating on one character as a reflector,
entering the consciousness of that one character and seeing events
largely focused through that point of view.

Conditional narrative. Faulkner developed a technique (for example,
in *Sanctuary* [1931]) in which the narrative shifts from consciousness to consciousness; the thoughts of characters are revealed to
us, but they do not connect together into a seamless web of
narrative. The consensus becomes ungraspable.

Absent narrator. A third-person narrative, with no overt first-person narratorial or metadiegetic comment, and with fairly limited oracular generalized statements, has also been widely used in the twentieth-century novel. Description in some cases is cut down so that only what is necessary for the setting of a scene is given. In extreme versions of this style, characters are presented only from the outside, there is no going into their minds or speculating on motives (an often cited example is Hemingway's short story "The Killers" [1928]).

Mixed Modes

Although we may separate out various kinds of narrator and narrative for the purposes of description, it is important to recognize that the novel is a constant field of experiment, where interesting mixed modes are found. Dickens gives part of *Bleak House* (1852–53) in first-person narrative, part in third (and, unusually, the third-person part is narrated predominantly in the present tense). Conrad's *Nostromo* generally uses an impersonal third-person narrative, telling the history of a silver mine in an imaginary South American country, but suddenly introduces chapter 8 in an entirely different way:

> THOSE of us whom business or curiosity took to Sulaco in these years before the first advent of the railway can remember the steadying effect of the San Tomé mine upon the life of that remote province. The outward appearances had not changed then as they have changed since, as I am told, with cable cars running along the street of the Constitution, and carriage roads far into the country.
>
> (Joseph Conrad, *Nostromo*, 1904, pt. 1, chap. 8)

In a few sentences an individual narrator is suddenly dramatized, as "one of us" who visited the country before the history being described. We are forced to consider that this is not a history told by an objective observer, but by someone who was there either on business or for curiosity—that is, someone who is implicated (as all modern readers are) in the process of capitalistic exploitation.

Effects of this kind are disturbing, and may disrupt our smooth consumption of the work of fiction, but there is, after all, no reason why we must immerse ourselves constantly in the illusions of any one form of narrative technique. Just as, when we see Shakespearean plays, we can move in and out of different levels of dramatic illusion (watching plays within plays—watching characters watching them—watching actors briefly destroying the illusion they have created), so novel readers find it quite possible to switch from level to level, watching what the text is doing and what they themselves are doing to understand it. A playfulness between and around narrative techniques is, indeed, one of the strongest characteristics of postmodern writing.

Paul Auster in *City of Glass* provides us with a third-person narrative about a novelist called Quinn, who uses a dramatized narrator (called Max Work) in crime novels that he writes under a pseudonym. Quinn is awakened in bed by the telephone:

> "Yes?"
> There was a long pause on the other end, and for a moment Quinn thought the caller had hung up. Then, as if from a great distance, there came the sound of a voice unlike any he had ever heard. It was at once mechanical and filled with feeling, hardly more than a whisper and yet perfectly audible, and so even in tone that he was unable to tell if it belonged to a man or a woman.
> "Hello?" said the voice.
> "Who is this?" asked Quinn.
> "Hello?" said the voice again.
> "I'm listening," said Quinn. "Who is this?"
> "Is this Paul Auster?" asked the voice. "I would like to speak to Mr Paul Auster."
> "There's no one here by that name."
>
> (Paul Auster, *City of Glass*, 1985, chap. 1)

Can we actually imagine a voice that is distant, mechanical *and* filled with feeling, and without gender? Such a "voice" might be that of a text with an absent narrator. But the voice claims it is looking for Paul Auster—accuses Quinn of being Paul Auster. The text plays not only with narrative expectations, but with conversational habits. Although it is standard American English to ask, "Who is this?" on reflection the question sounds illogical—*that* would be more appropriate. The voice asks, "Is *this* Paul Auster?" and of course in one sense it certainly is—the whole novel *is* Paul Auster. These questions don't really make sense, and yet within the context of the dialogue they almost do so.

Implied metadiegetic commentary on questions of narratology is being mixed by Auster with a confusion of the identity of narrator and author in an elaborate game. But that does not mean, surprisingly enough, that we are unable to imagine the scene. Simply we might agree with Quinn, when he puts down the phone: "I must learn to think more quickly on my feet."

Part IV

The Language of the Text

When we decide to start analysis of a literary text, we do so in the hope that it is possible to observe the features of the text in a reasonably stable way, and to discuss them. As we have already seen, there will always be differences in our readings, because we do not share complete and coherent systems of value, but our discussions become most fruitful where there is common ground for a starting point.

One of the chief areas in which we should be able to find such common ground is in the detailed analysis of the language of the text. The language is what is "there on the page." Not everyone agrees it is worth close examination in the case of the novel. T. S. Eliot, for example, wrote that novels "obtain what reality they have largely from an accurate rendering of the noises that human beings currently make in their daily simple needs of communication; and what part of a novel is not composed of these noises consists of a prose which is no more alive than that of a competent newspaper writer or government official."[1] But it is not difficult to find novelists who have taken language seriously. Maurice Blanchot points out that "the events, the characters and the dialogues of this world of fiction we call the novel are necessarily impregnated with the particular nature of the words on which their reality is based." The words of a novel, Blanchot thinks, do not "disappear into their meaning."[2]

Analytic reading, then, should pay attention to language. But having agreed on this as a general principle, how should we proceed? Rules about how language works at a local level are not simply transferable to the full text, or "global level" of the text: we cannot shift from one level to the other by a simple process of extension. There is, as A. Culioli explains, a "theoretical rupture" between local and global analysis.[3]

As readers of novels we are concerned with meaning, and meaning cannot be separated from context. If we think of a verb like *to sneeze*, which can be classified for the purposes of the *Concise Oxford Dictionary* as an intransitive verb and defined as "make explosive sound in involuntarily expelling anything that irritates interior of nostrils"; then a sentence like "John sneezed Mary the football" should be impossible. And "He sneezed his way into the room" should be nonsense. Rules of use that work at the local level would classify these sentences as ungrammatical. But is quite possible to imagine both sentences being used in a literary context.[4]

Our capacity to contravene rules does not, however, indicate that there is endless slippage in the signification of words, or that their combination in sentences is free of constraints. There must be conventions operating, or there can be no communication, but the conventions are radically affected by context.[5] Meaning, usage, and even truth-value depend upon context. A sentence like "France is a hexagon" is found to be true in certain situations (in a school geography lesson, for example, or in a newspaper article)—but not always. Its "factuality" is limited to situations where we are accustomed to quick, inaccurate sketch maps.[6] As Thomas Pavel points out, "global truth is not simply derived from the local truth-value of the sentences present in the text."[7] Our point of departure and return in this book is the novelistic text at its global level, and the methods of analysis we employ need to take this into account.

The texts we are looking at are nothing if not heterogeneous, so we cannot expect them to conform to any one pattern throughout. As we have already seen, the novelistic text may use (and interweave) narration, description, and dialogue, as well as explication and argumentation. One important context for our reading of any particular passage becomes the novel itself (perhaps more precisely called the *cotext*).

We can, then, find the stability necessary for discussion if we try to keep in mind that our analysis of a local part of a text will also be affected by other factors:

- What we see as the situation of its production (or enunciation)
- The reference we think it has to the world (in the case of fiction, a suspended reference)
- The sequence it forms with other parts of the text

It should be possible to note regularities and dominant forms at the level of language in a text—just as it should be possible to note irregularities and exceptions. Although these will not invariably determine each reading we make, they will have affected our reading, and it is therefore appropriate to ask how they come about (that is, on what basis they come to be seen as distinctive features) and to consider their function in a particular text.

When Henry James was asked if he was famous for the use of dashes in his novels, he replied: "Dash my fame. . . . And remember, please, that dogmatizing about punctuation is exactly as foolish as dogmatizing about any other form of communication with the reader. All such forms depend on the kind of thing one is doing and the kind of effect one intends to produce."[8] Joseph Conrad said that "half the words we use have no meaning whatever and of the other half each man understands each word after the fashion of his own folly and conceit."[9] Modern cognitive linguistics would suggest that Conrad overstates his case. Words *do* have meaning, but they are not like building bricks: they do not build up meaning in a simple way one on top of another. Our discussion, then, needs to consider language, but to focus on language as it is used in the novelistic texts, which are our primary field of study.

11

Sentence Structure and Connection

According to traditional views of language, the sentence is a basic unit that is, as the *Oxford English Dictionary* says, "grammatically complete." Since we are concerned with the analysis of texts, however, we must be cautious about considering sentences in isolation as separate units. In traditional terms, the sentence is something that may contain a proposition or propositions, and if we are to grasp the information in a passage, we need to understand the meaning of the propositions it contains. But propositions are not independent of form and context. Moreover, the information we gain from novels is not simply propositional, and we are as much concerned with what sentences evoke as what they encode. (There is in any case no clear boundary between evoking and encoding.)[1]

Fictional Sentences

A sentence conventionally contains a main verb, and so is very often a unit of narrativity. But we cannot say that sentences as such are necessary for narrative: comic strips and films narrate stories through images, and dispense with sentences. Only when we try to give an account of these narratives in language are we forced to use sentences.

There is no single underlying sentence pattern specifically found in sentences in works of fiction. Some sentences typically found within novels do, however, indicate fictionality, particularly those where there is an adverb suggesting the present and a verb suggesting the past:

> **And now Anna's heart was sinking under the heavy conviction which she dared not utter, that Gwendolen would never care for Rex.**
>
> (George Eliot, *Daniel Deronda* [1876], book 1, chap. 7)

> Now, as if he too were remembering that other time, he insisted on buying a drink, and pursed his lips disapprovingly when I asked for a gin.
>
> (John Banville, *The Book of Evidence* [1989], 36)

Sentences such as these mix "now" and past tenses, creating time-schemes that are illogical at the local level. They sidestep into the past in a way that is quite acceptable in fiction.[2]

Dividing Text into Sentences

From one point of view the use of customary sentence structure might be considered simply as a way of dividing up a text into manageable parts. We cannot read long texts without pauses, and so cut them into chapters, paragraphs, sentences, clauses, and phrases. The sentence unit gives us something to focus on, provides a frame for attention (with a capital letter at the start and full stop at the end).

Looked at in this way, the sentence is simply a convention of the modern book, which can be expanded, contracted, or even dispensed with if necessary. Samuel Beckett's *The Unnamable* ([Fr. 1953] 1958) attacks the convention by ending with a huge sentence several pages long, and his *How It Is* dispenses with sentences entirely. Beckett originally intended to publish *How It Is* as one long unbroken text, but then split it up into paragraphlike fragments. The narrative is told by an *I* who is in some kind of primeval mud and is going over the details of his relationship with a character called Pim:

> here then part one how it was before Pim we follow I quote the natural order more or less my life last state last version what remains bits and scraps I hear it my life natural order more or less I learn it I quote a given moment long past vast stretch of time on from there that moment and following not all a selection natural order vast tracts of time
>
> part one before Pim how I got here no question not known not said and the sack whence the sack and me if it's me no question impossible too weak no importance
>
> (Samuel Beckett, *How It Is*, [Fr. 1961] 1964)

At first glance this may seem incomprehensible. After a time it becomes possible to read: the phrases, or groups of words, separate off and provide us with sense, though we cannot quite be sure what is connected with what. Link words have been dropped along with punctuation, and with no breaks inside the paragraphs we are unsure where to focus our attention. Conventional division into sentences is obviously not an absolute necessity for the novel, but it is certainly a convenient device that makes texts easier to read. It gives us a sense of the structure of information, and helps us guess what is most significant.

Coherent Forms

To focus on the pattern of the sentence as a device for cutting up texts is only one way of looking at the matter. Cognitive linguistics has suggested that sentence and clause units are used to add *coherent forms* to language. Language first provides us with *lexical units* (words or groups of words), but a limitless development of new lexical units would be impossible to manage, so to convey information we present the lexical units in conventionalized coherent forms. The regularities of these forms correspond to what we think of as grammar.

As we begin to speak or write, we select possible forms, slot them in, and arrange patterns. This is largely done by habit, unconsciously, though in the process we also sometimes consciously take note of the acceptable styles of our period, or the needs of an audience, or the demands of "gatekeepers" (editors, publishers, and censors). It may sometimes be done with the self-conscious aim of writing an artwork. In any case, it is always a question of choices. As Bernard, one of the characters in Virginia Woolf's *The Waves* (1931), says: "Whatever sentence I extract whole and entire from this cauldron is only a string of six little fish that let themselves be caught while a million others leap and sizzle"(220).

Obviously most writers use a variety of coherent forms. Some contemporary writers, for example, choose short sentences in order to communicate swiftly, but short sentences produce a rhythm that is repetitive, so writers almost always vary their use. Other writers try to develop longer sentences, even aiming for the sense of an unfolding narrative at sentence level, or for the effect of a sentence that has "a capacity to be read two ways" and that "continues to haunt" the reader with its sense of possibility.[3] George Moore praised the writing of Hall Caine because he could write a sentence "three inches long" (presumably referring to length down, not across the page).[4] Walter Pater was interested in the long complex sentence as a way of enforcing slow reading: "To really strenuous minds there is a pleasurable stimulus in the challenge for a continuous effort on their part, to be rewarded by securer and more intimate grasp of the author's sense."[5]

There are three basic models for assembling coherent forms as sentences in English: *the simple sentence, the complex sentence,* and *the compound or loose sentence.*

Simple Sentences

Short, simple sentences are much favored in genre fiction and journalism. They come in four forms:

1. Subject, transitive verb, and object.
2. Subject and intransitive verb (possible adverb).
3. Subject, the verb *to be,* and predicate.
4. Subject, a link verb (*feels, seems,* or *becomes*), and predicate.

We can scan simple sentences quickly: they do not need what J. M. Coetzee calls the "heroic attentiveness" demanded by Beckett of his readers.[6] Their use in novels may evoke boldness and strength, an effect no doubt stemming from their association with the hard-boiled crime story and Hemingway's fiction. But they have other effects: they may equally give the impression of crude tabloid journalism, or (as in Evelyn Waugh's satiric accounts of modern society) capture the feel of a world drained of emotional depth.

The Hook

It is particularly common to start off chapters or significant passages with a simple sentence, or sentences, to hook the reader into the text. A paragraph in Doris Lessing's The *Grass is Singing* starts:

> **She went out. The men were silent. Dick's face was averted from Charlie, who, since he had never become convinced of the necessity for tact, gazed intently at Dick, as if trying to force him into some explanation or statement.**
>
> (Doris Lessing, *The Grass Is Singing,* 1950, chap. 10)

The short sentences here set up an opposition between the woman and the men. In general, we quickly pick up suggestions of parallelism in a series of simple sentences, needing only the slightest of hints (as here: A went out. B and C were silent.). The parallelism helps to establish the opposition between the action of the woman, on the one hand, and the reaction of the men, on the other. This opposition then serves as a frame for a description of the complex interreaction between Dick and Charlie.

Asyndeton and Parataxis

Simple sentences are often placed so as to suggest a sequence ("I opened the door. He came into the room."). If there is no linking conjunction, but an obvious sequence, this is known as *asyndeton*. In such cases we could easily link the sentences with *and*. We also find examples where connection would not be so easy, again with no linking words. ("He came into the room. I had opened the door.") This is known as *parataxis*.

But even when presented with parataxis, we inevitably begin attempting to find coherence—thinking of the events described in order of time (or perhaps linked by cause and effect), or following slight parallelisms and variations in pattern that provide a rhythm for our reading. Colm Tóibín starts off a paragraph in this way:

> **He waited in the ante-room. It was still not time. He felt excited at the prospect of getting away. Soon, he would be twenty-five years on the bench and he remembered this last day's waiting more vividly than the humdrum days or the significant or difficult cases.**
>
> (Colm Tóibín, *The Heather Blazing*, 1992, chap. 1)

Here we have two simple sentences, then a more complex one, and then a longer sentence joined by a linking word. The pattern can be described as parataxis with closure (as when we close a sequence: A, B, C, D, *and E.*) Use of parataxis gives the impression of a certain pseudo-objectivity: the writer presents the "simple facts." But parataxis with closure gives a satisfying neatness to the series, and allows the pseudo-objective note at the start to shift effortlessly into suggestions of subjectivity and psychological depth.

The Child's-Eye View

Simple sentences seem appropriate in writing from a child's-eye view. For example, Roddy Doyle produces the effect of a small child looking at his large father:

> **My da's hands were big. The fingers were long. They weren't fat. I could make out the bone under the skin and the flesh. He had one of**

his hands dangling over the chair. He was holding his book with his other hand. His nails were clean—except for one—and the white bits at the top were longer than mine. The wrinkles at his knuckles were a bit like the design of a wall, the cement between the bricks up and across. There weren't many other wrinkles but the pores were like hollows, with a hair for every pore. Dark hair. Hair came out from under his cuff.

The Naked and the Dead. That was what the book was called. There was a soldier on the cover with his uniform on. His face was dirty. He was American.

(Roddy Doyle, Paddy Clarke: Ha Ha Ha, 1993)

One of the assumptions behind this passage is that the child responds to the world differently from adults. He notices things that adults take for granted, and responds to the details of things. We start off with simple sentences, but by the middle of the paragraph we have moved to longer ones—communicating now an imaginative ability to make unusual comparisons (between "wrinkles" and "the design of a wall"). The longer sentences are then pulled up short by a descriptive phrase ("Dark hair."). And we move back to the dominant pattern of simple sentences.

At first sight the second paragraph appears even more transparent and simple. But it is in fact jokily allusive. The title of Norman Mailer's book *(The Naked and the Dead)* is presented as a sentence, and this leads on to a rather knowing pastiche of an American (Hemingwayesque) style: "His face was dirty. He was American." Doyle's writing represents naivete here, but is not itself naive. The literary allusions are there to appeal to adult, educated readers.

Even within passages dominated by short sentences, then, we are faced by the heterogeneity of the novelistic text. Although when read in one way Doyle seems to be giving an unmediated replication of a child's thought processes, the text is self-consciously allusive within the field of the novel.

Complex Sentences

According to traditional grammar there are two fundamental ways of making longer sentences. One is by adding clauses onto one another (coordination); the other is by using subordinate clauses:

1. Coordination: Jack plays golf *and* Julia plays tennis.
2. Subordination:
   a. The man who is playing golf must be Jack.
   b. Everyone hoped that Julia would learn to play tennis.
   c. You must finish your homework before you play golf.[7]

In traditional terminology, coordination produces *compound sentences,* and subordination produces *complex sentences.* The important difference is that the compound sentence provides us with pieces of information of approximately equal value. The complex sentence, in contrast, by subordinating one clause to another, ensures that we create hierarchies of information. In 2a, "The man . . . must be Jack" is the main clause, "who is playing golf" is subordinate.

Complex sentences are not necessarily more difficult than compound ones: indeed, they may be simpler to understand, because they order information for us and indicate what to concentrate on. In this respect they are obviously more appropriate for communicating a large amount of information. On the other hand, they do also require us to keep different pieces of information in mind at the same time, and may cause us to postpone our sense of what the sentence is about until we get to the last part. Subordination is typical of classical usage in Greek and Latin, and it has been argued that a key step was made in giving variety and rapidity to written English style when William Tyndale cut down on subordination in his 1534 translation of the Bible, preferring to connect clauses with *and.*[8]

While the fundamental difference described here can easily be grasped and picked out in isolated sentences, it is by no means always clear in the real language situation of a long text. Sentences of both kinds are commonly mixed together, and different parts of one sentence may show coordination and subordination.[9] If coordination adds on information, subordination may pick up and develop information, so that by using them together, the writer can produce sentences that deepen and unfold before us. An example is the famous last sentence with which Thackeray ends his account of the Battle of Waterloo in *Vanity Fair:* "Darkness came down on the field and city; and Amelia was praying for George, who was lying on his face, dead, with a bullet through his heart" (no. 9 chap. 32). Both subordination and coordination are used here: the general effect is a *fanlike structure,* opening out as we proceed, stage by stage, to the end.

Dominant Structures

Just as it is obvious that some modern writers favor the short sentence, it may be possible, when looking at a passage in a novel, to suggest that one of the longer forms is dominant. Many early novels, for example, add on clause after clause, sometimes with little indication that the stream of prose needs to stop at all. Sentences of this kind (often mixing in some subordination with their series of coordinations) are referred to as having a loose structure:

> There is no pain, my dear *Octavio*, either in Love or friendship like that of doubt; and I confess my self guilty of giving it you in a great measure by my silence the last Post, but having business of so much greater concern to my heart than even writing to *Octavio*, I found my self unable to pursue any other, and I believe you cou'd too with the less impatience bear with my neglect having affairs of the same nature there; our circumstances and the business of our hearts then being so resembling, methinks, I have as great an impatience to be recounting to you the story of my Love and Fortune, as I am to receive that of yours, and to know what advances you have made in the heart of the still charming Silvia! . . .
>
> (Aphra Behn, *Love-Letters Between a Nobleman and His Sister*, 1684–87, pt. 2)

There are subordinate clauses of various kinds here, but the most striking aspect of the sentence (which continues for some lines after the quotation) is the way in which it piles on new clauses with *and* and *but*, or uses semicolons when most writers would bring the sentence to a close. Janet Todd describes the novel it comes from as "a heady mixture of history, propaganda, journalism, letters, farce and romance." The use of enormously long sentences, and their confusing way with problems of order and value, play an important role in creating such a style.[10]

Use of compound structure in English always has the effect of bringing the prose back toward an informal colloquial style, as in Raymond Carver's stories, where we find sentences like: "Sandy and her husband sat at the table and drank whiskey and ate the chocolates" ("Preservation" [1983]). This reads as we might say it in an informal account. Some modernist writers have also been attracted to compound or loose structure to try to represent the flow of the mind:

But how strange, on entering the Park, the silence; the mist; the hum; the slow-swimming happy ducks; the pouched birds waddling; and who should be coming along with his back against the Government buildings, most appropriately, carrying a despatch box stamped with the Royal Arms, who but Hugh Whitbread; her old friend Hugh—the admirable Hugh!

(Virginia Woolf, Mrs Dalloway, 1925)

Woolf deliberately uses semicolons where other writers would use commas or break up the sentence with full stops. This allows her to focus on impressions rather than rational connections, and to create the sense that brief flickering perceptions (interspersed with stereotyped phrases like "her old friend Hugh") are the fundamental material of our mental lives.[11]

Inversion

With shorter sentences it is fairly obvious which are the important parts. The customary pattern for sentences in English is for the topic (usually information that is familiar) to be placed at the start, and for the weight of the sentence (the new information) to be placed at the end. With a sentence such as "The man was standing on the street-corner," the sentence is about the man: he is familiar to us (he is called "*the* man"). The new information is that he is on the street-corner.

With longer sentences there are certain tricks of style that can reorganize our processing of information and make parts stand out for attention. In literary texts it is common to reverse the familiar order of words in some part—that is, to use *inversion*—to draw attention to a word or phrase. Thus, chapter 11 of Jane Austen's *Sense and Sensibility* does not start with: *Mrs. Dashwood and her daughters had little imagined when they first came into Devonshire that so many engagements would arise.* Rather it makes the word "little" prominent, by starting: "Little had Mrs. Dashwood or her daughters imagined, when they first came into Devonshire, that so many engagements would arise." "Little" becomes the focus of the first part of the sentence, giving a strong contrast with "so many" and emphasizing the difference between what the Dashwood family had imagined and what actually took place.

Balanced Pairs

Another way of giving focus to sentence elements is by balancing them in pairs (often involving a repetition of some parts.) Again in *Sense and Sensibility*, we read:

> Like half the rest of the world, if more than half there be that are clever and good, Marianne, with excellent abilities and an excellent disposition, was neither reasonable nor candid. She expected from other people the same opinions and feelings as her own, and she judged of their motives by the immediate effect of their actions on herself.
>
> (Jane Austen, *Sense and Sensibility*, 1811, vol. 2, chap 9)

Balancing and contrastive pairs appear here with adjectives ("clever and good"), with adjective + noun groups ("excellent abilities," ""excellent disposition") and with clauses ("she expected from other people," "she judged of their motives"). Such reliance on balanced pairs to create a measured and fair description is characteristic of late eighteenth- and early nineteenth-century prose (a habit reflected even in the titles of Jane Austen's novels), and it can give form to the whole sentence. Balance used so extensively can indeed be further seen as one facet of a widespread contemporary attempt to impose or find order in a disorderly world—comparable to the heroic couplet of Augustan poetry, or the ordered symmetry of Georgian architecture.

Triads

Balanced sentences are particularly associated with Enlightenment prose, but we find triads more widely used in English as a way of giving focus and emphasis. Listing things in threes is an old trick of classical rhetoric, and it is attractive and useful enough to survive in modern English, particularly in formal summations. In *Sense and Sensibility* we find: "Could he ever be tolerably happy with Lucy Steele; could he, were his affection for herself out of the question, with his integrity, his delicacy and well-informed mind, be satisfied with a wife like her—illiterate, artful and selfish?" (vol. 1, chap. 23). This is the end of a paragraph of free indirect discourse—and the repetition of triad patterns helps to indicate a temporary closure, or summing up. That is how Lucy *is*: "illiterate, artful and selfish." It is not so much a fair, or balanced, judgment as a decisive one.

The Periodic Sentence

One important ideal sentence for classical rhetoric was the periodic sentence, described by Hugh Blair in his eighteenth-century advice manual on rhetoric as "the most pompous, musical, and oratorical manner of composing."[12] Blair cites as his example a sentence from Sir William Temple:

> If you look about you, and consider the lives of others as well as your own; if you think how few are born with honour, and how many die with the name of children; how little beauty we see, and how few friends we hear of; how many diseases, and how much poverty there is in the world; you will fall down upon your knees, and, instead of repining at one affliction, will admire so many blessings which you have received from the hand of God.

Obviously, there is a great deal of repetition here, but the key point is that several ideas are suggested or started off by the different clauses of the long sentence ("If you look," "if you think," "how few," "how little," "how many") and then are all *integrated* ("so many blessings . . . from the hand of God"). The end of the periodic sentence was seen as providing a "perfect union" and a "cyclical" conclusion of what had been suggested at the start.[13] Another way of describing such sentences would be to suggest that they start off several ideas and make us anticipate an impressive ending: we are anticipating a climax, it is delayed by new information, but the ending finally gives us what we have expected all along.

Although this sentence structure was so much admired in the eighteenth century as a way of giving dignity to prose, and was thus an important prototype for elegant writing, it is not that common in its pure form in the novel. Novelists are more likely to build up a few ideas, as they would for a periodic sentence, then (having narrative development in mind) allow the sentence to go on loosely to something else. When the full periodic sentences does come into view, however, it gives drama and rhetorical grandeur, draws special attention to a passage, and gives the passage its own premature closure.

Melville was unafraid to draw on thunderous rhetorical devices, and has a magnificently long sentence in *Moby-Dick* on the subject of sharks:

> Though amid all the smoking horror and diabolism of a sea-fight, sharks will be seen longingly gazing up to the ship's decks, like hungry dogs round a table where red meat is being carved, ready to bolt down

every killed man that is tossed to them; and though, while the valiant butchers over the deck-table are thus cannibally carving each other's live meat with carving-knives all gilded and tasselled, the sharks, also, with their jewel-hilted mouths, are quarrelsomely carving away under the table at the dead meat; and though, were you to turn the whole affair upside down, it would still be pretty much the same thing, that is to say, a shocking sharkish business enough for all parties; and though sharks also are the invariable outriders of all slave ships crossing the Atlantic, systematically trotting alongside, to be handy in case a parcel is to be carried anywhere, or a dead slave to be decently buried; and though one or two other like instances might be set down, touching the set terms, places, and occasions, when sharks do most socially congregate, and most hilariously feast; yet there is no conceivable time or occasion when you will find them in such countless numbers, and in gayer or more jovial spirits, than around a dead sperm whale, moored by night to a whale-ship at sea.

(Herman Melville, *Moby-Dick*, 1851, chap. 64)

All that we find in this sentence could have been explained much more simply, but then simplicity is not the point. The point is to take up the life of the whaler and endow it with heroic status. The heroism is not to be an austere heroism, it is to be one that encompasses rich, exotic detail: slaves, jewels, gilding, tassels. The act of killing is turned into a "hilarious" feast, redolent of biblical histories and fantasies of oriental splendor, and all this is to symbolize man's reckless effrontery in the face of the real powers of the natural world. The periodic sentence thus dignifies what is being said.

Parenthesis

Long sentences may contain one or more parentheses, set off by brackets, dashes, or commas. A parenthesis is inserted into a sentence, and need not be structurally related to the rest, so that we are no longer confronted by a uniformly structured unit.

We—your great-grandfather and I—were in the office, Father sitting at the desk totting up the money from the canvas sack and matching it against the list of freight bills which I had just collected around the Square; and I sitting in the chair against the wall waiting for noon when I would be paid my Saturday's (week's) wage of ten cents and we would go home and eat dinner and I would be free at last to overtake

(it was May) the baseball game which had been running since breakfast
without me: the idea (not mine: your great-grandfather's) being that
even at eleven a man should already have behind him one year of paying
for, assuming responsibility for, the space he occupied, the room he
took up, in the world's (Jefferson, Mississippi's anyway) economy.

(William Faulkner, *The Reivers*, 1962, chap. 1)

Parenthetical remarks here are introduced both with dashes and parentheses. The effect is to slow down the pace of reading and create a second
perspective behind the main sentence. The narrator gives us a memory
monologue about what *I* would be doing in the office in his childhood.
The parenthetic phrases make information precise, directly addressing a
you assumed to be listening. They produce a kind of backstage information, so that we are able to imagine both childhood and adult versions of
the narrative in parallel.

Apposition

Another important way of adding interest to long sentences is through
apposition. This is where a noun, noun phrase, or clause is added as a kind
of second chance at saying something. In its simplest form it is used with
names ("the ship *Titanic*," "my Uncle Jack"). We find it in longer sentences like: "They went back to the university, their alma mater, the place
where they had learned all the worst and best things they knew." Sometimes apposition is marked by expressions such as *namely* or *that is*: "their
university, namely, their alma mater."

George Moore is fond of apposition as a way of lengthening sentences.
In *The Lake* (1905 [1921]) we find: "Mrs. O'Mara's scandalous stories,
insinuating lies, had angered him till he could bear with her no longer,
and he had put her out the door" (chap. 6). "Scandalous stories" and
"insinuating lies" are not both strictly necessary; if "insinuating lies" is
right, then it could have been substituted for the former phrase. But adding the second phrase gives the sense of a precision growing as we read.

Apposition is useful in loose sentence structure, linking information in
intricate but flowing patterns, allowing the impression to emerge of a search
for the right word or phrase. The dust-jacket of Barbara Pym's novel *A
Few Green Leaves* tells us that it is a "beautifully written" comedy. Inside
we read sentences like the following:

> As the unmistakable end of summer approached—misty mornings, the
> first falling leaves, the days inexorably drawing in—Graham found him-
> self coming to the conclusion that as far as Emma was concerned he
> had 'bitten off more than he could chew', to quote a phrase his mother
> sometimes used (even his academic attempts at L.S.E. had come into
> that category, he remembered). Yet he had not exactly bitten anything
> off, it had been thrust at him in the form of Emma writing to him after
> the TV appearance.
>
> (Barbara Pym, *A Few Green Leaves*, 1980, chap. 22)

The appositives at the start ("misty mornings, the first fallings leaves") are
from one point of view simply a reiteration of clichés, but their use by
Pym seems to stem from the sense that after all clichés or stereotypes are
all that is available to us. She does not aim to be startlingly original, simply
to find the available phrase that does most justice to the situation. The
first sentence is like the famous periodic sentence in that it introduces
several pieces of information—but quite *unlike* the periodic sentence in
that it allows the topic to drift off at the end into the question of "his
academic attempts." It is not quite an attempt at registering impressions
in the Virginia Woolf style, but explores both the constraints and the possibilities of language. The literariness is brought home to us when the
next sentence picks up the cliché "bitten off more than he could chew,"
and begins to reexamine or reconsider the words. These are easy, undisci-
plined thoughts about the season, the weather, the man's mother, his relationship with a woman, a foregrounded topic with backstage comments
in parentheses—yet the text manages also to seem literary, to read as though
it were exploring the medium of language in its modest way.

A. S. Byatt is perhaps thinking of a style not unlike Pym's when she
talks of the "good *modern* sentence": "A good modern sentence proceeds
evenly, loosely joined by commas, and its feel is hypothetical, approximate, unstructured and always aiming at an impossible exactness which it
knows it will not achieve."[14]

Linking Words

How things are connected is, as David Bordwell points out, important for
our understanding of narratives: "For perceivers of all ages, texts with
reordered story events or ambiguous causal connections tend to reduce
understanding. Causal connections are especially important in remembering stories."[15] We can go further than this, and say that sequential linking

is one of the basic characteristics of a text. We decide something is a text when the things within it have been put together in some relation or linked together.[16]

There are a variety of ways in which texts can be connected at the sentence level. We have seen how they may be put together in parataxis, in compound, or complex sentence structure: they may also be connected by linking words, which borrow the feel of a logical, or at least coherent, argument. Mikhail Bakhtin pointed out the use of *consequently* in Dickens, to give the feel of a "pseudo-objective motivation."[17] Such words not only add on new information, they also indicate a necessary or rational connection between one sentence and another, or between one part of a sentence and another. Elizabeth Deeds Ermarth talks of the importance of clauses starting with *meanwhile* in realist fiction: they enable the novelist to bring the action in one plot into synchrony with another.[18]

We can observe how such links are set up in a text like William Golding's *Darkness Visible* (1979), which provides us with a narrative that is difficult for the reader to swallow—of an angel who comes to modern England in the form of a badly injured child, and then manages to save an elderly pedophile from his own nature by carrying him off in a cloud of flame. Unbelievable things happen, but Golding pushes the narrative on with *linking adjuncts* that encourage us to see everything as fully caused and reasonable. In the course of two pages we have sentences starting "*So* they put Matty by and sent for Mr. Pedigree"; "*Nevertheless*, Mr. Pedigree did come down"; "*So* Mr. Pedigree screamed at him"; "*So* the headmaster, who had an account . . . "; "*So* he sat and thought and wondered."

We might contrast this with the frequent use of simple conjunctions by Anthony Trollope in *Castle Richmond* (1860). This is a novel about rich young families in Ireland at the time of the famine, and their problems over love-matches and inheritance of money. Paragraph after paragraph, and sentence after sentence, starts with a conjunction. In chapter 5, for example, twelve out of the thirty-eight paragraphs begin with either *and* or *but*. On one page of this chapter alone we find three paragraphs beginning: "And then it was discovered . . ."; "And then other enquiries . . ."; "And the search was not at an end . . ." Conjunctions are traditionally used *within* sentences, not (except for special emphasis) at the start. Trollope's usage seems to reflect a need to make the text smooth and seamless, his fear of losing the attention of his readers. In general he protested that he was not good at plots, but at the sentence level he is careful to pull us along with him, not to have us stop and think. We are not to stop and question the incongruity between this story of money and love among the rich, and the narrative of the Irish famine outside.

Ellipsis and Rupture

At the opposite pole to links in texts are points of *ellipsis* (gaps in the sentence), or even of *rupture* (where a text temporarily breaks down).[19] These may be indicated by a series of periods (. . .), dashes, a blank in the page, or simply by a break in syntax. Modern usage suggests that there should be no punctuation introducing an ellipse, but it appears in eighteenth- and nineteenth-century texts (for example, ! . . . or :— or .—).

Ellipsis contributes to a sense of the inadequacy of language, but also allows the suggestion of communicating what is, for one reason or another, inexpressible—like religion or sex. The gap in the text does not mean that we simply jump over such indications. As E. H. Gombrich has pointed out, breaks in a pattern are "points of maximal information content" that we focus upon.[20] Rupture is more interesting than continuity and promises greater depth of meaning.

The Hindu ceremony in E. M. Forster's *A Passage to India* represents something that cannot be fully grasped within Western language or the Western mentality. Forster ends the chapter as follows:

> **The singing went on even longer . . . ragged edges of religion . . . unsatisfactory and undramatic tangles . . . 'God si Love.' Looking back at the great blur of the last twenty-four hours, no man could say where was the emotional centre of it, any more than he could locate the heart of a cloud.**
>
> (E. M. Forster, *A Passage to India*, 1924, chap. 36)

The phrase "God is Love," popular in Christian ritual, has become mangled here to "God si Love," but this is only the climax of a breakdown in language signaled by the earlier ellipses. Forster himself is responsive to the demands of Western convention, and so does not end the chapter with broken syntax. He gives us instead a conventional sentence that sums up the problem in Western fashion, with a literary comparison to "the heart of a cloud."

Ellipsis is notoriously used for sex (in colloquial terms, *dot, dot, dot* at the end of a chapter). This is not always prudish or conventional: it can be a good deal more erotic than anatomical detail. Nonetheless its presence very often represents the frustration writers in the nineteenth century felt at not being able to speak out.

In Meredith's *Diana of the Crossways*, the husband of Diana's best friend, Sir Lukin, makes a pass at her while they are out on a walk together in the countryside:

> Her reproachful repulsion of eyes was unmistakeable, withering; as masterful as a superior force on his muscles.—What thing had he been taking her for?—She asked it within: and he of himself, in a reflective gasp. Those eyes of hers appeared as in a cloud, with the wrath above: she had the look of a Goddess in anger. He stammered, pleaded across her flying shoulder—Oh! horrible, loathsome, pitiable to hear! . . . "A momentary aberration . . . her beauty . . . he deserved to be shot! . . . could not help admiring . . . quite lost his head . . . on his honour! never again!"
>
> (George Meredith, *Diana of the Crossways*, 1885, chap. 4)

The text indicates the fury of Diana, at what she thinks is an inexplicable betrayal by Sir Lukin of his wife, the confused embarrassment of Sir Lukin, and the undercurrents of sexual excitement, which were (as Meredith often complained) unmentionable. The paragraph develops from fairly orderly prose to exclamations and incomplete phrases. The dashes around "What thing had he been taking her for" indicate a shift in the level of discourse: the sentence is what she asked "within" herself, but the problems of articulating what has happened become more and more severe, and repeated ellipses lead to a breakdown in normal sentence structure, with some free indirect speech ("he deserved to be shot") appearing inside quotation marks. Meredith could not be open about sexuality in the novel, but he found ways of making punctuation suggest much that lay below the surface.

In analyzing sentence structure, the point is not simply to look for regularity. Our interest is rather in noting dominant forms, and then in considering methods of linkage and rupture. Literary texts often establish their most interesting effects in varying expected forms, by transgressing syntactic rules, or testing limits. Gertrude Stein tells us that she found, when at school, that "the really completely exciting thing" was the grammar lesson, and analyzing sentences: "I really do not know that anything has ever been more exciting than diagraming sentences."[21] Not everyone shares quite her excitement (and not everyone goes on afterward to attempt the "destruction of syntax"), but since we so often read without paying close attention to the coherent forms of sentences, there is almost always some interest to be gained by shifting focus to look at sentence structure, and re-reading sentence structure in the light of cotext and context.

12

Verbs: Tense, Time, and Voice

Novels contain narratives, and narratives involve time. Verbs are obviously important to narratives, since as Aristotle pointed out, the verb is a word "involving the idea of time."[1] Vladimir Propp's analysis of narratives suggests that "verbs or actions are more structurally significant than nouns or characters."[2]

Verbs are not the only words that refer to time, but they give us a sense of actions, processes, and states in time. The grammatical forms or tenses of verbs seem (at least to native speakers of the language) to correspond to our concept of time. But we cannot assume a simple correspondence: for example, narrative often describes past events by using the present tense. Paul Ricoeur points out that a tense system is "a storehouse of distinctions, relations and combinations from which fiction draws the resources for its own autonomy."[3]

The *aspect* of verbs (the way they signify how an event is viewed) is also important. Some events are seen as completed or fixed in relation to where we stand, while some are in progress or indefinite. If we use perfect aspect in the past indefinite form (as in "Mr. Smith has made a fortune"), we give a general contour of time: we know Mr. Smith's making a fortune happened in the past, but we cannot specify when. (We would need to think up a particular and unusual situation of enunciation to produce the sentence "Mr. Smith has made a fortune on June 5, 1985"—though within a literary text this could certainly be done.)

The syntax of verbs used in conventional ways does shape our narratives and their location in time. As we have seen in chapter 11, there are also prototypical fictional sentences where we find usages in which the system of tenses and their relation to time is disturbed. In the context of fiction we readily accept a mixture of past verbs and adverbs referring to the present: "Today he roamed throughout Europe"; "This evening he intended to play the flute." Käte Hamburger points out that because of the fictionality of a text, "the grammatical past tense loses its function of informing us about the past-ness of the facts reported."[4] Sentences of this kind are not only found in novels; they can also occur in nonfiction works—for example, in histories that are attempting to make things vivid—but we respond even there by reading them as fictionalizing sentences. We take it that the writer is trying to make an account of the past come to life "like a novel."[5]

Conventional Past-Tense Narrative

If fiction can contain apparently anomalous sentences that confuse the handling of time, it works more generally with a pattern of tenses that allows us to coordinate a fictional narrative as a discrete unit. Conventionally this is done with a system of verb tenses that locate narrative in the past. ("He went into the house. He found something he had not expected to find.") And this is true even of science fiction, which is supposed to describe the future: "We were in the spaceship at last. It was June 5, 2050. We had escaped the aliens."

There are various ways in which classic fiction breaks out of the domination of the past tense, but its customary use may have had wider implications. As Elizabeth Deeds Ermarth says: "By the apparently innocent gesture of accepting the past-tense narration . . . we have accepted several rather more complex ideas: that time is a single continuum; that temporal continuities extend beyond the arbitrarily limited horizons of the text; that events point beyond themselves to a coordinating system."[6]

Tense and Time

Old-fashioned grammars of English, based on the patterns of Latin paradigms, combined tense and aspect to produce a large number of possible verb forms—twelve might be a conservative estimate. We can, however, simplify matters (following Seymour Chatman) by suggesting that English is capable of indicating four temporal stages:

1. anterior time   (had gone, had eaten)
2. past time   (went, ate)

3. present time   (go, eat)
4. future time   (will/shall go, will/shall eat)

Traditionally, a novel sets what Chatman calls the "story-NOW" in the second time, using the simple past tense.[7]

What we might expect in the simplest case is what we get from the incipit of Arnold Bennett's *Clayhanger* (1910): "Edwin Clayhanger *stood* on the steep-sloping, red-bricked canal bridge, in the valley between Bursley and its suburb Hillport." Or the incipit of Frank Norris's *McTeague* (1899): "It *was* Sunday, and according to his custom on that day, McTeague *took* his dinner at two in the afternoon at the car conductors' coffee-joint on Polk Street." The simple past used in this way is never likely to be sustained for long. It may be the main tense in which a classic novel is told, but backward and forward movement begins from this starting point, with the use of verbs suggesting anterior time, or continuous, iterated, or timeless actions. Dickens's *A Christmas Carol* starts off:

> MARLEY was dead: to begin with. There is no doubt whatever about that. The register of his burial was signed by the clergyman, the clerk, the undertaker, and the chief mourner. Scrooge signed it: and Scrooge's name was good upon 'Change, for anything he chose to put his hand to. Old Marley was as dead as a door-nail.
>
> Mind! I don't mean to say that I know, of my own knowledge, what there is particularly dead about a door-nail. I might have been inclined, myself, to regard a coffin-nail as the deadest piece of ironmongery in the trade. But the wisdom of our ancestors is in the simile; and my unhallowed hands shall not disturb it, or the Country's done for. You will therefore permit me to repeat, emphatically, that Marley was as dead as a door-nail.
>
> (Charles Dickens, *A Christmas Carol*, 1843)

We find simple past tenses here, but also present, past perfect, modal auxiliaries (that is, auxiliaries such as *can, may, might, must, ought to, should, would*), and even future tense. Dickens has opened the story with a mixture of *discours* and *récit*. The *discours* is based on the present, and can accommodate a future concerned with itself: "You will . . . permit me." The *récit*, on the other hand, is set in simple past tense: "Marley was dead."

The combination of *discours* in the present and *récit* in the past is, as we have already seen, quite usual—but it has particular importance here, since Dickens wants to blend a tale based on the figure of Scrooge (a representative character of the miser drawn from folk-literature) with comment on modern London life and urban poverty. To do this, the narrative has to switch between an image of Scrooge in a typical story world ("Once upon a time . . . . old Scrooge sat busy in his counting-house") and a narrator who is here with us, telling us about how it *is* for those who work on "'Change" in the City of London.

Past and Present

Verb tenses, then, not only represent a particular time, they set up that negotiation between past and present which became so complex and productive in the mid-nineteenth-century novel. If we find, as Kathleen Tillotson pointed out, an important shift in this period from the overtly historical novel (of the type Walter Scott wrote) to "the use of the past in novels of private life," then verb tenses play a significant role in that shift.[8] *The Mill on the Floss* has already established its *récit* when we read:

> **Mr. Tulliver was speaking to his wife, a blond comely woman, in a fan-shaped cap (I am afraid to think how long it is since fan-shaped caps were worn—they must be so near coming in again. At that time, when Mrs. Tulliver was nearly forty, they were new at St. Ogg's, and considered sweet things.)**
>
> (George Eliot, *The Mill on the Floss*, 1860, bk. 1, chap. 2)

One way of looking at this would be simply to see a comment by an "intrusive" narrator breaking into a historical narrative, but a more nuanced reading might point out how the text has gone from a simple past in the previous paragraph ("said Mr. Tulliver"), to a progressive past ("was speaking"), to a present ("I am afraid"), to a modal auxiliary in the belief mode ("must be"), and then back to simple past again. The main narrative of the novel is set about thirty to forty years before its date of publication (the date not exactly specified), but these temporal transitions establish a framework of what the novel itself calls "memory" which is "still half passionate and not merely contemplative" (bk. 6, chap. 9).

Present-Tense Narration

If the story-NOW is traditionally set in the past tense, there are some occasions, even in the classic novel, when it is not. Summaries of narrative, such as chapter headings in eighteenth-century novels, use the present. Chapter 2 of Henry Fielding's *Tom Jones* (1749), for instance, is headed: "In which Mr Jones *receives* many friendly Visits during his confinement; with some fine Touches of the Passion of Love, scarce visible to the naked Eye." We also find examples in classic novels of what Dorrit Cohn calls an evocative present—where writers forget about time and recount as if things were happening before their eyes.[9] In Aphra Behn's *The History of a Nun* (1689) the heroine "pretended" to be asleep in bed, and "resolved" to think things over, but then the tense shifts without warning: "she brings reason on both sides . . . she argues that she was born in sin." Epistolary novels use an impossible present. (It is all happening *now* for the letter writers, but when do they get the time to write?)

The *récit* of a novel may make a longer switch from past to present, as Dickens does from the middle of chapter 2 in *Our Mutual Friend* (1864–65). We have been reading about a man called Twemlow and his friends, the Veneerings, in a narrative that uses the past tense. Dickens then changes mid-chapter to the use of the present: "This evening the Veneerings *give* a banquet. . . . Mrs Veneering *welcomes* her sweet Mr Twemlow. Mr Veneering *welcomes* his dear Mr Twemlow. Mrs Veneering *does not expect* that Mr Twemlow *can* in nature *care* much for such insipid things as babies, but so old a friend *must* please *look* at baby." The present tenses then continue until the end of the chapter and recur when the Veneerings are the subject of later chapters.

If the evocative present is usually a way of "dramatic heightening" that "puts the reader in the place of someone actually witnessing the events as they are described,"[10]—this does not seem quite to fit *Our Mutual Friend*. The Veneerings are caricatured throughout: "bran-new people in a bran-new house in a bran-new quarter of London." The present tense used for them is like the present tense in stage-directions, or in the instructions for a toy theater.[11] In the context of a novelistic narrative, it contributes to the *unreality* of the scene.

The usage of the present in this novel is not consistent. Dickens does sometimes shift scenes with other characters into the present—as where Mr. Venus talks with Mr. Boffin and Silas Wegg. Here the tag phrases certainly give us a kind of stage-direction: "Mr Wegg opens the gate, descries a sort of brown paper truncheon under Mr Venus's arm, and remarks, in a dry tone . . . " (bk. 2, chap. 7). Dickens, we might conclude, has a large repertory of effects. There is not much evidence of planning their use in advance: he seems to be inventing opportunities to use them, and improvising new effects as he goes along.

Present as Main Narrative Tense

Use of the present tense for the main narrative tense, as Christine Brooke-Rose has pointed out, has become "very current" in the contemporary novel. This has different implications from occasional use, and as Brooke-Rose says, causes considerable problems. The present may seem a natural tense to use, because people do use it to make narrative vivid in conversation (and because of its "presentness"), but "at every sentence, it excludes easier slidings, and forces the writer to find an alternative."[12] William Trevor's *Felicia's Journey* starts off:

> **She keeps being sick. A woman in the washroom says:**
>
> **"You'd be better off in the fresh air. Wouldn't you go up on the deck?"**
>
> **It's cold on the deck and the wind hurts her ears. When she has been sick over the rail she feels better and goes downstairs again, to where she was sitting before she went to the washroom. The clothes she picked out for her journey are in two green carrier bags; the money is in her handbag. She had to pay for the carrier bags in Chawke's, fifty pence each. They have Chawke's name on them, and a Celtic pattern round the edge. At the *bureau de change* she has been given English notes for her Irish ones.**
>
> (William Trevor, *Felicia's Journey*, 1994)

Present is the dominant tense in this novel, but not all the usages are the same. "She keeps being sick" is an iterative present (like "I always go on Thursdays"). "They have Chawke's name on them" is a timeless present (like "England is a small country"). "A woman in the washroom says" is the instant or punctual present, which gives an action in the present—the story-NOW of the text.

Present dominates, but it is noticeable how easily the narrative slips back into the past ("where she was sitting," "she picked out") and how complex this interplay rapidly becomes. Trevor is not making it easy for himself in using the present—but then that is presumably not his aim. The uncertainties of the relation between past and present, and the tendency to base present actions on confused misunderstandings, or memories of narratives, come indeed to constitute a major subject of Trevor's novel.[13]

A dominant present tense can work in a quite different way, to couple quiet menace with extreme banality. Lise in Muriel Spark's *The Driver's Seat* is on her own in a hotel in Italy:

> Lise slides open the cupboard, pulls down a wooden hanger and throws it across the room with a clatter, then lies down on the bed. Presently she looks at her watch. It is five past one. She opens her suitcase and carefully extracts a short dressing-gown. She takes out a dress, hangs it in the cupboard, takes it off the hanger again, folds it neatly and puts it back. She takes out her sponge-bag and bedroom slippers, undresses, puts on her dressing-gown and goes into the bathroom, shutting the door. She has reached the point of taking a shower when she hears voices from her room, a scraping sound, a man's and a girl's. Putting forth her head from the bathroom door, she sees a man in light brown overalls with a pair of steps and an electric light bulb, accompanied by the maid. Lise comes out in her dressing-gown without having properly dried herself in the evident interest of protecting her hand-bag which lies on the bed.
>
> (Muriel Spark, *The Driver's Seat*, 1970, chap. 4)

The punctual present here becomes slightly formal (as though everything were being listed in a catalogue), or perhaps mesmeric, a kind of searching through unconscious memories with the narrator saying, "She does this. Then she does that. Then she does that again." Sentence after sentence opens with a clause that follows the order of subject + verb + predicate, and produces a mechanical regularity of rhythm. The novel can be read as a series of instructions to a performer—perhaps a long film scenario. We have the sense that every action is definite and fixed, preordained either by Lise or by some agent controlling her.

From the start of *The Driver's Seat* there have been indications that something terrible is about to happen, there will be blood and murder—though it is still not quite plain whether it is Lise who is planning to do something, or whether something will be done to her. The forward movement of the narrative follows a detective-story pattern, in which our attention is fixed on the sequence of actions, as though they held some clue. But this is not a conventional detective story, and it is extremely difficult to judge the seriousness with which we are supposed to be decoding the actions. The verb aspect can change ("She has reached the point") to draw attention to an instant in time. The immediacy of the present makes us think that something important is about to happen, but it is only someone coming to change a lightbulb. The overall effect (as with Dickens and the Veneerings in *Our Mutual Friend*) is of distance rather than immediacy.

Active Voice and Style

F. Scott Fitzgerald wrote to his daughter: "All fine prose is based on the verbs carrying the sentences. They make sentences move."[14] Verbs are thus associated not only with time but with action, and it is a common modern assumption that "good writing" will contain strong active verbs.

This is a question both of the choice of the active mood, and the selection of a range of verbs, rather than the repetition of a few old favorites. (It is often assumed that phrasal verbs, such as *catch on, turn up, blow up, take off, break down* are weaker and less colorful than one-word verbs.)

The dreadful narrator of the second part of J. M. Coetzee's *Dusklands* is an active and vigorous explorer in mid-eighteenth-century South Africa. He is captured by "bushmen" and then released, along with his farm worker Klawer, who becomes sick and is left to die. He writes:

> I was alone. I had no Klawer to record. I exulted like a young man whose mother has just died. Here I was, free to initiate myself into the desert. I yodelled, I growled, I hissed, I roared, I screamed, I clucked, I whistled; I danced, I stamped, I grovelled, I spun; I sat on the earth, I spat on the earth, I kicked it, I hugged it, I clawed it.
>
> (J. M. Coetzee, *Dusklands*, [1974] 1988, p. 95)

Coetzee's novel as a whole is deeply disturbing in the way it confronts us with the limitations of our own responses. Here we can partly understand the narrator's relief at being alone, but his assumption that his feelings of exultation are like those of a young man whose mother has just died are hard to stomach. The fictionalizing sentence ("Here I was") leads us into an extraordinary bombardment of verbs, all predicated on the repeated and inescapable *I* of the narrator. The ordering of these verbs, their listing and grouping into units of noise and then action, split off by commas and semicolons, would itself be worth examination; in this context we can simply point to how the variety of active verbs communicates the intense energy of the narrator. However much we may loathe him, we stand in awe of his energy and inventiveness.

Passive Voice

Coetzee is undoubtedly aware of what he is doing in the passage quoted above, because he has written elsewhere of the significance of the passive voice in English. A common assumption is that the passive produces weak, depersonalized English, associated with the colorless prose of bureaucracy or scientific reports. Instead of "the drunken driver drove the car into a brick wall," we use the passive to say, "The car was driven into a brick wall." By using the passive, the agent and the question of responsibility are somehow removed. We can of course add a "by" clause: "The car was driven into the brick wall (by the drunken driver)." But this is optional. And the *Handbook on Writing Well* (by William Zinser) thus recommends that we "use active verbs": "the difference between an active-verb style and a passive-verb style—in pace, clarity and vigor—is the difference between life and death for a writer."[15]

Coetzee, however, argues that this view of the passive stems from too much attention to the verb on its own, and too little attention to what the verb does in the whole sentence or how the sentences relate to the rest of a text. Passives allow us to talk about acts without mentioning agents, but it does not follow that the writer then conceives of acts without agents. The passive may be used to show an "interplay" between "various unnamed agents." It may question what agency is, suggest unconscious motivation, or, in texts using irony, may block out the agent in such a way that agency "will be inferred (recovered) with fair accuracy" from the context.[16]

The main text of Charles Brockden Brown's *Wieland* (1798) begins with predominantly active verbs: "I *feel* little reluctance in complying with your request. You *know* not fully the cause of my sorrows. . . . Yet the tale I *am going* to tell is not intended as a claim upon your sympathy. In the midst of my despair, I *do not disdain* to contribute what little I *can* to the benefit of mankind" (italics added). We have, however, already encountered a paratext (the "Advertisement") that brings agency into question: "The power which the principal person is said to possess can scarcely be denied to be real." "It must be acknowledged to be . . ."; "It will not be objected that . . ."; "It will be necessary to add . . ."; "It may likewise be mentioned . . ." These are the stylistic tricks of modern science, placed here and there throughout the text in such a way that the narrative establishes itself as a series of questions, or oppositions: "Was this the penalty of disobedience? this the stroke of a vindictive and invisible hand? Is it a fresh proof that the Divine Ruler interferes in human affairs . . .? Or, was it merely the irregular expansion of the fluid that imparts warmth to our heart and our blood . . .?" (chap. 2). Agency is thus not deleted from *Wieland*—it is put in question.

Weak Verbs at Work

Is there then something to be said for the passive voice? And perhaps for weak verbs too? Writers of handbooks would generally disagree. Virginia Tufte boldly assures us: "Verbs are action words. Verb phrases are action phrases. These generalizations hold true more for good writing than for any other kind, and they apply not only to the main predicate verb but to verb phrases in other positions as well."[17] "Good writing" seems, however, not always to follow prescriptions of this kind, and to have other ends in view. There are ranges of meaning that are verbal but not active.

Anthony Powell's prose, for example, is almost a parodic version of crippling inaction on the page. Powell's narrator in *A Buyer's Market*, moving across London, is on his way to dinner with his school friend Widmerpool, and thinks to himself that he does not want to go:

> There is a strong disposition in youth, from which some individuals never escape, to suppose that everyone else is having a more enjoyable time than we are ourselves; and for some reason, as I moved southwards across London, I was that evening particularly convinced that I had not yet succeeded in striking a satisfactory balance in my manner of conducting life. I could not make up my mind whether the deficiencies that seemed so stridently to exist were attributable to what had already happened that day, or to a growing certainty in my own mind that I should much prefer to be dining elsewhere. The Widmerpools—for I felt that I had already heard so much of Widmerpool's mother that my picture of her could not be far from the truth—were the last persons on earth with whom I wished to share the later part of the evening. I suppose I could have had a meal by myself, thinking of some excuse later to explain my absence; but the will to take so decisive a step seemed to have been taken physically from me.
>
> (Anthony Powell, *A Buyer's Market*, 1952, chap. 3)

We start off with the weak existential "There is,"— which leaves the subject position of the sentence vacant. Then we have weak linking verbs ("seemed," "felt," "suppose"); negatives ("never," "not yet," "could not," "not far from"); passives ("deficiencies . . . were attributable," "the will . . . seemed to have been taken"); a general sentence structure slowed down by hesitation, parenthesis, and a lexicon that indicates over-elaborate precision. Almost nothing moves the traffic-jam of self-conscious suppositions.

But this is not uncalculated. Powell's linguistic effects neatly indicate the kind of young man the narrator is. He is pompous and timid. He is also lonely; can't make up his mind; never initiates anything; can't free himself from his washed-up social context. The people he is opposed to in the novel (the Widmerpools) are power-hungry, insensitive, and greedy. Because the novel is told in the first person, the reader can never quite be sure how much Powell intends to criticize his narrator. Other characters, however, do criticize him. He meets a tough young woman called Gipsy Jones, who asks him: "Why are you so stuck up?" He replies weakly that he is "just made that way." The character is built up through these linguistic effects, through a rejection of bold straightforward movement, and an endlessly indecisive series of impressions.

We may agree with Propp, then, on the importance of verbs, but it is not helpful to prejudge their choice or the way in which they are to be used. The global sense of a text constantly releases new possiblities for the individual elements.[18]

13

Adjectives

The novelist in one of A. S. Byatt's stories thinks about words as she walks along the street: "It was mostly adjectives. Elephantine bark, eau-de-nil paint on Fortnum's walls, Nile-water green, a colour fashionable from Nelson's victories at the time when this street was formed." Searching for adjectives in this way sounds a little contrived and precious. Henry James called them "the sugar of literature," and Chekhov advised writers, "when you read proof, take out adjectives and adverbs wherever you can."[1] Adjectives can add precision to nouns and register affect. Their control, as well as their deployment, is obviously one aspect of a writer's technique.

Classifying and Nonclassifying

We can make a crude distinction between classifying and nonclassifying adjectives.[2] *Classifying adjectives* are definable independently of particular situations in which the words have been used, and permit one to delimit a class (for example, "the scientific book"). Color adjectives are particularly important in literary descriptions, and form a special group of classifying adjectives.

Nonclassifying adjectives are more subjective, and gain their meaning from the context in which they figure. They may identify qualities (like "happy" or "pretty"), or they may emphasize feelings ("complete," "absolute"). There is no class of "pretty" objects or "absolute" disasters.

Surplusage

M. E. Braddon, in *Phantom Fortune,* gives us a description of a woman in her new dress that piles on details, and uses a mixture of classifying and nonclassifying adjectives:

> Lesbia's Chamount costume was a success. The women praised it, the men stared and admired. The dark-blue silken jersey, sparkling with closely studded indigo beads, fitted the slim graceful figure as a serpent's scales fit the serpent. The coquettish little blue silk toque, the careless cluster of gold-coloured poppies, against the glossy brown hair, the large sunshade of old gold satin lined with indigo, the flounced petticoat of softest Indian silk, the dainty little tan-coloured boots with high heels and pointed toes, were all perfect after their fashion; and Mr. Smithson felt that the liege lady of his life, the woman he meant to marry willy nilly, would be the belle of the racecourse.
>
> (M. E. Braddon, *Phantom Fortune*, 1884, chap. 30)

The effect here is like one of those huge nineteenth-century pictures of English life, where the painter includes as much as possible in every corner of the canvas, and ends up producing a jumble of images. It is what Walter Pater calls "surplusage."[3]

All the same, the description is rich in details, and we may wonder why they fail to cohere. Part of the problem is the repetitive three-part patterns ("dark-blue silken jersey," "slim graceful figure," "glossy brown hair"). The principal problem is that there is just too much to take in: we have to imagine not only *all* the colors ("dark-blue," "indigo," "blue," "gold," "tan"), but also shapes, materials, and subjective evaluations.

Braddon was a hugely popular writer in her time, and some of our modern difficulties with passages of this kind may stem from the fact that we no longer buy clothes as people did in the nineteenth century. We are used to illustrations in photographs, or to buying ready-made clothes, so we do not have much practice at visualizing details from written descriptions. It may also be that the description is intended to be ironic. Braddon's pictures of middle-class life never quite take themselves seriously.[4]

The Controlled Palette

One of the lessons the modern novel learned from Flaubert was that adjectival details should in some respect *count* in the narrative. It is no good for a novelist to stick things in because "they might be there in real life":

anything might be there in real life. Careful writers work with a controlled palette. They use what Henry James called the "challenge of economic representation," which is so "intensely interesting to meet." [5] Through restriction of color adjectives they can achieve a play on colors of the kind we saw in Joyce's "A Painful Case."[6]

James describes the appearance and dress of Daisy Miller:

> **The young lady meanwhile had drawn near. She was dressed in white muslin, with a hundred frills and flounces, and knots of pale-coloured ribbon. She was bare-headed; but she balanced in her hand a large parasol, with a deep border of embroidery; and she was strikingly, admirably pretty.**
>
> (*Daisy Miller*, 1878 [1909], chap. 1)

"White" is the dominant color adjective, motivated by its connection with youth and virginity (and death), and moving us on to the frills, flounces, and "pale-coloured" ribbons. Daisy has "a hundred frills and flounces," and this registering of excess is sustained by the nonclassifying adjectives "large" and "deep." Anne Hollander points out that dress in fiction is usually "tacitly supplied": it is assumed that the general outline would be known to writer and reader—and therefore an outfit is best conveyed by "one or two strokes" or by brief contrasts.[7] The details provided in *Daisy Miller* are strongly influenced by the subjectivity of the narrator: Daisy exemplifies for him what Europeans of the period saw as American extravagance (as well as American innocence).

In the final sentence the focus is on the adjective *pretty*—this time placed on its own in a predicative position: "she was . . . pretty." *Pretty* is precisely chosen: Daisy is not beautiful, for all her frills and flounces. The slight hesitation between the modifiers before *pretty* ("strikingly, admirably") registers the ambivalence of the narrator: her appearance is a little ostentatious, and yet it is also admirable. James has been sparing with colors, and has picked up only a few details to describe, but they contribute significantly to the themes of the story.

Impressionist Adjectives

At the turn of the twentieth century aesthetic prose used adjectives in a way that can be related to impressionist painting, and a desire to record impressions rather than facts. Writers of this period wanted prose to be unashamedly art prose, and one obvious means to this end was a lavish array of adjectives (often in unfamiliar contexts). They used adjectives not for accurate description, but to evoke impressions and sensations. George Levine talks of Conrad's "vaguely evocative and menacing adjectives," such as *inconceivable* and *impenetrable*.[8] In Oscar Wilde's *The Picture of Dorian Gray* (1891) we read that Sybil Vane has "a little flower-like face, a small Greek head with plaited coils of dark-brown hair, eyes that were violet wells of passion, lips that were like the petals of a rose" (chap. 4). There is no attempt to limit the color range here, or to make the details fictionally descriptive: the surplusage is as evident to modern readers as it is in M. E. Braddon.

Synesthesia

One of the most important adjectival effects (again developed at the end of the nineteenth century, and often associated with the influence of French writers like Baudelaire) is that of *synesthesia,* the confusion of senses—talking of the *colors of sound*, or the *perfume of a color*.

Writers use synesthesia when they want to shift description into the evocation of sensation. George Moore writes in *The Lake* ([1905] 1921) of how, after a fox has been around, "a thick yellow smell hung on the still air." Susan, in Virginia Woolf's *The Waves* (1931), says, "I sit among you abrading the silver-grey flickering quiver of words with the green spurt of my clear eyes" (184). And when Patrick White's Theodora Goodman plays the piano in *The Aunt's Story* (1948), we find her "beating out the icy bars of a nocturne" (28).

Adjectives in general, then, reveal the writer being literary: their ostentatious deployment frequently reminds us that we are being given artwork, not a functional guidebook. At the end of a chapter of Esther Freud's *Hideous Kinky*, set in Morocco, we read:

> **I turned around. The sun was a smouldering crescent, lying on the edge of the world. Fingers of light streamed away from it up through a wafer-thin purple cloud and into the dome of the sky.**
>
> (Esther Freud, *Hideous Kinky*, 1992, chap. 11)

The tricks of aesthetic prose are apparent here: the *-ing* form of adjective ("smouldering"); the unusual adjective for a cloud ("wafer-thin"); and the favored color range of the *fin de siècle* ("purple"). But this is not writing from the 1890s, it is from a contemporary novel. And, oddest of all, it is a first-person narrator recalling her impressions of Morocco at the age of five. Could we expect a five-year-old to have registered a scene in this way? Obviously not. Adjectival evocation creates here a dissonance and distance in the narrative. All first-person accounts of childhood face some of the same problems of distance, but the particular style used here produces acute disjunctions, which make the text both unsettling and interesting to read. It would be too easy to criticize the passage as amateurish or over-written. It has its effect, but we need to consider the choice and use of lexicon to see how it achieves it.

14

Figures: Metaphor, Metonymy, Irony

Metaphor

The traditional view of metaphor, from Aristotle to the present day, has been that it is a deviant use of words, or *trope*, which achieves a special literary or poetic effect. In recent years cognitive linguistics has called this into question, suggesting that metaphor is not an unusual device in language, but common and necessary. Since our conceptual system is "fundamentally metaphorical," it is through metaphor that we do much of our thinking.[1]

We use metaphor, for instance, to talk about abstract topics, such as love, time, life, ideas, or the emotions. We talk of being *crazy about* someone, of time *stretching out in front* of us, of life *in its last stages*, of *incisive ideas*, or of someone being *cold* toward family and friends. These are familiar expressions, but they are not literal ones. It has been customary to consider most of our language as literal, some conspicuous metaphors as "creative," and the majority, like those cited above, as conventional, or "dead." But cognitive linguists have pointed out that this is confusing. Just because metaphors are conventional, it does not follow that they are inoperative as metaphor: they continue to shape the way in which we think and talk about things. "Those [things in our cognition] that are most alive and most deeply entrenched, efficient and powerful are those that are so automatic as to be unconscious and effortless."[2]

Metaphor is used for thinking and talking about things, for developing our ideas. Metaphors are handy tools that function in the processes of communication. This is as true in the sciences as the humanities (recent discussions of the "selfish" gene provide a noteworthy example), and it is an unavoidable aspect of discourse. When a metaphor has been set up, or "primed," elaboration or extension can take place on its basis. For example, if someone says, "These colors are not particularly close," and the reply comes, "Well, there's not that much distance between them," we are extending the metaphor of closeness as similarity. "The selfish gene," we are told, "wants to" optimize conditions for its reproduction.

Concepts before Words

The underlying assumption of the new cognitive approach is that metaphor is a matter not just of words, but of concepts. As George Lakoff and Mark Johnson explain, "the essence of metaphor is understanding and experiencing one kind of thing in terms of another."[3] In order to think about some conceptual domain, we use the structure of another domain and the corresponding vocabulary. Thus we talk about TIME AS SPACE:[4] "Christmas is approaching"; "summer is around the corner."[5] We talk, for instance, about COMPLEX SYSTEMS AS PLANTS: "They are preparing the ground for future projects"; "the university has been cultivating links with industry."[6] It is extremely difficult for us to discuss abstract topics without relying on metaphors. We frequently use the concept of war, for example, to understand and perform (and talk about) argument. We can be said to map the concept of war onto the concept of argument when we produce sentences like these: "He attacked all the weak points in my argument." "What you say is indefensible." "He's won that argument!" "Why don't you just fight it out between you?" Lakoff and Johnson argue that such expressions can be easily understood because they stem from the basic conceptual metaphor ARGUMENT IS WAR. This may perhaps be culture-specific (not all cultures evaluate belligerence in the same way), but endless variations on the theme are understood in English, because we are accustomed to the mapping of war onto argument.

Literary texts (like all other texts) offer us innumerable examples of conventional metaphors. Since, according to the tradition derived from Aristotle, the invention of metaphors by a writer could be seen as a "sign of genius,"[7] we may also find writers building them up, experimenting with and augmenting them in unusual ways. In *Vanity Fair*, there is an argument between Becky Sharp and Miss Pinkerton. The narrator comments:

> **Worthy Miss Pinkerton, although she had a Roman nose and a turban, and was as tall as a grenadier, and had been up to this time an irresist-**

ible princess, had no will or strength like that of her little apprentice, and in vain did battle against her, and tried to overawe her.

(William Thackeray, *Vanity Fair*, (1847–48) 1848, no. 1, chap. 2)

All that has actually happened in the argument is that Becky has refused to work without payment, and has laughed at the pretensions of Miss Pinkerton, but it is mapped onto the domain of war as a "battle." Because of this mapping, Thackeray can insert references to Miss Pinkerton's "Roman nose" and "turban," or comparisons with a grenadier guard and the princess of fairy stories. The logic of such comparisons would fit the domain of war, but they are too many and too disparate to be appropriate for this small domestic squabble. They seem to overextend the blending of the two domains. Thackeray is mocking the metaphor even as he establishes and elaborates on it, and making Miss Pinkerton look the pompous, self-important ass she is.

It is not always so easy to decide on the implications of metaphor in literature. In Trollope's *Castle Richmond*, Owen Fitzgerald is protesting that his rival in love has stolen his fiancée. He says, speaking of his desire for the young woman:

Shall I see the prey taken out of my jaws, and not struggle for it? No, by heavens! you must fight me; and I tell you fairly, that the fight shall be as hard as I can make it.

(Anthony Trollope, *Castle Richmond*, 1860 [1873], chap. 30)

Owen is portrayed as a not very bright young squire, whose main interests in life are hunting and gambling, so it is not too surprising that, when inspired to strong emotion, he should speak in this way. Such metaphors for love as hunting and fighting, distasteful though they may be on close examination, are not uncommon in English or other languages.[8] Having been primed, they contribute to the framework of discussion, and where they are used, they will suggest that fighting and male pursuit are more important than women's happiness, or indeed than a relationship on equal terms.

Does Trollope see this? And how much are we intended to criticize Owen for using such metaphors? Answers to these questions are not easy, since the words are attributed to Owen as speech in a stretch of dialogue, and do not receive direct narratorial commentary. Owen's fiancée actually decides to reject him, and claims the right to make up her own mind, so the plot development does work against Owen. But even if Trollope's plot implies criticism of the treatment of women as prey, or as breeding-stock in a marriage market, it still makes Owen something of a romantic hero. There is a residual affection and admiration for the metaphorical framework within which Owen conceives the world.

Concept and Culture

One major problem that has emerged from the cognitive account of metaphors is the extent to which they derive from (and are reinforced by) individual experience, or depend upon the usages of the cultures in which we live. Lakoff and Johnson argue that there are hundreds of "primary metaphors," based on our sensorimotor experience of the world. Examples are MORE IS UP (which produces such statements as "prices are high"; "it's too hot, turn the heating down"; "my salary rose this year"). Or IMPORTANCE IS BIG ("he has been a huge influence"; "it's a big day"; "it has made an enormous difference to me"). Language, according to their view, is not a set of abstract symbols, but is motivated and grounded in experience. Our experiences give rise to image-schemas (like UP-DOWN, CONTAINER, PATH) which we map onto other domains. "Each of us is a container, with a bounding surface and an in-out orientation. We project our own in-out orientation onto other physical objects that are bounded by surfaces."[9] We see rooms as containers (with things *in* them), also gardens and countries. We see categories as containers, and arguments as containers ("a leaky argument"; "he blew a hole in my argument"). We see texts as containers ("stick to what's in the text!") as well as sentences, words, and instances of language in general ("this contains some fundamentally good things").

However, not all languages, and not all people, end up expressing things in the same way. We must conclude that our use of metaphor becomes affected by the culture in which we live, as well as by the conventions of the language we happen to speak (and its history of development). The question of how exactly our embodied concepts come to be affected by cultural practices is still problematic in cognitive linguistics.

Image Metaphors

Within literary texts making metaphors has been highly esteemed as an indication of literary talent. As a result we also find metaphors that seem a long way from conventional usage, but which are nonetheless striking.

The cognitive approach has been to suggest that these are special cases, based on a comparison of images, or unusual "one-shot" metaphors:

His intentions burnt on the dark an almost invisible trail.

(Elizabeth Bowen)

Purple silence petrified the limbs of trees and stood crops upright in the fields.

(Shirley Hazzard)

We find, very frequently, mixtures of metaphor and comparison, or simile (indicated by *like* or *as*):

The very air in which he speaks hangs listless as a sheet.

(J. M. Coetzee)

The silence was swelling like a tumour at my back.

(John Banville)

The mapping of domains is slightly odd at first sight in these cases (though perhaps no odder than the familiar and conventional "grim reaper" metaphor for death, which has been analyzed by Mark Turner).[10]

Arresting mixtures of this kind have proved useful for communicating high emotion in the novel, particularly when writers wish to avoid the supposed banality of the literal, as in sex scenes. D. H. Lawrence, in *Lady Chatterley's Lover*, despite his more famous use of colloquial four-letter words in dialogue, turns to a very literary combination of simile and metaphor to describe Connie's feelings about her orgasm:

And it seemed she was like the sea, nothing but dark waves rising and heaving, heaving with a great swell, so that slowly her whole darkness was in motion, and she was ocean rolling its dark, dumb mass.

(D. H. Lawrence, *Lady Chatterley's Lover*, [1928] 1960, chap. 12)

Although this is still, in Lakoff and Johnson's phrase, experiencing and understanding one thing in terms of another (that is, orgasm as sea), it includes not just the simple blending of concepts, but the construction of developed images and the employment of appropriate rhythm.

When there is self-conscious use of metaphor in literary texts, we may move rapidly between the familiar and the one-shot. James's *The Golden Bowl* tells us about Maggie:

> **This situation had been occupying for months and months the very centre of the garden of her life, but it had reared itself there like some strange tall tower of ivory, or perhaps rather some wonderful beautiful but outlandish pagoda . . . She had walked round and round it—that was what she felt.**
>
> (Henry James, *The Golden Bowl*, 1904 [1909], vol. 2, chap. 1)

Life is mapped onto the concept of the garden as container. But then one-shot comparisons are made with a "strange tall tower of ivory" and an "outlandish pagoda," and integrated into the garden metaphor ("She had walked round and round it"). Metaphor is being used as an aid to understanding here, but in a complex and unusual way.

Self-consciously literary writers reach for different kinds of metaphor, both to describe and to develop their understanding of the situation they are attempting to represent. In Graham Greene's *The End of the Affair*, Sarah writes in her diary:

> **Sometimes I get so tired of trying to convince him that I love him and shall love him for ever. He pounces on my words like a barrister and twists them. I know he is afraid of that desert which would be around him if our love were to end, but he can't realize that I feel exactly the same. What he says aloud, I say to myself silently and write it here. What can one build in the desert? Sometimes after a day when we have made love many times, I wonder whether it isn't possible to come to an end of sex, and I know that he is wondering too and is afraid of that point where the desert begins. What do we do in the desert if we lose each other? How does one go on living after that?**
>
> (Graham Greene, *The End of the Affair*, 1951, book 3, chap. 2)

Various metaphors are at work at different levels here. The sentence "He pounces on my words like a barrister and twists them," for instance, obviously contains nonliteral elements. The description of the man as "like a barrister" might seem a simple comparison—but when put with "pounces" it participates in the blending of concepts of a predatory animal and the legal system. The man is imagined as a barrister (which, by profession, he is not), and as one who attacks viciously. The image of the "barrister," however, allows metaphor to take off in another direction—when Sarah says he "twists" her words. Speech or language is conceptualized as a kind of rope. The barrister (or legal system) twists the words to catch (or hang) the prisoner. At this level Sarah is a victim of a merciless system of attack associated with her lover.

But the metaphor that threads through most of the passage is LIFE IS A JOURNEY. Life is conceptualized as a journey with various stages, and it is assumed that love is a journey through a garden or zone of pleasure, so that life without or beyond love is a desert. This metaphor gives the idea of "the point where the desert begins" and of getting lost in the desert, but the idea of a desert also has more definite religious connotations within the culture of Christianity. It recalls a famous image from the Gospel of St. Matthew, which talks of the foolish man who knows the words of Christ but does not act on them, and thus "built his house upon the sand" (12.27). The question in the passage, "What can one build in the desert?" refers both to the woman's fear of being alone at the end of her affair and to the theme that is to become increasingly important in the novel, of her gradual return to the Catholic Church.

We do not find, then, and should not expect to find, that the metaphors used by a writer like Greene are necessarily new or different—indeed their resonance and echo of other uses gives them depth within the passage. What we find in a literary text is that the metaphors are deployed in new ways—and deployed here to give the impression of a self-conscious search for the right expression.

Linked Metaphors

Much of what has been said so far about metaphor applies in general to literary analysis, not just to analysis of the novel. But with regard to the novel, it is of key significance that, as Gilles Fauconnier says, "our conceptual systems are dominated by intricately linked networks," and "the mappings we use routinely in our everyday thinking and talking will be at various stages of conceptual interaction."[11] Within a long prose text we may find mappings and linkages that are not foregrounded by the writer, but which nonetheless run through the text.

In Anita Brookner's novel *A Private View* the hero, George Bland, answers his telephone, and realizes that he is talking to a woman he has seen from time to time in his block of flats:

Mrs Lydiard, he reflected, laying down the receiver. Was she that rather handsome woman with the silver curls and the tall narrow body, always so well dressed, whom he sometimes crossed in the lobby or met at the lift? If so, then he approved of her, as he approved of all women who continued to fly the flag, decking themselves out bravely for a visit to the shops, never to be encountered in less than perfect order. He approved all the more of Mrs Lydiard inasmuch as she appeared to live alone, like himself, and did not seem to have been driven mad by it. He had never seen her in the company of a man, although there might of course be a bedridden husband upstairs. Somehow he doubted it. Mrs Lydiard, for all her careful glamour, had something resolute about her, as if there were no one to share in the mighty task she faced in keeping herself afloat. She was brave, of that there was no doubt. He had no idea of her age, having never given much thought to the matter. He supposed she might be the same age as himself, or a few years older. With women it was difficult to tell. These flats served as an unofficial retirement home for the elderly. She appeared embattled, largely because she gave the impression of having taken the matter of her own survival in hand.

(Anita Brookner, *A Private View*, 1994, chap. 2)

In this narrated monologue Mrs Lydiard, who has no obvious connection with the navy (though her name might contain a faint echo of *dockyard* or *lanyard*), is constantly described using terms that link her metaphorically with the sea, or with ships and naval battles. She "flies the flag," is one of those women who "deck themselves bravely." She keeps herself "afloat" and she appears "embattled." The naval metaphors seem to be related through a *network of connotations*, with terms like "brave" used in relation to her, or the "something resolute" about her, and her "mighty task." The image of her as someone George Bland "sometimes crossed," makes her sound like a ship whose path crosses his in mid-ocean. There is no naval theme in the novel that might account for such analogies, and there is an obvious ironic distance implied in George Bland's reflections on her: he "approve[s] of Mrs Lydiard" but does not want to get too close.

Some of this use of naval terms may simply reflect conventional habits in English. Frank Boers has pointed out that while French and English both use path metaphors frequently, "the additional imagery in English is more often that of ships and sailing."[12] But whether conventional or not, the metaphors are also related at some level to the theme of the possibilities of heroism in modern life (inspired by Baudelaire's view of the dandy as modern hero), which Anita Brookner traces through the lives and actions of apparently ordinary middle-class people living in London flats. In this respect the linked metaphors in the novel may be said to have a hermeneutic function, guiding readers to deeper meanings, even against the current of surface meaning.

Metonymy

Metonymy is traditionally associated with metaphor as a figure or trope, but contrasted with it in its form. It is described as a kind of *name change* or shift in reference. The name of something is replaced by the name of something commonly related to it or an attribute of the thing. Thus "the White House" is metonymic for the U.S. presidency; "the tomb," for death.

In metonymy, cause can be replaced by effect ("a Shakespeare" instead of "the works of Shakespeare"). An instrument replaces the user of the instrument ("a fluent pen" for "a productive writer"); the container replaces the contained ("to down a glass" instead of "to drink some beer"; "all London" for "all the people in London"): clothes, or the characteristics of clothes, replace the people wearing them (the "All Blacks" for the New Zealand rugby team that wears black sports kit).

The cognitive account of metonymy suggests that it works similarly to metaphor, but "involves only one conceptual domain, in that the mapping or connection between two things is within the same domain."[13] Lakoff and Johnson maintain that this leads to an important difference: "Metaphor is principally a way of conceiving one thing in terms of another, and its primary function is understanding. Metonymy, on the other hand, has primarily a referential function, that is, it allows us to use one entity to *stand for another*."[14]

Metonymic Modes, Things, and Names

Because metonymy sticks within the same conceptual domain, and because it works as a way of referring to things, it obviously plays a significant role in the realist novel. One of the fundamental methods of realism has been to assume that some *thing* or event can stand for a larger domain to which it would conventionally belong: the schoolboy's cap stands for the schoolboy; the single house for the street; the street for a whole social class; the hasty swallowing of a glass of whisky for the problem of alcoholism. David Lodge refers to the use of such things or events in modern realist style as a "metonymic mode."[15]

When we read in Theodore Dreiser's *Sister Carrie* (1912) that Minnie could not sympathize with her sister's thoughts because she "was too busy scrubbing the kitchen wood-work and calculating the purchasing power of eighty cents for Sunday's dinner" (chap. 4), we readily assume that Minnie would not only have scrubbed the kitchen woodwork, she would have cleaned the entire apartment. And she would not only calculate the price of Sunday dinner, she would have to calculate the price of food for the family in general. Minnie's scrubbing and poverty-stricken calculations stand in metonymic relation to the way of life of her whole class, and that is why they are described here in the novel. They form a contrast to the consumer fantasies that drive her sister Carrie onward into a more glitzy world.

As an example of the way in which specific *things* can be given metonymic function, we might take the file that Pip steals in Dickens's *Great Expectations* and gives to Magwitch. When a stranger visits The Jolly Bargeman pub and buys drinks for Joe and Mr. Wopsle, he looks at Pip and "makes his shot":

> It was not a verbal remark, but a proceeding in dumb-show, and was pointedly addressed to me. He stirred his rum-and-water pointedly at me, and he tasted his rum-and-water pointedly at me. And he stirred it and he tasted it: not with a spoon that was brought to him, but *with a file*.
>
> He did this so that nobody but I saw the file; and when he had done it he wiped the file and put it in a breast-pocket. I knew it to be Joe's file, and I knew that he knew my convict, the moment I saw the instrument.
>
> (Charles Dickens, *Great Expectations*,
> (1860–61) 1861, vol. 1, chap. 10)

The file is, in traditional literary-critical terms, "symbolic"—but it is not just an arbitrarily chosen symbol—or a religious or cultural symbol. It is not figurative: it *is* the file that Pip stole; it is also the file the convict needed iin order to get free; it stands for and participates in both criminality and breaking free from imprisonment.

In a similar way names can function metonymically, referring to larger domains. In Elizabeth Gaskell's *Cranford*, the conservative Miss Jenkyns is an admirer of Samuel Johnson's prose, Captain Brown is an admirer of Dickens's fiction. They argue over the relative merits of the two authors and read aloud passages. Miss Jenkyns feels affronted by Captain Brown's dismissal of Johnson's style:

> **She drew herself up with dignity, and only replied to Captain Brown's last remark by saying, with marked emphasis on every syllable, "I prefer Dr. Johnson to Mr. Boz."**
>
> **It is said—I won't vouch for the fact—that Captain Brown was heard to say, *sotto voce*, "D—n Dr Johnson!"**
>
> (Elizabeth Gaskell, *Cranford*, (1851–53) 1853, chap. 1)

"Dr. Johnson" stands here for an old-fashioned, polished, and classical style, not just of writing, but of general conduct, which Miss Jenkyns determinedly tries to keep alive in Cranford and to barricade round with pomposity and snobbery. Captain Brown is opposed to her. "Mr. Boz," the pseudonym used by Dickens for journalism and for his *Pickwick Papers*, represents an openness to thoughts and feelings of those outside one's own social class—in short, modernity. Captain Brown, as an admirer of Dickens, is warm-hearted to the poor, and associated with the new railway (which kills him). The two names work as reference to more substantial domains in an important conflict over tradition and the encroachment of the modern.

As with metaphor, then, we can say that metonymy and the metonymic work at various levels. Behind the use of the figure lies that impulse Raymond Carver described: "to write about commonplace things and objects using commonplace but precise language, and to endow those things—a chair, a window curtain, a fork, a stone, a woman's earring—with immense, even startling power."[16]

Irony

In the discourse of our everyday lives we are accustomed to dealing with certain rhetorical figures, such as *hyperbole* (obvious exaggeration) or *litotes* (understatement.) When they are used, we do not discount what the other person has said or written as a complete lie, but we make appropriate adjustments and recognize that a double sense, or double reading, is necessary. Irony similarly requires us to give texts a double reading, but is often more complex (and more difficult to interpret) and is signaled to readers in a variety of ways. It requires reference not only to the words in the text, but to the contextual situation in which the statement is made.

Irony and Antiphrasis

Traditional definitions of irony as a rhetorical device suggested that it consists in saying the opposite of what one really means *(antiphrasis)*.[17] But simply saying the opposite is not enough to define the device. As Raymond W. Gibbs Jr. says, irony is a device for concealing our intentions, for avoiding responsibility for statements: it is associated with play and mockery, but it can be recognized as a gambit "only when participants are sure they share the same beliefs and knowledge."[18]

In E. M. Forster's *A Passage to India,* after the incident that takes place while the characters are on a picnic, when Miss Quested is thought to have been assaulted by Dr. Aziz, Forster begins chapter 20:

> **Although Miss Quested had not made herself popular with the English, she brought out all that was fine in their character. For a few hours an exalted emotion gushed forth, which the women felt even more keenly than the men if not for so long. 'What can we do for our sister?' was the only thought of Mesdames Callendar and Lesley, as they drove . . . to inquire.**
>
> (E. M. Forster, *A Passage to India*, 1924, chap. 20)

Forster does not, in fact, think that the reaction of the English shows what "was *fine* in their character": he thinks the reverse. They are demonstrating their character as imperialists and racists. He assumes that his readers share his dislike of jingoistic nationalism. When he writes of "*exalted* emotion," he does not expect us to think that it is truly "exalted": on the contrary, it is self-righteous and disproportionate. Nothing terrible has happened to Miss Quested, simply her dignity has been threatened by a confusion. "Mesdames Callendar and Lesley" are described as thinking of Miss Quested as their "*sister*." But they do not truly think of her a sister; they do not even like her. She is a different kind of Englishwoman, and they are simply indulging in racist panic. All this antiphrasis can work only if we share (at least to some extent) Forster's view of the English in India.

Unstable Irony

To communicate by saying what we do not mean, however, is always problematic, and it is never certain that readers will agree or understand. It may not be clear exactly what the opposite is, or exactly why it is wrong. If I say of someone "He is really clever!"—intending my statement to be ironic—I may mean that he is stupid, or I may mean that I disapprove of his sharpness. Only the context of enunciation can reassure us about ironic meanings.

Thus, Jane Austen's *Northanger Abbey* begins:

> No one who had ever seen Catherine Morland in her infancy, would have supposed her born to be an heroine. Her situation in life, the character of her father and mother, her own person and disposition, were all equally against her. Her father was a clergyman, without being neglected or poor. . . . A family of ten children will always be called a fine family, where there are heads and arms and legs enough for the number; but the Morlands had little other right to the word, for they were in general very plain, and Catherine, for many years of her life, as plain as any. She had a thin awkward figure, a sallow skin without colour, dark lank hair, and strong features;—so much for her person;—and not less unpropitious for heroism seemed her mind. . . .
>
> Such was Catherine Morland at ten. At fifteen, appearances were mending; she began to curl her hair and long for balls; her complexion improved, her features were softened by plumpness and colour.
>
> (Jane Austen, *Northanger Abbey*, 1818)

Some of this is straightforward antiphrasis, easily identifiable as Austen's irony (few readers are going to take seriously the idea that a family of ten children will always be called fine when there are enough heads, arms, and legs). But the ironic import of statements like "No one who had ever seen Catherine Morland in her infancy, would have supposed her born to be an heroine" is more difficult to grasp. Is it that we should not expect prettiness and romantic circumstances from heroines? That ordinary girls can be heroines? Or is it that talk of heroines is foolish in the first place? We cannot be sure that we share Austen's beliefs, and the irony thus becomes unstable.

This does not necessarily detract from the value of the novel as a literary text. Although we may feel some uncertainty about our reading, we are still able to see the text as repository of possible meanings: indeed the undecidability may contribute to its interest, giving the impression of untappable depth.

Markers of Irony and Language at Second Degree

From the point of view of analysis, one of the major problems is to say exactly what features make us decide in the first place that a text is ironic. In heavy irony, particularly in the kind of antiphrasis used in informal communications, the device is marked with inappropriate hyperbole ("This is *tremendously* interesting"), or an exclamation mark ("I really like your friend!" [when it is obvious from the context that I don't]). There are other markers that indicate a withdrawal from what is being said, like "*sic*" or "evidently." (The quotation from Forster's *Passage to India* underlined its irony by using the French word "Mesdames" about English women in India.)

Irony of this kind does not contain simple usages of language, but "mentions" of language.[19] In irony in general, it can be said that language is being used *at second degree*, so that our attention is drawn to the way in which the use does not fit the contextual situation and the way the author evades responsibility for what is said. (Thus novels like *Jane Eyre*, which give us the impression that the writer *is* taking responsibility for what is said through the first-person narrator, are written at first degree and are not ironic.) Irony relies on a context of mutual agreement, but since it uses statements that controvert what the author actually intends to say, it can be seen as a device that produces what Mikhail Bakhtin called *heteroglossia*, or the "double-voiced" in the novel.[20]

15

Words and Meanings

A novel is a finite text and contains a finite number of words. What can we gain simply from examination of the words it contains?

In ordinary circumstances we often assume that words considered on their own have fixed and stable meanings. We isolate the words we use for objects and translate them into other languages. We give definitions of single words in dictionaries. We use single words as titles for texts (like Kipling's "If" or Henry Green's *Caught*). We use "key words" to sum up ideas in culture (like "the picturesque"). But our common assumptions do not bear much examination. Word-for-word translation between languages turns out in practice to produce nonsense; dictionaries are notoriously unsatisfying (they can never decide whether they should be just telling us how to use a word, or giving us information about the concept referred to by the word—or how much information we are likely to need). And single-word titles or key words can only be understood by those who already know the context.

Words, we can say, bring a potential for meaning. They *can* be identified as the same in different contexts—but the "initiative of meaning" passes over finally to the sentence and to the text. We must always be conscious, then, of what Paul Ricoeur calls the "reciprocal interplay between the word and the sentence"—and the text.[1]

Polysemy

We think we know what we mean by a word, but most of the words we use, perhaps all, are *polysemous* (they can have many meanings), and we only know which meaning is relevant when we know the context. For instance, a "duck" may be a bird, or a score in the game of cricket, or a nod of the head, or (in British English) a term of endearment. The meaning is usually plain when the word is used—though if someone simply shouts "Duck!" at us from a distance, it is not always obvious what is meant.

The context of use produces constraints on meaning. Once we are given a context, we are able to dismiss irrelevant possibilities. Evelyn Waugh's *Officers and Gentlemen* (1955) describes the arrival of a course at a banquet: "At this moment the piper put an end to the conversation. He was followed by the butler bearing a huge joint which he set before the host" (bk. 1, chap. 7). "Joint" here does not refer to marijuana. The word may be used in that way in modern English, but (apart from the fact that other sentences make plain that it refers to a piece of meat) it was not used with such a meaning in British English in 1955. Only by moving the sentence to a different context could it be read in such a way.

Distinctions, however, are not always so clear. When we read in a Raymond Carver story: "Sandy's husband had been on the sofa ever since he'd been terminated three months ago" ("Preservation" [1983]), the context makes fairly plain that *terminate* refers to losing his job, but the use of the word as a euphemism for killing, or the more abstract sense of "brought to an end," are difficult to dismiss from our minds, especially when we read that "he'd come home looking pale and scared." There is no point in trying to specify what the word *really* means. The word has a potential for different meanings, and whether we consider those meanings seriously or not will depend on whether we are prepared to accept other possible contexts. In this case, the fact that it is a literary text predisposes us to play with possible (and perhaps unintended) meanings, which seem to have some relevance to the wider context.

Monosemy

It is the aim of certain kinds of discourse to restrict possible meanings to a single meaning, and thus to suggest *monosemy*. Science aims to give precise definitions of words, limiting them in this way: the law tries (fruitlessly) to construct firm limits to the use of terms like *murder* or *tort*. In literature, polysemy and monosemy may intersect in an interesting way, as when the discourse of science or law intrudes into the world of a novel. In Wilkie Collins's *The Woman in White*, a novel that plays with sensational adventures and their recounting in different styles, the hero is offered a quasi-legal contract for a job, in which his friend says "the writing . . . speaks with a tongue of trumpets for itself." One of the articles of this contract stipulates:

> **Thirdly, That the terms offered to the person who should undertake and properly perform these duties, were four guineas a week; that he was to reside at Limmeridge House; and that he was to be treated there on the footing of a gentleman.**
>
> (Wilkie Collins, *The Woman in White*, [1859–60] 1861, epoch 1, chap. 3)

In the legal discourse intended by this contract, *gentleman* would be monosemic, and "the footing of a gentleman" would have fairly specific implications (that he eats with the family, and uses the same rooms.) But *gentleman* is connected for many Victorians specifically with a social class whose members are not employed on a contractual basis to teach art, and who do not enter into this kind of contract for money. A gentleman is someone who is defined by birth, or indifference to money. Although *gentleman* is polysemic, it is being pushed here into a monosemic legal context. This suggests trouble in store, and helps explain why the narrator is unwilling to accept the engagement, though he knows that the offer is financially attractive, and he does need the money.

Lexicon

At any given time a writer's language can be thought of as a kind of personal dialect, or *idiolect*. We can also imagine a personal word list, or *lexicon*, that a writer customarily draws upon. From the reader's point of view, the characteristics of this lexicon help to construct an idea of a writer's "voice." The whole lexicon will never be available in one book, and there will always be certain conscious or unconscious choices. Prevailing ideologies will limit the repertory of available choices—so that what the writer produces becomes part of a *sociolect* (a dialect of a particular group in a society).

The Mise en Texte

We are chiefly concerned here with the analysis of particular literary texts rather than problems of general discourse, so the most pertinent questions are those concerning the *mise en texte*—the *placing* of language in the novel we hope to analyze.

Exhaustive analysis of a writer's supposed lexicon is not going to be a feasible task, as there is no limit to the questions that could be asked. But we can start with general impressions or striking effects, and then move on, where appropriate, to try more systematic approaches. It is always worth asking, for example, whether the writer seems to favor concrete or abstract terms, whether there is an attempt to show respect for the norms of traditional grammar and usage, whether the writer likes to use rare words or tries to imitate a more familiar, or oral, style.

Without undertaking a complete analysis, we can note local effects. A shift from one range of terms within the lexicon to another, for example, can often be an important marker. In Evelyn Waugh's *A Handful of Dust* there is a riding accident that kills the hero's young son, John Andrew:

> **At that moment the motor bicycle, running gently in neutral gear, fired back into the cylinder with a sharp detonation. . . . Miss Ripon's bay, rearing and skidding, continued to plunge away from the bus.**
>
> **"Take a hold of him, Miss. Use your whip," shouted Ben. "The boy's down."**
>
> **She hit him and the horse collected himself and bolted up the road into the village, but before he went one of his heels struck out and sent John into the ditch, where he lay bent double, perfectly still.**
>
> **Everyone agreed that it was nobody's fault.**
>
> (Evelyn Waugh, *A Handful of Dust*, 1934, chap. 3, pt. 5)

We jump here suddenly from a detailed description in concrete terms to a stark and isolated one-sentence paragraph: "Everyone agreed that it was nobody's fault." The universal pronouns ("everyone," "nobody") create indefiniteness and abstraction. On the one hand, there is detail of motor bicycles, the "cylinder" and the "sharp detonation"; on the other, there is vacuous generality. A death has occurred, and nobody will take the blame. The contrast points up how, although the world of the novel may contain precise modern *things*, it is a world empty of valid ethical concepts or notions of responsibility. By manipulating his lexicon in this way, Waugh is able to indicate fierce moral disapproval—without using any conventional terms of direct moral condemnation to do so.

Lexicometry

The systematic analysis of lexicon has traditionally been a question of focusing on a few key terms, noting expressions that deviate from "general usage" and the contexts in which they occur. This kind of study, of which Leo Spitzer was the pioneer, has been developed more recently by J.-P. Richard, who looks not only at the trajectory of a word in a text, but also at its variations.[2]

If we decide to attempt the Spitzer method, how can we know which terms to focus on? The answer is, quite simply, that we have no objective guide. Spitzer says that one must "read and reread, patiently and confidently in an endeavour to become, as it were, soaked through and through with the atmosphere of the work. And suddenly, one word, one line, stands out."[3] He then tries to support his intuitive judgment by demonstrating how often the word is found, in what contexts, and with what wider implications.

That the Spitzer method must rely first on intuition has led some critics to distrust it, along with any form of word-counting, or *lexicometry*. It has been claimed that such techniques add a pseudo-scientific gloss to a circular, self-confirming process. If this were a truly scientific method, it is maintained, there would be some way of predicting which words count and how many occurrences are needed to make a literary effect—and there is not.

Objections of this kind seem powerful at first glance, but they take an unrealistic view of the way in which explanations arise in the human sciences: lexicometry does not have to pretend to be anything more than precise observation, confirming or highlighting aspects of the reading process. It can accept that words become interesting or significant only in a particular context and that there are many possible variants in reading a text. Its insights are not absolute, but (within obvious limitations) stable. This is, moreover, an area of study in which computers prove useful to the student of the novel. Word-counts are considerably speeded up by putting the texts of novels into a computer file, and performing word-searches on them.[4]

Obviously not all words are usefully counted. We do not learn much from a count of articles, conjunctions, or auxiliary verbs (unless, like Henry Green with his suppression of articles, the writer intends some special effect).[5] A mechanical count of repetitions of words is often not enough; we may need to convert plurals, or convert different verbal and adjectival forms to the simple dictionary forms *(lemmatization),* before we make any general statements. Once a count has been made, it is most useful to ask what combinations the lexical items occur in, and if they occur in negative or positive contexts. Exercises of this kind are convincingly performed on whole texts, but there is no essential reason why lexicometry of chapters or short passages cannot also be useful and interesting.

To take an example of a full text, we can start by noting that some abstract nonpersonal pronouns often used by Henry James (such as *something, everything, nothing, anything*) are particularly striking in *The Spoils of Poynton*. The novel concerns a struggle over some beautiful antique objects contained within a house (the "spoils"), and the complications of its plot derive from the fact that the people involved in this struggle (the owner's widow, his son, the son's fiancée, and a friend of the owner's widow) are unsure exactly what they are struggling to get. In a typical exchange we read:

> Her mother, to make up for this, broke out universally, pronounced everything 'most striking,' . . . she jarred upon Mrs. Gereth by her formula of admiration, which was that anything she looked at was 'in the style' of something else. This was to show how much she had seen, but it only showed she had seen nothing; everything at Poynton was in the style of Poynton. . . .
>
> (Henry James, *The Spoils of Poynton*, 1897, chap. 3)

The key terms come up again and again in the novel, often in conjunction with one another (as in the quotation above), and also with adverbs of indefinite frequency, like *ever* and *never*. In a short work of less than two hundred pages, we can make the following count of occurrences:

everything	(89)
something	(85)
nothing	(100)
anything	(55)
ever	(23)
never	(80)

A focus on these words is useful because, although there is so much discussion in the novel of the value of "everything" at Poynton, we learn very little about what the spoils actually consist of. The abstract terms of description thus fill a variety of functions: they allow us freely to imagine what the beauties of the house are, but also to realize that material objects only have their value in relation to other things (in relation to their history, styles, market prices, or to the life that is possible—as at Poynton—

among beautiful objects). The "spoils" of Poynton *could not* be precisely described—except by an act of distortion (as it would be, for example, to give their prices in a sale catalogue).

The abstract terms used to describe these "spoils" are terms that do not just have their meaning in relation to objects. We read, for example:

> [Mrs. Gereth said] "Yes, I did tell you a while ago that for you I'd do it. But you haven't told me yet what you'll do in return."
>
> Fleda thought an instant. "Anything in the wide world you may require."
>
> "Oh, 'anything' is nothing at all! That's too easily said." Mrs. Gereth, reclining more completely, closed her eyes with an air of disgust, an air indeed of inviting slumber.
>
> Fleda looked at her quiet face, which the appearance of slumber always made particularly handsome. . . . "Well then, try me with something. What is it you demand?"
>
> (Henry James, *The Spoils of Poynton*, 1897, chap. 11)

In such exchanges, and in such slippage of terms ("anything" becoming "nothing" then "something"), James is able to suggest that the objects in the house are only a substitute for deeper emotions that the characters cannot themselves fully understand or describe. The terms are used not just for denotation, but as part of a network of connotations that spreads through the text. The desires and longings, urges to control and manipulate the emotions of others, which are constantly present in the novel, are secret, hidden, and difficult to grasp; they disappear into these evasions about "something" and "nothing" when forced into words.

Sometimes the use of such terms in this novel can seem like an over-refinement, a squeamishness about admitting bourgeois greed for material objects, in which James colludes. But the use of the words that come up so often—*everything, nothing*, and *never*—can also be read as a skillful way of indicating the inability of the characters in the novel to make compromises. They are locked in a cruel dance of desires because they cannot settle for anything half-hearted: they desire "everything." If *nothing* is the most frequently used of the key terms, then that also is highly appropriate, since at the end, "nothing" remains. The material objects did not have permanence: the house burns and all the things in it are lost to everyone. The human relations, too, remain completely uncertain: perhaps there was "nothing" there after all.[6]

Lexical Field

A *lexical field* is a group of terms referring to the same reality, theme, or concept. In the representative descriptions of realist novels writers often draw on a recognizable lexical field from a social class or workplace. Thus, in Arnold Bennett's *The Old Wives' Tale* Mr. Povey decides to make new sales tickets for the draper's shop:

> Tickets ran in conventional grooves. There were heavy oblong tickets for flannels, shirting, and other stuffs in the piece; there were smaller and lighter tickets for intermediate goods; and there were diamond-shaped tickets (containing nothing but the price) for bonnets, gloves, and flimflams generally. The legends on the tickets gave no sort of original invention. The words "lasting," "durable," "unshrinkable," "latest," "cheap," "stylish," "novelty," "choice" (as an adjective), "new," and "tasteful," exhausted the entire vocabulary of tickets. Now Mr Povey attached importance to tickets, and since he was acknowledged to be the best window-dresser in Bursley, his views were entitled to respect. . . . When Mr Povey suggested circular tickets—tickets with a blue and a red line round them, tickets with legends such as "unsurpassable," "very dainty," or "please note," Mr Chawner hummed and hawed, and finally stated that it would be impossible to manufacture these preposterous tickets, these tickets would outrage the decency of trade.
>
> (Arnold Bennett, *The Old Wives' Tale*, 1908, bk. 1, chap. 5)

Obviously much of the vocabulary here relates to drapery ("bonnets, gloves, and flimflams"). It suggests an early twentieth-century commercial sociolect, and is marked off by quotation marks from the writer's own idiolect. Within the lexical field used in this commercial world, Bennett wants us to notice fine differences. Certain terms are acceptable to the old generation ("lasting," "durable," "unshrinkable"), while others indicate a new generation of drapers ("unsurpassable," "very dainty," and "please note"). The lexical field of drapery is set off from the narrator's own lexicon by the use of such expressions as "the *legends* on the tickets," or "the *entire vocabulary* of tickets," where the focus is on the language used and not on discussion of drapery as such.

Overall these are ironic mentions of terms rather than straightforward usages.[7] But if the narrator mocks the conflict over the language of drapery, he does take seriously the idea of generational change, and conveys that such terms might be of considerable significance to the people involved. Mr. Povey, we are told, had been "granted a minimum share of imagination," but had "nevertheless discovered his little parcel of imagination in the recesses of being, and brought it to bear effectively on tickets." His concern is thus "effective," even if the arguments about price-tickets seem ridiculous to outsiders. The slightly pompous, academic phraseology surrounding this discussion allows the narrator to retain a certain distance from Mr. Povey. He reserves his right to look down on the characters in the novel and find them comic.

Some of the approaches described in this chapter, particularly lexicometry, represent exactly what many readers dislike in methodical analysis. This is not entirely surprising, since if lexicometry tries to establish abstract formulas of word frequency in literary texts, it can become a waste of time. It is not a waste of time, however, when it is used more simply to confirm (or question) our readings.

The writer/narrator in Italo Calvino's *If on a Winter's Night a Traveller* is overawed by a young student who tells him that her computer can list all the words in his texts, and give her an "already completed reading . . . with an incalculable saving to time." He complains that when he tries to write after talking to her, he sees the words spinning round in an electronic brain, ranked according to frequency: "Perhaps instead of a book I could write lists of words, in alphabetical order, an avalanche of isolated words which expresses that truth I still do not know, and from which the computer . . . could construct the book."[8] Computers can do a great deal to speed up analysis, but it will be a long time before they autonomously construct books.

16

Repetition and
Figures of Construction

Texts in general use repetition, and fictional texts are no exception. Repetition works in part to establish order or pattern: as E. H. Gombrich points out, we need principles of categorization of information to survive: "We could not function if we were not attuned to certain regularities." Our sense of repetition enables us to construct the schemata through which we try to imagine a text overall or recall its most striking parts. But repetition in texts also becomes redundancy, of the kind that we are used to scan out in our readings: continuously repeated things sink below the threshold of our attention. Too frequent repetition, indeed, makes things meaningless: "If a word is repeated long enough it appears to be drained of meaning and becomes a mere puzzling noise."[1] Order and meaning thus interact in a complex fashion.

In a text such as a novel, repetition works in a variety of ways. Apart from the pattern of lines repeated on the page, which we take largely for granted, words are repeated, as are sounds, phrases, names, images, and narrative effects in general. Exact repetition is, of course, impossible. Novelistic texts are extended through space, and so the position and context of a repeated element will always make it slightly different from a first occurrence. Moreover, if repetition is something read (or rather, remembered), the context of reading will produce differences for the reader. "It is very like a frog hopping," Gertrude Stein says, "he cannot ever hop exactly the same distance or the same way of hopping at every hop."[2] This does not prevent us, however, reading some things *as* repetition, or reading others *as* discontinuity and variation.

Russian formalist critics preferred to talk of repetition as *parallelism*.

Viktor Shklovsky maintained that "in general any work of art is created as a parallel and a contradiction to some kind of model." A work of art is read always against a background of other works of art, and its form is "determined by the relation to other forms existing before it."[3] Prototypical novels, in such a view, would be works like *Don Quixote, Northanger Abbey,* or *Madame Bovary,* which parallel, but also distance themselves from, and criticize, earlier fictions.

Certainly, narratives often repeat conventional patterns. They range, Ricoeur says, "between the two poles of servile repetition and calculated deviance." On the one hand "popular stories, myths, traditional narratives in general, stay closer to the pole of repetition."[4] Novels tend toward the other pole, emphasizing their calculated deviance from what has gone before (though there are times when, as Steven Connor says of the contemporary British novel, "telling [becomes] compulsorily belated, inextricably bound up with retelling, in all its idioms: reworking, translation, adaptation, displacement, imitation, forgery, plagiarism, parody, pastiche").[5] Deviance in any case is not a total break with models—some form of repetition must always be implied somewhere for the deviance to be noticeable.

Framing Repetition and Isotopy

Repetition is at its most obvious when a text simply offers some part of itself to the reader again. George Moore's novel *Esther Waters* begins:

> SHE stood on the platform watching the receding train. A few bushes hid the curve of the line; the white vapour rose above them, evaporating in the pale evening. A moment more and the last carriage would pass out of sight. The white gates swung forward slowly and closed over the line.
>
> An oblong box painted reddish brown and tied with a rough rope lay on the seat beside her. The movement of her back and shoulders showed that the bundle she carried was a heavy one, the sharp bulging of the grey linen cloth that the weight was dead. She wore a faded yellow dress and a black jacket too warm for the day. A girl of twenty, short, strongly built, with short, strong arms.
>
> (George Moore, *Esther Waters*, 1894)

Moore's naturalist style establishes itself here with a description of a woman among the contingencies of ordinary life, standing in a railway station after getting off a train. Three hundred or so pages later, when we have gone through forty-five chapters (in which Esther has been seduced, become pregnant, lost her job, suffered poverty, been married, and then lost her husband), chapter 46 gives an exact repetition of the novel's incipit: "SHE stood on the platform watching the receding train. A few bushes hid the curve of the line; the white vapour rose above them evaporating in the grey evening. A moment more and the last carriage would pass out of sight." Only in the second paragraph does it change: "An oblong box painted reddish brown lay on the seat beside her. A woman of seven or eight-and-thirty, stout and strongly built, short arms and hard-worked hands, dressed in dingy black skirt and a threadbare jacket too thin for the dampness of a November day."

A naturalist style, then, does not entail a transparent text simply describing things as they happen: it allows a patterned text that may draw its own design to our attention. One way of describing how this has been done is to use a spatial analogy, and see it as a kind of picture-frame round the novel. Perhaps because the narrative is naturalist, and rejects the familiar shape of drama or myth, it needs a framing device to separate it from the continuum of ordinary life. In this view, the reiteration can be said to give structure to the novel.

But repetition is also always accompanied by difference, even in a narrative frame. From a "girl of twenty" Esther has now become a "woman of seven or eight-and-thirty." She has gone through eighteen years of hard experience. There are slight differences in the setting: the "pale" evening has become a "grey" evening; the yellow and black clothes have turned to a "dingy black skirt and a threadbare jacket." Esther is still "strongly built"—she is not of the leisured classes—but she is now "stout." The warmth of the earlier day (which, we have learned in reading the novel, was in June) has turned to the "dampness of a November day." In a symbolic pattern, the year, the novel, and Esther's active life are all drawing to a close (a little early at age thirty-eight, one might think, but that is what the novel seems to suggest).[6]

Repetition has thus added levels of meaning (or polysemy) to this text. For this reason A.-J. Greimas prefers to talk of repetition in texts as *isotopy.*[7] Meanings are added at each recurrence, while the sense of pattern produced contributes to the overall coherence of the text. Greimas sees it as a general tendency of texts as they become extended to close in upon themselves, to offer less and less information, with more levels of meaning. As Edith Wharton said of her novels: "My last page is always latent in my first."[8]

Realism and Repetition

David Bordwell has shown how in the cinema "repetition can heighten curiosity and suspense, open or close gaps, direct the viewer toward the most probable hypotheses or toward the least likely ones, retard the revelations of outcomes."[9] All this is also true of novels. Repetition, which seems on the face of it to be part of the artificiality of texts, can heighten our sense of the real. In *Robinson Crusoe* we are given an account of Crusoe's early days on the island, and then read:

> **But having gotten over these things in some Measure, and having settled my household Stuff and Habitation, made me a Table and a Chair, and all as handsome about me as I could, I began to keep my Journal, of which I shall here give you the Copy (tho' in it will be told all these Particulars over again) as long as it lasted, for having no more Ink I was forc'd to leave it off.**
>
> (Daniel Defoe, *Robinson Crusoe*, 1719)

What follows this passage is a transcript of Crusoe's journal, which does indeed repeat incidents we have already read about, though in slightly different terms. It is in one sense simply dull to read about these events all over again, except that the journal seems to add authenticity, and there are slight variations. Use of the journal draws attention to the narrative as narrative, but by its very repetitiveness also seems an assurance that it is the real thing, that all this really happened to Crusoe and was recorded as written (though we happily keep somewhere in mind, even as we read it, that the whole thing is a work of fiction).

Motifs

The repeated mention of things or images, or the repeated use of certain phrases, produces in novels what are usually referred to as motifs. *Motif* (or *motive*) is not just a literary term, it is also used with reference to architecture and sculpture, where it can mean either a repeated ornament or a structural principle. It is also important in relation to music, particularly Wagnerian opera, where a recurrent motif heard from time to time represents an idea, or is associated with a particular character. Talk of repeated motifs in a work of literature partly draws on these other fields. It suggests some kind of organizing design or structure, and at the same time is often related to leading ideas or themes said to be contained in the work.

Why should we consider a repeated motif to be structural, or organizing? Gestalt psychology shows that when presented with a randomly organized picture, with many signals competing for our attention, we find it difficult to know how or where to focus.[10] Putting things in an ordered pattern (organizing repeating or symmetrical motifs) makes it easy for us to "rest our gaze" and see the picture as a whole. For this to happen we do not need to articulate to ourselves that we understand the organization of the pattern: it is simply that we find tidied-up patterns easier to apprehend and remember.

The concept of a literary motif assumes that repetition can work in an extended literary text in a similar way. The repeated elements are there and (it is thought) help readers, though not everyone will spot motifs at work.[11] But when we attempt a methodical reading of the text, we hope that we will notice them and that they will indicate the ideas "contained" in the text.

We can take Peter Walsh's pocket-knife in Virginia Woolf's *Mrs Dalloway* (1925) as an example. Walsh brings it out on many occasions when he appears in the novel, "always playing with a knife," fidgeting with it frequently, "stealthily fingering it," and "par[ing] his nails with it." Other characters think of him "with that knife, opening it, shutting it. 'Just as he always was, you know.'" "That was his old trick, opening a pocket-knife, thought Sally, always opening and shutting a knife when he got excited." The novel as a whole provides a series of contingent events on a single day in London, happening to a disparate collection of characters, often (though not always) fitting things together in a way that does not conform to our usual idea of a plot. Peter Walsh's knife provides one way for the reader to grasp an image of the man that can be sustained through his appearances on the single day, and can also link him up with various characters' recollections of the past. The knife may also have other implications. Does it suggest that he lives dangerously? Or is his always opening and shutting it a sign that he is too hesitant, too unsure of himself? Clarissa Dalloway, we note, is active with her scissors while he is playing with his knife, and it is she who "sliced like a knife through everything." The motif both provides coherence *and* has a potential for suggesting ideas.

Dickens's novels are more conventional in their plot patterns, but they are long and full of characters, and we need help in converting our reading experience into cohesive recollections of a novel. The repeated motifs found in his mature novels work in such a way: images of prisons, rivers, fog, or dust heaps may recur through a novel, linking characters and events into a pattern, encouraging different generalizations and having a wide thematic resonance. It seems, in *Little Dorrit* {(1855–57) 1857} that, although only one set of characters is actually in the Marshalsea debtors' prison, everyone is in a prison of one kind or another. Mrs. Clennam, for instance, "stood at the window, bewildered, looking down into this prison as it were out of her own different prison" (bk. 2, chap. 31).

Other writers achieve similar effects by the use of repeated words and phrases. As David Lodge points out, key words in Joseph Conrad's fiction, such as *darkness* in *Heart of Darkness, youth* in *Youth*, or *material interests* in *Nostromo* "are kept reverberating in our ears by conscious contrivance."[12] Some novels give the effect of motifs through an extended play on colors—as red recurs through Arnold Bennett's *The Old Wives' Tale*,[13] or contrasts of red and white run through *Jane Eyre*. In the case of *Vanity Fair*, Elizabeth Deeds Ermarth has suggested that the color green constantly recurs, and also "seeds" other words including *green* (*Mr. Green, greengrocer, green schoolboy*) in what she describes as "dozens of different incarnations" and "paratactic patterns."[14]

There have been many objections to the tracing of motifs in novels. It can be questioned whether they really affect our reading processes, whether they are simply projections of the reader onto the text, or whether they really do lead us to ideas "contained" in the text. Nonetheless, as long as we wish to say something that covers the whole text, we are going to have to use some organizing idea of this kind.

Figures of Construction

Repetition does not, after all, have to be conscious on the part of the writer, and its use will always be open to a variety of explanations. One traditional way of describing it has been through the terms of rhetorical analysis; some of the classic terminology remains relevant when we need to describe what is going on in a text, particularly when it is used to create rhythmical effects, or the sense of a characteristically literary description. Such figures can be called *figures of construction*.[15]

Epizeuxis and Hypozeuxis

In reading any novel by Dickens we are confronted by descriptions like the following:

> It was wretched weather; stormy and wet, stormy and wet; and mud, mud, mud, deep in all the streets. Day after day, a vast heavy veil had been driving over London from the East, and it drove still, as if in the East there were an Eternity of cloud and wind.

> (Charles Dickens, *Great Expectations*,
> (1860-61) 1861, vol. 2, chap. 20)

There is some highly self-conscious patterning here, and we need rhetorical terms to describe it. The simple repetition of a word in one part of a phrase ("mud, mud, mud") is called *epizeuxis*, and is traditionally identified with the attempt to communicate strong or intense feelings.

In Dickens the epizeuxis contributes to the feeling of a poetic prose, but perhaps the most common use of epizeuxis in contemporary prose is simply in swearing: "Oh christ, oh fuck sake, oh fuck, fuck fuck, oh fuck" (James Kelman, *The Burn* [1991]). Kelman, however, breaks up the repetitions—presumably in an attempt to get closer to the patterns of real speech.

We also find, in the passage from Dickens, repetition of a phrase: "stormy and wet." This is called *hypozeuxis*, and is conventionally identified with lyricism or an incantatory tone. The repetition in the passage functions not only to communicate strong feeling about the weather, but also to indicate to readers that this is poetic description: the narrator is foregrounding his technical literary skills to add rhythm and color, to counterbalance what might otherwise have been simply a depressing wet London scene. And, of course, he wants to give the impression that this bad weather just goes on and on without a break.

Anaphora

The most frequently used form of repetition, and one that is easy to pick out in all kinds of novelistic prose, is *anaphora*: repetition of a word, or a group of words, at the start of a series of sentences (or at the start of syntactic groups). D. H. Lawrence very often uses the device, as in the novella "Daughters of the Vicar." One of the two daughters of the vicar in this story marries a man who is a vicar, like her father, although she does not feel sexual or emotional attraction toward him. Lawrence wants to emphasize that her decision to marry is an act of will:

> Mary, in marrying him, tried to become a pure reason such as he was, without feeling or impulse. She shut herself up, she shut herself rigid against the agonies of shame and the terror of violation which came at first. She *would* not feel, and she *would* not feel. She was a pure will acquiescing to him. She elected a certain kind of fate. She would be good and purely just, she would live in a higher freedom than she had ever known, she would be free of mundane care, she was a pure will towards right. She had sold herself, but had a new freedom. She had got rid of her body. She had sold a lower thing, her body, for a higher thing, her freedom from material things. She considered that she paid for all she got from her husband. So, in a kind of independence, she moved proud and free. She had paid with her body: that was henceforward out of consideration. She was glad to be rid of it. She had bought her position in the world—that henceforth was taken for granted. There remained only the direction of her activity towards charity and high-minded living.
>
> (D. H. Lawrence, "Daughters of the Vicar," 1914, sec. 5)

In this passage, sentence after sentence follows the same anaphoric pattern of *she* + verb + predicate. "She had . . ." is repeated at the start of three sentences: "She had sold herself"; "She had got rid of"; "She had sold a lower thing." The anaphoric patterns take various forms ("she shut herself" twice; "she would not" twice; "she would be" twice; "she had sold" twice. One sentence starts with hypozeuxis ("She *would* not feel and she *would* not feel"), where the repetition is further emphasized by the use of italics.

Repetition is picked up within sentences ("a lower thing . . . a higher thing . . . material things"). There is also a repetition of *free* in "higher freedom," "free of mundane care," "a new freedom," "free from material things," "proud and free."

All these repetitions can seem over-insistent (and do indeed annoy some readers of Lawrence), but the passage is not written without a deliberate aim of producing a certain style. Lawrence defended his "pulsing, frictional to-and-fro" as a way of representing "every natural crisis in emotion or passion or understanding."[16] The passage could be read as free indirect discourse. It represents self-persuasion, a struggle to find the right words and the exact right expression. It is as though we are to follow thought processes as they are recorded, and nothing is to be changed in retrospect. Language is used to foreground its own process of production.

Elegant Variation

Unmotivated repetition seems to indicate a poverty of vocabulary, and it is customary to try to avoid it. But avoiding repetition *per se* leads to the problem of *elegant variation*. Traditional guides to good writing, like Fowler's *Modern English Usage*, sternly advised against the "infirmity" and "literary fault" of this "incurable vice," found among "the minor novelists and the reporters." There is nothing wrong in repeating words, we are told, when the things referred to are the same.

Nevertheless, most of us try somehow to avoid it. (Roget's *Thesaurus* is just as popular a deskbook as Fowler's *Modern English Usage*.) Even major novelists may be anxious that their work should not be thought tedious.[17] Ian Watt, in his celebrated "explication" of the first paragraph of Henry James's *The Ambassadors* pointed out the frequent use of elegant variation by James, and justified it as part of his "tendency to present characters and actions on a plane of abstract categorizations." These variations could be connected, Watt decided, to the "multiplicity of relations" in the novel.[18]

Phonetic Repetition and Seeding Effects

Repetition in prose, as in poetry, may be important on the phonetic level—to communicate the sense that this is a key moment of strong emotion, or to give lyrical effect. Through rhyme and rhythm, for instance, we have the impression in Thomas Hardy's work that, as Adam Piette says, the "prose seems to be remembering poetry."[19]

The most obviously noticeable trick is *alliteration*—the repetition of consonants (particularly those at the start of words). Dickens cannot resist alliteration in his set-piece descriptions, like that of the ship in *Martin Chuzzlewit* {(1843–44) 1844}: "Onward she comes, in gallant combat with the elements, her tall masts trembling, and her timbers starting on the strain" (part 6, chap. 15). Philippe Hamon suggests that, in such cases, a thematic word functions to "seed" a succession of words starting with the same letter, or a group of anagrams.[20] Presumably the use of alliteration is quite often unconscious on the part of the writer: it is simply a question of reaching for an appropriate word—and the "seeding" effect leading to a train of repetitions.

Assonance is the repetition of similar vowel sounds. We find both alliteration and assonance in George Eliot's description of the flood at the end of *The Mill on the Floss*:

> Some wooden machinery had just given way on one of the wharves, and huge fragments were being floated along. The sun was rising now, and the wide area of watery desolation was spread out in dreadful clearness around them—in dreadful clearness floated onwards the hurrying, threatening masses.
>
> (George Eliot, *The Mill on the Floss*, 1860, bk. 7, chap. 5)

Repetition here is both of phrases and letters. Apart from alliteration with *w*, there are eye-rhymes in *oa* and *ea*. Assonance conveys the *spread* of water, the *threat*, and the *dreadfulness* of the flood. All these effects contribute to the sense of a poeticized or marked section of text. As in *Esther Waters*, they repeat the opening of the text and signal the imminent closure of the novel.

Alliteration can sometimes seem ridiculous in prose fiction, as though the writer were using the tricks of the wrong genre. Henry James had a good deal of fun criticizing the "inveterate bad taste" of the fashionable novelist Harriet Elizabeth Prescott, citing her "childish attempts at alliteration" in descriptions like that of blackberry leaves, "damasked with deepening layer and spilth of colour, brinded and barred and blotted beneath the dripping fingers of October, nipped by nest-lining bees."[21] But heavy alliteration is not always considered in bad taste. There are times in fiction when we accept that the prose draws attention to itself, particularly in moments of closure. James Joyce's story "The Dead" ends with a celebrated lyrical passage:

> It had begun to snow again. He watched sleepily the flakes, silver and dark, falling obliquely against the lamplight. The time had come for him to set out on his journey westward. Yes, the newspapers were right: snow was general all over Ireland. It was falling on every part of the dark central plain, on the treeless hills, falling softly upon the Bog of Allen and, farther westward, softly falling into the dark mutinous Shannon waves. It was falling, too, upon every part of the lonely churchyard on the hill where Michael Furey lay buried. It lay thickly drifted on the crooked crosses and headstones, on the spears of the little gate, on the barren thorns. His soul swooned slowly as he heard the snow

> falling faintly through the universe and faintly falling, like the descent
> of their last end, upon all the living and the dead.
>
> (James Joyce, "The Dead,"Dubliners, 1914)

The exact implications of this ending have been the cause of much argument, but there is little disagreement that it is impressive. It is overtly lyrical, employing, for example, inversion of usual word order ("watched sleepily the flakes") and rhetorical figures like *chiasmus* (a repetition of two or more words with the order reversed: here, "falling softly . . . softly falling" and "falling faintly . . . faintly falling"). The word *falling* is repeated in the passage seven times—giving us not only the sense of snow falling but the impression that the word has some symbolic significance—if only that it brings the story and the collection of stories to an end on its falling note. At the end there is an accumulation of *s* sounds ("soul swooned slowly"), finishing with a pattern of *d* sounds ("descent," "end," "dead"). The overall effect for most readers is that of a harmony of sound and meaning, though this does not mean that the sounds actually reproduce the sounds of the scene (what does falling snow sound like, anyway?). Rather, the connotations of the words used, and the connotations of associated words with *s*, *f*, and *d* lead us to imagine resemblances between their sound and what they describe.

Banality, Modernity, and Repetition

Modernist art sometimes challenges our patience by a repetition of repetitions. Beckett's Watt complains: "And the poor old lousy old earth, my earth and my father's and my mother's and my father's father's and my mother's mother's and my father's mother's and my mother's father's and my father's mother's father's . . ." And so on, for fifteen lines of text, until he concludes: "An excrement."

Analysis has to approach texts like this differently: repetition here is obsessional list making, producing something we are severely tempted to skip as redundancy or "noise." The text can be enjoyed only at second degree, in a kind of complicity with the writer against other, less agile, readers. We learn little or nothing directly, but we can admire how the writer insists on continuing his lists and repetitions, up to his own sense of a limit, without any concession to the attention span of the reader. Repetition here is a demand for a different way of approaching texts, and an exploration of the continuing possibilities of meaning.

Contemporary "dirty realism" also uses banal repetition. For example,

James Kelman gives us a conversation between men after an unsuccessful attempt at burglary:

> **Okay Lecky . . . ?**
> **Aye—fuck. Lecky grinned: Close, eh?**
> **Aye.**
> **Fucking close alright, muttered Ray, Fucking lucky.**
> **Aye.**
> **John winked at Lecky. We're aye fucking lucky, int we?**
> **Aye.**
>
> (James Kelman, "Unlucky," *The Burn*, 1991)

Repetition is used here partly on the assumption that it equals verisimilitude. Kelman wants his fiction to represent the real thing, or as close as possible (thus the experiments with dialect and odd punctuation). But the repetition also does provide a minimalist pattern, which shapes the work and textualizes the banality of communication in a marginalized, nonintellectual social class. The authorial narrator (who is obviously himself literate, intelligent, well read, and a conscious artist) conceals himself behind a textual world that seems to owe nothing to polite or conventional discourse. Banal repetition, he insists, is how the world *is*—though, as Gilles Deleuze reminds us, we are not in fact confronted by the world, we are confronted by a text.

17
Lists

Lists fill textual space: they are descriptive, they classify things, and yet they may function instead of arguments. Students in composition classes are taught that lists should always be drawn from the same category of things (thus, "books, magazines, newspapers" or "blue, green, yellow, and pink" are fine, but "cats, dogs, hamsters, and Labradors" or "London, Milan, the Atlantic, and Tokyo" are not). Novelists, of course, do not need to obey such rules: they may have good reason for unusual associations.

Lists are, in effect, collections of words, and collectors, as José Saramago points out, are those who "cannot bear the idea of chaos being the one ruler of the universe, which is why, using their limited powers and with no divine help, they attempt to impose some order on the world, and for a short time they manage it."[1]

When we read for analysis, our aim should be to look for the organizing logic of the list. We need to ask not just why things are there, but if there is a particular order. Lists in novels may follow a focalizor's attention moving through some place (listing things as they are seen), or they may reflect a logic of association—of ideas or rhymes and rhythm.

The following list looks randomly chosen at first:

> Seems a pity somehow, I thought. I looked at the great sea of roofs stretching on and on. Miles and miles of streets, fried-fish shops, tin chapels, picture houses, little printing-shops up back alleys, factories, blocks of flats, whelk stalls, dairies, power stations—on and on and on.

Enormous! And the peacefulness of it! Like a great wilderness with no wild beasts.

(George Orwell, *Coming Up for Air*, 1939, pt. 1, chap. 3)

Orwell's narrator is describing an English landscape, an area of the urban working class, and he emphasizes through phrases like "on and on" and "miles and miles" how vast this area is. Alliteration is not particularly important (though there is some in fried fish, factories, and flats; picture houses, printing shops, and power stations). This is a description of where people live and work—and at the heart of it we are given the key places: "blocks of flats" and "factories." It opens with the "fried-fish shops," "tin chapels," and "picture houses," which sum up the cheap pleasures of the people who live in this area. The food they eat is fried, and no doubt unhealthy; their religion is a cheap version of the "opium of the people"; and their imagination is fed by the fake glamor of Hollywood in "picture houses." But there are also "little printing shops up back alleys"—traditional workshops where radical political thinkers might meet. After the factories and flats come the "whelk stalls," last remains of a distinctive working-class culture and working-class taste in food, then dairies and power stations—sources of energy in differing ways in the peaceful English scene. The list is framed by a repetition. From a general picture of the "sea of roofs" it has moved in to focus on details, and then moved out again—emphasizing the endlessness of the modern urbanization with "on and on and on."

Overall, this list embodies an ambivalent reaction to the English social landscape. The narrator will not pass over what he sees as the depressing features of modern cut-price civilization, but at the same time he discovers human qualities, which are not without charm. He is expecting war (what was to be World War II), and this mixed landscape functions as a counter-image to fascist dreams of inhuman order: it is a "wilderness" perhaps, but one with "no wild beasts." Instead of regularity or beauty, he sees "the peacefulness of it."

Orwell's list describes a landscape; a list in Elizabeth Bowen's *Heat of the Day* evokes a way of life:

Balanced upon the bales, a tribe of tray-shaped baskets invited Stella's inspection of their contents so carefully sorted out—colourless billiard balls, padlocks, thermometers, a dog collar, keyless key-rings, a lily bulb, an ivory puzzle, a Shakespeare calendar for 1927, the cured but

unmounted claw of a greater eagle, a Lincoln Imp knocker, an odd
spur, lumps of quartz, a tangle of tipless tiny pencils on frayed silk
cords.

(Elizabeth Bowen, *The Heat of the Day*, 1949, chap. 9)

The heroine of this novel is visiting the Republic of Ireland, newly independent at the time, and neutral during World War II. In a large Anglo-
Irish house, symbolic of the old colonial order, she comes upon these
baskets containing odds and ends. The things are a jumble, but a jumble
that tells about people's lives. The people who once lived here were interested in games. They played billiards—a sign of upper-class life in the
Edwardian period. Perhaps they played card games (since they had the
kind of pencils on silk cords that are used for scorecards). Or perhaps the
young women in the household went to balls, and used the pencils to
mark their program of dances. They probably enjoyed hunting, since they
have a spur, an eagle's claw, a dog collar. The padlock might have been
used to close a stable-door, but was certainly used to protect property.
Obviously they were of the property-owning and leisured classes. They
were also interested in gardening, as they have a lily bulb. They collected
stones: a piece of quartz. Although they lived in Ireland, their lives were
directed, like many Anglo-Irish lives, toward England, since they had a
Lincoln Imp knocker and a Shakespeare calendar. Their life is a kind of
island out of time—the calendar is from 1927, and this is the 1940s. Some
slight alliterations occur through the list (billiard balls, tangle of tipless
tiny pencils), but most significant are the three words ending with the
suffix -*less*: colour*less*, key*less*, and *tipless*. The effect created by the list is of
a world drained of meaning, time, color, and coherence, a world that is
now life*less* and use*less*.

Modernist Lists

Lists in the detective or suspense story are associated often with decoding.
We must puzzle out their significance in terms of the hidden elements of
plot. In modernist fiction they may form the basis of stylistic experiment,
and foreground the textuality of the work. James Joyce or Samuel Beckett
took a delight in lists that seem at first to be repetitious or confusing, that
challenge the patience of the reader. The narrator in Beckett's *Watt* (1953)
tells us: "Personally of course I regret everything. Not a word, not a deed,
not a thought, not a need, not a grief, not a joy, not a girl, not a boy, not
a doubt, not a trust, not a scorn, not a lust, not a hope, not a fear, not a

smile, not a tear, not a name, not a face, no time, no place, that I do not regret, exceedingly" (pt. 1). The point of this list is presumably its surface banality—it contains cliché after cliché in a series of pairs (for example, grief-joy, girl-boy.) But it is also constructed in a pattern of alternating rhyme words: *deed—need, joy—boy, trust—lust, fear—tear, face—place*. And it is a play on negatives. All the instances of *not* (19) and *no* (2), in an exuberant concord of negativity, are in effect simply saying what the previous sentence manages to say with an affirmative: "I regret everything." Life, as he goes on to say, is "ordure, from beginning to end"—but there is obviously some interest to be gained from experimenting with language on the way.

A contrast to Beckett is represented by the enthusiastic lists of Georges Perec: lists of furniture, pictures, objects, memories—the things people live among, construct their lives from, remember and delight in. Perec foregrounds lists like modernists, but does not use them to problematize communication: his lists note our communal experience of the world. Novels such as *Life: A User's Manual* (1978) are in effect *constructed* out of lists, rather than the usual patterns of narrative. Perec's lists have the fascination of the act of classification behind them. As with all novels, however, we can still fruitfully ask why things are on Perec's lists, what order they come in, and what connects one to another.

Part V
Endings

As readers, Frank Kermode suggests, we partake of some "abnormally acute appetites"—in particular, "we hunger for ends and crises."[1] Part V of this book is concerned with the question of endings. If we hunger for ends, how do novels actually satisfy that hunger? How do they wrap things up when they get to the last page?

A character in Jorge Luis Borges's story "The Immortal" suggests that *as the end approaches . . . there are only words.* The narrator comments: "Words, words, words taken out of place and mutilated, words from other men—those were the alms left him by the hours and the centuries."[2] We certainly have to pay attention to words if we are to produce a reading that does justice to a text. But the challenge remains for us to say something about how the words are organized, how they contribute to our sense that this is a text. In looking at endings, then, we are looking at words on the borderline, in one of the important boundary areas of the text.

18
Endings

Although novels are often long, they are finite texts, they come to an end. As we have seen in chapter 8, closure is fundamental to narrative. Novels contain narratives, and we therefore read them as directed toward various kinds of closure. In our reading we have, as Frank Kermode points out, "considerable investment in coherent patterns"—the desire for a predictable ending and for the "satisfying consonance" of things.[1] We read patterns back into the novel when we have reached the end, though the conclusions of the final chapter do not constitute the novel, and may indeed contradict much of what we have gained in the progress of our reading. If there is some danger in looking at novels through the prism of their endings, it is still inevitable that we do so. Endings, like incipits, are obvious points of reference from which analysis often starts.

From the writer's point of view the ending of the classic novel is only too often a matter of compromise with the demands of readers, publishers, and circulating libraries. According to Anthony Trollope, he had no idea how his novels would end: "When I sit down to write a novel I do not at all know and I do not care very much how it is to end."[2] But it does not then follow that Trollope's endings are surprising: he consents to what he thinks the reading public demands, even as he complains about it; his plots converge into predictable patterns, into the moral and conventional.

Many novels end with the promise of marriage. "Who can be in doubt of what followed?" the last chapter of Jane Austen's *Persuasion* (1818) begins. "When any two young people take it into their heads to marry, they are pretty sure by perseverance to carry their point." Many novelists of the nineteenth century were plagued by the demands of readers for some version of providential narrative—by the need for the novel to show the working out of divine providence in the individual life, for things to seem to conform with the workings of God in nature. At its crudest this simply led to moralistic optimism: "The good ended happily, and the bad unhappily," Miss Prism says of her attempt at novel-writing in Oscar Wilde's *The Importance of Being Earnest*. "That is what Fiction means" (act 2). Nineteenth-century novel endings needed to suggest that love, money, and moral problems would all be resolved—what Henry James called the "distribution at the last of prizes, pensions, husbands, wives, babies, millions, appended paragraphs, and cheerful remarks."[3] But when everything and everyone is provided for in this way, a novel comes too close to myth for modern tastes: many readers of realist fiction would also like some falsification of their expectations, some suggestion of disappointments in an imperfect world. Realism, as George Levine points out, should lead "not to closure but to indeterminacy."[4]

We know the ending is coming in a novel when we see, in Jane Austen's words, "the tell-tale compression of the pages," indication "that we are all hastening together to perfect felicity" (*Northanger Abbey* [1818], vol. 2, chap. 16). We might also, of course, be all hastening to damnation. Endings quite often use the great symbols of the apocalypse: everything in flames, "the sky tall with scarlet" (Elizabeth Bowen, *The Last September* [1929]); "all collapsed" (Herman Melville, *Moby-Dick* [1851]); leaving a promise of "the earth's new architecture, the old brittle corruption of houses and factories swept away" (D. H. Lawrence, *The Rainbow* [1915]). If not actually apocalyptic, the end may imply the loss of innocence, Adam and Eve going out from the garden of Eden into the world, couples who "join hands" and walk away (Thomas Hardy, *Tess of the d'Urbervilles* [1891]), to the "great beginning" of "the home epic" (George Eliot, *Middlemarch* [1871–72]) when "the world's all before us," though the world is "a mighty sea," where we float "in fathomless waters" (Henry James, *Portrait of a Lady* [1881]).

In modern realism the end may simply be metonymic: an exit. Final exits in novels frequently take place over thresholds, with a character about to enter or leave the house, or close the door on a room: "But she turned to the door, and her headshake was now the end" (Henry James, *Wings of the Dove* [1902]).

General Characteristics

Claude Duchet has pointed out that we can look at the endings of fiction to find some combination of the following characteristics:[5]

1. The ending of the plot or intrigue.

2. The closing of the text-world of the novel. A fictional world has been presented to us with a certain time and space, and the ending seals this off. In the Victorian novel it is often a question of finally uniting *discours* and *récit*, of saying how things are now in the writer's world, of tying up all the threads in a "comprehensive epilogue."[6]

3. The closing of the text as text. Works of fiction are not like sonnets, which end after fourteen lines, or geometric proofs, which end with the demonstration of the theorem: they do not have a fixed way to end, but they do use stylistic effects. They may have rhyming and lexical effects of ending (as we have seen in James Joyce's "The Dead"), or thematic endings (marriage, apocalypse, death), or repetitions of the incipit (as in George Moore's *Esther Waters*, or Vladimir Nabokov's *Pnin* [1957]), or they may simply represent the end of the text in typographic terms—a separated paragraph, a sentence in italics, a sequence of dots that comes to an end.

4. A moral or message. An ending is the point of finality of a novel, where a certain position has been taken. Endings quite often give us morals or messages. As a reaction to such endings, morals may also be denied, and the whole work revealed as ludic. Finality in this way connects the text to its paratext: it is a kind of addition to the textual world that reminds us we are reading a text.

5. A suggestion of closure, but also of infinity. Although we leave the text, the world inside it is still going on—perhaps endlessly repeating itself, perhaps moving on to new events undescribed. If we say that texts themselves are finite, and must close, there are ways in which, once opened, they cannot close. As long as there are readers who read them, the life within them is imagined to proceed.

Effects of closure are not limited to the end of a novel—a narrative within the novel may close before the end, and novels contain constant minor closures of chapters or sections, or moments of resolution of plot— (like that when Jane Eyre realizes that St. John Rivers is her cousin, and says, "I stopped. . . . Circumstances knit themselves, fitted themselves, shot into order: the chain that had been lying hitherto a formless lump of links, was drawn out straight—every ring was perfect, the connection complete"[vol. 3, chap. 7]).[7] We should try to be aware of how narratives are cut into shape while the novel progresses, but all the same it is in the final chapter and on the last page that we find effects of closure that are typical of the genre.

E. M. Forster concludes *Howards End* (1910) with a chapter that jumps fourteen months after the end of the main plot and moves the narrative into a pastoral mode, of hay and summertime and children playing in the meadows. Instead of a world of contingencies, it suggests a world of reiterated events "year after year." The final sentences are:

> **From the garden came laughter. "Here they are at last!" exclaimed Henry, disengaging himself with a smile. Helen rushed into the gloom, holding Tom by one hand and carrying her baby on the other. There were shouts of infectious joy.**
>
> **"The field's cut!" Helen cried excitedly—"The big meadow! We've seen to the very end, and it'll be such a crop of hay as never!"**
>
> *Weybridge*, 1908–1910

The main intrigue has already ended before this section, but here the small narrative of the last chapter is brought to a close with the end of the cutting of the grass in the big meadow. The closing of text as text is signaled on the thematic level by the ending of an action, and by the shouts and laughter that accompany this ending. On the lexical level cues are given by phrases such as "at last" and "to the very end." The body of the novel has been concerned with family life in a context of "telegrams and anger," impinged upon by the business world, with its sordid, disconnected morality. A moral point is thus being made in this ending, when the final event of the novel is a natural scene of harvesting, from which emerges the timeless group-image of a mother and children. The last sentence of the narrative neatly indicates closure and ending ("We've seen to the very end"), but it also suggests the infinitude of the world of the text, with its future tense ("it'll be such a crop of hay as never!"). Its theme of the fruitful harvest gives promise of endless renewal. The infinity of this world of the *récit*, however, is cut off with a brief paratextual note that connects it to the scene of writing: "*Weybridge*, 1908–1910." The place name, italicized and set after the main text, is a reminder to readers that we have been reading a novel and that the novel represents Forster's work from 1908 to 1910. In his contract with the reader he does not pretend to infinity; he accepts a precise time limit: *Howards End* is what the world seemed like then.

The last chapter of Thackeray's *Vanity Fair* offers another kind of shift between the text-world and the world outside. It is entitled "Which Contains Births, Marriages, and Deaths," and it seals off the intrigue of the novel. Becky has already had her come-uppance and been caught out by her husband, but now Amelia and Dobbin are brought together in marriage at last. As so often in Victorian novels, money matters have to be sorted out: we learn who has gained what, and how Becky has managed to get half of Jos's insurance policy. The time scheme of the narrative changes gear, and from past tense moves into present; *récit* and *discours* converge: "The Baronet lives entirely at Queen's Crawley. . . . She [Becky] has her enemies. Who has not? Her life is her answer to them." It seems that the text-world of the novel is going to be allowed to continue after the closing of the narrative, but then, in the last sentence of the main text, Thackeray cannot resist the temptation of a further act of closure. The narrator rounds off his comments with verbs in the past tense: "But he never *said* a word to Amelia, that was not kind and gentle; or *thought* of a want of hers that he did not try to gratify" (italics added). Then, after this, we shift narrative level and move to the famous final paragraph:

> Ah! *Vanitas Vanitatum*! Which of us is happy in this world? Which of us has his desire? or, having it, is satisfied?—Come children, let us shut up the box and the puppets, for our play is played out.
>
> (W. M. Thackeray, *Vanity Fair*, 1847–48)

The narrative level switches from that of Becky and Amelia to the authorial (dramatized) narrator, reminding us of the fictionality of the novel and sending us off into "this world." The lexical choice of the sonorously biblical phrase *"Vanitas Vanitatum"*[8] gives a feeling of ending and echoes the title of the novel itself. The rhetorical questions allow a sense of continuance—no answers are offered, we do not satisfy our endless desires, we continue. But the last part of the sentence does provide a closure, a playing out. We return to the puppets mentioned in the opening paratext of the novel, and to the scene shown on its title-page. The puppeteer's box is at last closed.

Thackeray's final paragraph troubles some readers, because it starts with religious reference and traditional morality, and ends with cynical pessimism, describing his readers as children and his characters as puppets. The narrator is revealed as self-parodic, the novel as play, an imitation that is not real life. Yet this ending is not superficial or ill-considered, since Thackeray as authorial narrator includes himself among the players: it is "*our* play." He suggests a strong desire for finality, for sealing things off, settling accounts, and ending the game, but at the same time echoes an important theme of the novel: that it is impossible, in the world in which we live and communicate, to locate the real and the sincere, the true or the worthwhile; that we lack, despite all our pretenses to the contrary, a fixed moral center, or a benign assurance of providence.

Breaking with Clichés

Early modernist, high modernist, and postmodernist novels try to break away from the clichés of closure, as they try to break away from narrative clichés in general. It is a search for what Johnson's *Rasselas* called a "conclusion, in which nothing is concluded." Alternative endings may be offered, as in John Fowles's *The French Lieutenant's Woman* (1969): the alternatives Fowles offers, however, are themselves conventional. We do not like things to end inconclusively, and it is difficult to avoid some final gesture of signing off.

In contrast to the conventions of "felicity" in the Victorian novel, a resounding pessimism is one possibility. Joseph Conrad ends *Victory* (1915):

> "And then, your Excellency, I went away. There was nothing to be done there."
>
> "Clearly," assented the Excellency.
>
> Davidson, thoughtful, seemed to weigh the matter in his mind, and then murmured with placid sadness:
>
> "Nothing!"
>
> *October, 1912–May, 1914*

Other novelists prefer a final affirmation. James Joyce's *Ulysses* (1922 [1960]), the great novel of modern iconoclasm, which broke all contemporary rules of propriety and polite writing, ends with Molly Bloom lying in bed thinking:

and then he asked me would I yes to say yes my mountain flower and
first I put my arms around him yes and drew him down to me so he
could feel my breasts all perfume yes and his heart was going like mad
and yes I said yes I will Yes.
Trieste-Zürich-Paris, 1914–1921

Joyce's ending has been much admired, as a positive note struck against
the general negativity of literary modernism: "Yes" is an affirmation of
life, of sexuality, possibly a coded reference to orgasm. But we should note
that it sounds uncannily similar to the performative response to a marriage
proposal: "Will you marry me?" "Yes I will. Yes." Joyce's ending, we might
say, reacts against, but to some degree depends upon, the familiar conventions of the marriage plot. We hasten toward perfect felicity—we end with
anticipations of married bliss.

Checklist of Questions
for the Analysis of a Passage

Where Is It From?

- Is this an incipit? Does it have the function of introducing the text-world to the reader?
- If it is from the middle of a text, is it description, narrative, character portrait, dialogue, monologue, or free indirect discourse?
- Is it an ending? Does it have the function of closure?

Pronouns

- What personal pronouns are used? Is it first-person narrative or third-person narrative? Is the reader addressed directly with second-person pronouns?

Names

- What proper names are used? What seems to be the motivation for the names?
- Are names used first and then pronouns, or are we expected to know from the start whom the pronouns refer to?
- Are the place names real or fictional?

Space

- How does the narrative set up the space of the novel? How does the focalizor move? (Try to follow the movement of the focalizor, or to work out where it stands.)
- Is there a sense of perspective? What is the logic connecting the things described?
- What is the geography of the text, and how does it change?

Time

- How is the time-scheme set up? (Look for direct references to time in the piece. Note the use of deictics.)
- What are the verb tenses used? (Look also for adverbs that indicate changes of time.)

Where Does It Start? How Does It Change?

- If this is an incipit, does the narrative start at the beginning of the story, or in the middle? What kind of jumps backward (analepse) and forward (prolepse) does it make?
- Are the things described meant to have happened once, or have they happened repeatedly?

Description

- If the passage is a description, what kind of description is it? Is it a thing or a process?
- Does it use hyperbole? Does it create an atmosphere reflecting the observer (expressive), or is it an encyclopedic description of the world (representative), or does it foreground its own production?

Character Portraits

- If the passage is a character portrait, what is included? Appearance? Background history? Mental traits? What aspects of the character are emphasized?
- What kind of character is this: a type or representative, or a character who will be presented as an individual or personality?

Dialogue and Monologue

- If there is dialogue in the passage, how is it represented? Is it direct, indirect, free indirect, or summary?
- Is there an attempt at dialect, or foreign languages?
- What frames the dialogue? What kind of exchange is taking place?

Type of Narrative

- Is it *récit* (using past tenses) or *discours* (emphasizing the act of writing and where the narrator is now)?
- Is this a main or an embedded narrative?

Narrators

- Is a narrator obviously present or absent? What kind of narrator, protagonist or observer?

- Is the narrator on a different level from the main narrative (intrusive or authorial narrator)? Is the narrator strongly dramatized?
- Is there a reflector or center of consciousness?
- What is the distance between the narrator and the events being narrated?
- Is the narrator reliable?

Sentence Type

- What kind of sentences are present? Is there a tendency to use short sentences? Complex or compound?
- Are the sentences in parataxis? Or is hierarchy and logic made plain?

Verbs, Adjectives, Link Words

- What kind of verbs are used? Are they active or passive?
- What kind of adjectives are used? Is there any play on color adjectives? Is the palette restricted?
- What kind of link words are used? Is there an attempt to make the passage strongly ordered or logical? Are there ruptures or ellipses? Are stage directions given in parentheses?

Comparisons

- What kind of metaphors does the passage contain? Is there any sign of linked metaphors or networks of connotation?

Irony

- Is there any use of irony? Is there obvious antiphrasis?
- Does the text use exaggeration? Is there hyperbole? Or paradox? Is language used at "second degree"?
- Is there an ironic distance between narrator and narrative?

Lexicon

- Does the text use abstract or concrete terms?
- Is the vocabulary in the passage chosen from a particular lexical field? Is there a network of connotations?
- Are there any words that seem a focus for attention?

Repetitions

- Are there obvious repetitions? Are they structural isotopes, or repetitions at the sentence, phrase, or word level? What function do they have?
- What oppositions does the text set up?

Lists

- If there are lists, what is their logic? Are things grouped to create a reality effect?
- Are the lists linked by rhyme or alliteration?

Endings

- If the passage is from an ending, how does it close the plot? Is there a final moral?
- What suggestions are there of the imagined world continuing after the end of the novel?
- How does the text close as text?

Appendix 1

Film and the Novel

The relationship between film and novels has been important for film-makers since the days of D. W. Griffith (who emphasized that novels were a good source of narratives).[1] Many modern readers come to novels because their interest has been attracted by a film version and, whether we like it or not, many modern discussions of novels are affected by the existence of a film version. Neglected novels may be brought into prominence by a good film. How many people would have read Thackeray's *Barry Lyndon*, if Stanley Kubrick had not made a magnificent film from the novel? Purists may want to go through a text for themselves before they see a film, but that is not always possible—and indeed one of the peculiarly modern pleasures for novel readers can be that of clearing away misconceptions first produced by the film.

Film Theory and the Novel

Film theory is by now a highly developed field, and it offers valuable insight into the problems posed by transferring texts into a different medium. The discussions of narrative and meaning in film by David Bordwell are particularly helpful, and there are interesting recent discussions of the relation of film and fiction by Jakob Lothe and Brian McFarlane.[2]

Without moving into film theory as such, it is worth bearing some simple points in mind when considering film versions of a novel.

A film version is a transfer of the novel into another medium, but it always embodies some kind of reading of a text. In the seventeenth and eighteenth centuries there was a fashion for publishing "imitations" of classic works, like Pope's version of Homer's *Iliad*, or of the poetry of

Chaucer. These were not strictly translations, but reshapings and rewritings. They were an act of homage to the original work, which attempted to make it palatable to a modern audience. Many film versions of classic novels are, in this sense, imitations. They aim to please wide audiences (though for this reason they may seem bland, and even patronizing, to those who have had the experience of reading the text for themselves.) John Huston's film of Joyce's "The Dead" is a good example: as Lothe says, it shows "meticulous respect for the literary original."[3] It makes minor changes to the story, adding a recitation of a poem and a character, and shifting third-person narration to a voice-over from the central character. It pleases audiences because of its tact and respect, but it does not say much new about the story.

Some film versions of novels show strong and unexpected readings, which tell even experienced readers things they may not have noticed before. To see an intelligent film version of this kind is like encountering a good work of criticism. We could argue, for example, that Iain Softely's film of Henry James's *Wings of the Dove* brings out undertones of sexuality in the novel that many readers have overlooked. It forces one to reconsider the novel.

Many readers are annoyed because they find that things are "left out" in a film, but this is not a reasonable complaint. A film cannot possibly show all that a novel contains. (For this reason some filmmakers prefer to work only with short stories or novellas, though even then there are bound to be omissions.)

Films also change things in novels, and this is to be expected. Film narrative, for example, cannot proceed in the same way as novelistic narrative—because we don't re-view scenes in the cinema as we do on the page. It may be necessary to reorder events to make film narrative more easily graspable. Narrators are dropped. Voice-overs can be used as a partial substitute, but they don't control focalization in the same way. It is interesting to note how such changes have been made in transferring novels to film, not just to complain about them.

Film versions tend to simplify issues that arise in novels. Films are costly to make and need a mass audience to recoup the investment involved, so they largely follow conventions that are considered appropriate for their market (upbeat endings, simple good and bad characters, celebrities playing themselves rather than actors in disguise, plenty of action, and so forth). The simplifications of films can produce banal readings of texts. The Merchant-Ivory films of E. M. Forster's novels, for example, present a "heritage" England that is saccharine in comparison with the England of the novels; BBC versions of Dickens's late novels turn them into dressy love stories. But some simplifications can also be interesting. Jane Campion's film of James's *Portrait of a Lady* does not represent the way everyone goes through the text, and it does simplify issues, but it nonetheless embodies a powerful feminist reading of the novel.

The question of whether a film gives a fully accurate representation of the world of the novel dominates many discussions by novel readers, and is usually a distraction. The representation on screen of characters or settings drawn from a novel will inevitably have weaknesses. What looks authentically eighteenth- or nineteenth-century when a film is made soon begins to look dated and anachronistic. Directors concentrate on getting the actors' hair right, or ensuring that dresses are the right style and color, but they always neglect something. After a few years it becomes obvious that actors are wearing modern make-up, or that their clothes are too clean. As Brian McFarlane demonstrates, in his illuminating discussion of the Bogdanovich version of *Daisy Miller*, insistence on accuracy has no limits and can produce distracting detail that clutters a film.[4] As far as criticism is concerned, it is best to try and understand what is being attempted, not simply demand that a film follow what we think the text "really" contained.

Some readers of novels accept that details will be changed, but worry about whether a film has been faithful overall to "the spirit" of the novel. The idea of the spirit of the novel, however, will vary from reader to reader. A film version is only ever going to be one possible reading.

We have to accept that filmmakers are not academics and are often out of touch with the latest studies of novels. They tend to rely on fashionable readings rather than to produce original readings of their own. But even within the weakest film versions (like the Schlöndorff film of Proust's novel *Swann in Love*) there may still be performances that add something to our reading of the text (like that of Ornella Muti in this film as Odette).[5]

Appendix 2:

Stereotype and Cliché

in the Novel

Readers who dislike a novel often justify their criticism by complaining that it is full of clichés, or stereotypical ideas. We should be careful, however, about criticism of this kind. Studies of the discourse of cliché, particularly those by Ruth Amossy, have shown how complex the use of cliché is in the novel, and how muddled attacks on it are.[1] We need to describe how cliché and stereotype are used, rather than simply reject them out of hand.

The idea of a cliché is itself modern, and derives from the nineteenth-century world of printing. Printers used to set up books from movable type, but when they had to produce books for a mass market, they started to make molds of whole pages (*clichés* in French, or *stereotypes* in English), which could then be used again and again. In the original sense, then, clichés and stereotypes were useful things: the terms only came to have unpleasant connotations because people felt threatened by mass production. *Cliché* came to mean words, phrases, or ideas that are habitually used by the mass of people. Clichés and stereotypes were identified with short-cuts to communication and with evasion of serious thought.

A general attack on the use of clichés is, however, hardly ever convincing. We all constantly pick up and repeat phrases and ideas that are used by others around us: we need to do this in order to communicate. Our languages and our ways of thought are codified, and we cannot escape the repetitions they involve. To criticize the use of cliché in a novel is not usually to give a precise description of a writer's linguistic habits; rather, it is a way for the critic to show that he or she belongs to a superior intellectual (or social) class. The implication is that the novelist being attacked belongs to the unintellectual, uneducated mass, to the class of people who are unthinkingly enthralled, and dominated, by cliché.

As far as analysis is concerned, it is important first to note that the repetition of fixed phrases and familiar ideas is accorded different values at different times and in different cultures. In premodern culture it was often admired as an endorsement of tradition, community, and unity of feeling. There was nothing wrong with saying what was often thought, or universally acknowledged, especially if one said it in a decorated style. There are still many cultures in the world in which literary skills include such things as chiming in with apposite proverbs, or repeating a complex mixture of traditional and elegant phrases.

The use of familiar phrases in Europe starts to change with the rise of industrialism and the breakdown of traditional society. Ruth Amossy and Elisheva Rosen have shown how Romantic "poetic" prose comes to use cliché in a new and interesting way. The poetic language is taken from a traditional public rhetoric, but modern writers want to innovate, to be personal and individual. When used by a writer like Charlotte Brontë, the poeticizing becomes (in a way that is riddled with contradictions) part of an intense and personal "harangue."[2]

Realist fiction in the nineteenth century, as we have seen, suspends reference to the real world, but relies nonetheless on our background sense that there is a real world outside the fictions of the novel. Clichés are often used by writers, as Amossy shows, to provide shortcuts between fiction and the real world outside. In George Eliot's *Middlemarch*, we read how Will Ladislaw, when he had seen Dorothea, "started up as from an electric shock" (chap. 39). Comparisons of love with electric shocks are already familiar by the 1870s, but the narrator goes on to explain that Ladislaw really did feel the shock—and this explanation then moves off into a general explanation of how passion works in the world, and how it is different for men and women. The verisimilitude of the text is reinforced by a little excursion into familiar territory.

Stereotypes can work in the same way, introducing characters who are assumed to be familiar in real life: "He was one of those men who . . ." Stereotypes are used to indicate simplified moral categories, and they contribute to the creation of novelistic melodrama: "She was a fallen woman." "He was a drunken rogue." As Peter Brooks has shown, this kind of melodrama provides a way of setting up ethical struggles in a world that has lost faith in a transcendent order.[3]

The use of stereotypes is frequently unpleasant (as when racial and gender stereotypes are used to malign people). But it would be wrong to suggest that it might be dismissed from all our discourse. It is not apparent how we can think of people in general terms at all without some form of stereotyping. We can't always discuss everything in terms of individuals.

If cliché is often used in the novel at first degree (for example, when a novelist assumes that the term "fallen woman" can refer to, and adequately describe, a character who is morally ruined), it is also often used at second degree—to mock the habits of usage, or the banal ideas, of others. Some of the most impressive social criticism in the novel (like the famous attack on reactionary English businessmen in the Podsnappery chapter of Dickens's *Our Mutual Friend*) is done through putting clichés into the mouths of stereotypical characters. Modernism and postmodernism also constantly use cliché as part of their critique of the world and our difficulties in describing it.

Analysis of cliché and stereotype should not, then, be dismissive: it should focus on how they function and whether they are used at first or second degree. Like the novelist character in Anita Brookner's *Hotel du Lac*, who spends half her time fitting people into mistaken stereotypes, we may need to give "prolonged attention" to some things that sound as if they are of the "utmost triviality."

If we start off by accepting that clichés and stereotypes are found in various forms in the novel, we can begin to ask what use has been made of them. And we can have a firmer grasp of why some novels may seem tediously full of cliché, but may have their admirers all the same.

Notes

Introduction

1. See Nathalie Albou and Françoise Rio, *Lectures méthodiques* (Paris: Ellipses, 1995).

2. Umberto Eco, *Six Walks in the Fictional Woods* (Cambridge, Mass.: Harvard University Press, 1994), 10.

3. See Michael McKeon, *The Origins of the English Novel* (1987) (London: Radius, 1988), 26–28.

4. Jacques Derrida, *Limited Inc.* (Paris: Galilée, 1990), 27.

5. Michael Riffaterre, *Fictional Truth* (Baltimore: Johns Hopkins University Press, 1990), 29.

6. See J. A. Downie, "Mary Davys's 'Probable Feign'd Stories,'" *Eighteenth-Century Fiction* 12, nos. 2–3 (January 2000): 310–26. See also Dorrit Cohn, *The Distinction of Fiction* (Baltimore: Johns Hopkins University Press, 1999), 12. Cohn points out that the term *fiction* is also used to mean "lies" or "abstractions."

7. Gérard Genette makes a useful distinction between constitutive literariness (works written as literature) and conditional literariness, which we accord certain texts, but which can always be withdrawn. Similarly, some texts are written as novels, some are conditionally called novels. See Genette's *Fiction and Diction* (1991), trans. Catherine Porter (Ithaca: Cornell University Press, 1993), vii.

8. A synchronic theory looks at something (such as language or art) as it appears at one time: it provides a kind of cross-section. This can be contrasted with a diachronic theory, which is historical and looks at a thing as it changes through time.

9. Italo Calvino, *If on a Winter's Night a Traveler* (1979), trans. William Weaver (San Diego: Harvest Books, 1981), 5.

10. Manfred Jahn, "Frames, Preferences and the Reading of Third-Person Narratives: Towards a Cognitive Narratology," *Poetics Today* 18, no. 4 (winter 1997): 441–68.

11. *Oulipo Laboratory*, trans. Harry Mathews and Iain White (London: Atlas Press, 1995), x.

12. See Jean Molino, "Pour une théorie sémiologique du style," in *Qu'est-ce que le style*, ed. Georges Molinié and Pierre Cahneé (Paris: PUF, 1994), 215–20.

13. These are guidelines, not objective divisions. The category of "period" is often open to question, and there are many literary works whose authors are not known.

14. Michael Riffaterre, *Text Production* (1979), trans. Terese Lyons (New York: Columbia University Press, 1983), 2.

15. As Patrick Charaudeau points out, it can still function quite adequately within a semantics-based grammar. See Charaudeau, *Grammaire du sens et de l'expression* (Paris: Hachette, 1992), 4.

16. One model has been the helpful combination of stylistic and rhetorical analysis in Catherine Fromilhague and A. Sandier-Chateau, *Introduction à l'analyse stylistique* (Paris: Dunod, 1996). See also Fromilhague, *Les Figures de style* (Paris: Nathan, 1995); and Patrick Bacry, *Les Figures de style* (Paris: Belin, 1992).

17. *Surviving: The Uncollected Writing of Henry Green*, ed. Matthew York (London: Chatto and Windus, 1992), 92.

18. Helen Vendler, *The Art of Shakespeare's Sonnets* (Cambridge, Mass.: Harvard University Press, 1998), xvii.

19. Gustave Flaubert, *Sentimental Education* (1869), trans. Robert Baldick (Harmondsworth, Middlesex, England: Penguin Books, 1964), 36, 61.

20. Ian Watt's *The Rise of the Novel* (1957) is a classic statement of this view for the English novel. The same view underlies Georg Lukács's *The Theory of the Novel* (1920). See Michael McKeon, "Ian Watt's *Rise of the Novel* within the Tradition of the Rise of the Novel," *Eighteenth-Century Fiction* 12, nos. 2–3 (January 2000): 253–76.

21. See Denis Donoghue, *The Practice of Reading* (New Haven: Yale University Press, 1998), 54–79.

22. Derek Attridge, "Closing Statement: Linguistics and Poetics in Retrospect," in *The Linguistics of Writing* (Manchester: Manchester University Press, 1987), 25.

23. Ford Madox Ford, "Henry James, A Critical Study," in *The Ford Madox Ford Reader*, ed. Sondra J. Stang (London: Grafton Books, 1987), 195.

24. James Phelan, "What Do We Owe Texts? Respect, Irreverence, or Nothing at All?" *Critical Inquiry* 25, no. 5 (summer 1999): 782.

25. Mieke Bal, *Narratology: Introduction to the Theory of Narrative* (1985), 2nd ed. (Toronto: University of Toronto Press, 1997), 13.

26. See John Sutherland, *Victorian Fiction: Writers, Publishers, Readers* (Basingstoke, Hampshire, England: Macmillan, 1995), ix.

27. Jorge Luis Borges, "Pierre Menard, Author of the *Quixote*," in *Labyrinths*, ed. Donald A. Yates and James E. Irby (1964) (Harmondsworth, England: Penguin Books, 1970), 66.

28. McKeon, "Ian Watt's *Rise of the Novel* within the Tradition of the Rise of the Novel," 253.

29. See Jean Ricardou, cited in Yves Reuter's valuable and informative *Intro-duction à l'analyse du roman* (Paris: Dunod, 1996), 22.

30. See Almuth Grésillon, *Éléments de critique génétique: Lire les manuscrits modernes* (Paris: PUF, 1994).

31. See Frédéric Regard, "Pour un retour à la 'vie de l'auteur': L'éthique du biographique," *Études anglaises* 3 (July–September 1999): 298–311.

32. Marcel Proust, *Against Sainte-Beuve and Other Essays*, trans. John Sturrock (Harmondsworth: Penguin Books, 1988), 12.

Part I
Openings

1. Henry James, "The Lesson of Balzac," in *Literary Criticism: French Writers Etc.* (New York: Library of America, 1984), 125.

1. Starting the Analysis

1. See Gérard Genette, *Paratexts: Thresholds of Interpretation* (1987), trans. Jane E. Lewin (Cambridge: Cambridge University Press, 1997).

2. See Philippe Lejeune, *L'Autobiographie en France* (Paris: Armand Colin, 1971).

3. *Serious Reflections during the Life . . . of Robinson Crusoe* (1720). See Michael McKeon, *The Origins of the English Novel* (1987) (London: Radius, 1988), 121.

4. See section on "the field of study" in Introduction for signs of fictionality given by Michael Riffaterre.

5. But the confusion as to whether the book was an autobiography or not apparently stopped it getting the Booker Prize for fiction. Although it was short-listed, it was rejected at the last stage by some of the judges, who decided it was not a novel.

6. The term derives from the Latin words used at the start of a manuscript in the Middle Ages, *incipit liber* (here the book starts). A precise definition of the length of an incipit is not particularly helpful, but for the purposes of discussion it can be assumed that it continues until there is a break of some kind in the narra-tive.

7. Umberto Eco, *Six Walks in the Fictional Woods* (Cambridge, Mass.: Harvard University Press, 1994), 95–96.

8. The distinction between these two kinds of opening is discussed in more detail in chapter 2, in the section on "two basic forms of narration."

9. Amos Oz, *The Story Begins: Essays on Literature* (New York: Harcourt Brace, 1999), 8–9.

10. The birth of the narrator would seem an obvious place to start a first-person narrative, but we are still left (as in Sterne's *Life and Opinions of Tristram Shandy* [1759–67]) with the problem of what moment at birth to choose.

11. Quoted in Ian Watt, "The First Paragraph of *The Ambassadors*," reprinted in *The Ambassadors*, Norton Critical Edition (New York: W. W. Norton, 1964), 481.

12. Paul Ricoeur, *Time and Narrative,* vol. 1 (Chicago: University of Chicago Press, 1984), 76.

13. It has been suggested by Mary Louise Pratt that there is a basic structure of oral anecdote that can be seen reflected in the novel: anecdotes start with an "abstract," or outline of the story, and then go on to an orientation in time and space. See *Towards a Speech Act Theory of Discourse* (Bloomington: Indiana University Press, 1977). It is easy, however, to oversimplify the relation between orality and written texts, and such structures are not found in all oral narratives. See Robin Tolmach Lakoff and Shirley Brice Heath, in *Spoken and Written Language: Exploring Orality and Literacy,* ed. Deborah Tannen (Norwood, N.J.: Ablex, 1982).

14. George Eliot, "Leaves from a Note-Book," cited by Miriam Allott, *Novelists on the Novel* (London: Routledge and Kegan Paul, 1959), 263.

15. *One* is considerably more important in French. In English it is associated with formality, and is avoided by some native speakers. See the section on *you* and *one,* below, in chapter 1.

16. See Émile Benveniste, *Problèmes de linguistique générale* (Paris: Gallimard, 1966), vol. 1, 225–66. Benveniste's analysis is significantly modified in Catherine Kerbrat-Orecchioni, *L'Énonciation: De la subjectivité dans le langage* (Paris: Armand Colin, 1980), 43–44.

17. Käte Hamburger insists that first-person narrative is always "feigned reality statement." She suggests that "it is an innate characteristic of every first-person narrative that it posits itself as non-fiction, i.e., as a historical document." See *The Logic of Literature,* 2nd ed. (1973), trans. Marilynn J. Rose (Bloomington: Indiana University Press, 1993), 312–13. This may be going too far, but it usefully indicates an important difference between first- and third-person narrative.

18. Thackeray, letter of 23 October 1847; Virginia Woolf, *Women and Writing* (London: Women's Press, 1979), 129; Henry James, preface to *The Ambassadors,* New York ed. (1909) (Fairfield, Conn.: Augustus M. Kelley, 1976), xix.

19. F. K. Stanzel, *A Theory of Narrative,* 2nd ed. (1982), trans. Charlotte Goedsche (Cambridge: Cambridge University Press, 1984), 93–94.

20. See Dorrit Cohn, *Transparent Minds: Narrative Modes for Presenting Consciousness in Fiction* (Princeton: Princeton University Press, 1978), 11–12.

21. It is also possible (though unusual) for narrators to refer to themselves in the third person, in the way mothers sometimes say to their children, "Do what Mummy tells you—she's very angry with you." The narrator of J. M. Coetzee's *Boyhood: Scenes from Provincial Life* (1997) refers to the boy who is obviously himself by using "he" throughout. But this is simply a way of making some distance from what is still fundamentally an I-position.

22. Stanzel, *Theory of Narrative,* 158–60. See also Yuri Lotman on Pushkin in *Universe of the Mind: A Semiotic Theory of Culture,* trans. Ann Shukman (London: I. B. Tauris, 1990), 66–67.

23. Steven Connor, *The English Novel in History 1950–1995* (London: Routledge, 1996), 11.

24. Monika Fludernik discusses the use of *one* and *you* in contemporary fiction in "Pronouns of Address and 'Odd' Third-Person Forms: The Mechanics of In-

volvement in Fiction," in *New Essays in Deixis*, ed. Keith Green (Amsterdam: Rodopi, 1995). *You* can also be used from time to time instead of *I* for self-reference in first-person narrative—as when the narrator of Tim Parks's *Destiny* (1999) says to himself, "You were compelled to leave your wife. But why?"

25. Quoted in David Lodge, *The Modes of Modern Writing* (London: Arnold, 1977), 55.

26. See, for example, George Eliot's oracular statement in *Felix Holt: The Radical* (1866), chap. 3, that "there is no private life which has not been determined by a wider public life."

27. See the discussion in Wolfgang Iser, *The Fictive and the Imaginary: Charting Literary Anthropology* (Baltimore: Johns Hopkins University Press, 1993), 248.

28. Names with *gg* seem to be particularly associated by some writers with characters who are unpleasant. For example, Anthony Powell has an opportunistic communist journalist called Quiggin, who is associated with Howard Craggs and published by Boggis & Stone (*At Lady Molly's* [1957]).

29. Franco Moretti, *Atlas of the European Novel 1800–1900* (London: Verso, 1998), 18.

2. Space and Time

1. See chapter 1, section on "proper names."

2. See Gérard Genette, *Figures II* (Paris: Seuil, 1969), 61–69; Émile Benveniste, *Problèmes de linguistique générale* (Paris: Gallimard, 1966), vol. 1, 237–50. The term *histoire* is also widely used for *récit*.

3. See chapter 12, section on "the present as main narrative tense."

4. Elizabeth Deeds Ermarth argues that the *récit* of nineteenth-century third-person narratives is told by a narrator who is not an individual, but who represents social consensus (*Realism and Consensus in the English Novel* [Princeton: Princeton University Press, 1983]). See chapter 10, section on 'the "Nobody" narrator.'

5. See Jakob Lothe, *Conrad's Narrative Method* (Oxford: Clarendon Press, 1989), 6.

6. Some modernist writers encourage this sense by laying all their emphasis on space, cutting out conventional plot development and juxtaposing one space against another. See Joseph Frank, *The Widening Gyre* (New Brunswick, N.J.: Rutgers University Press, 1963).

7. Preface to *The Portrait of a Lady*, New York ed. (1908) (Fairfield, Conn.: Augustus M. Kelley, 1977), x.

8. *Point of view* was a key analytic term in Percy Lubbock's *The Craft of Fiction* (1921). Seymour Chatman calls it "one of the most troublesome of critical terms" (*Story and Discourse: Narrative Structure in Fiction and Film* [Ithaca: Cornell University Press, 1978], 151). My discussion here, and in what follows, draws on Mieke Bal's account of focalization in *Narratology: Introduction to the Theory of Narrative*, 2nd ed. (Toronto: University of Toronto Press, 1997). Chatman makes plain that use of the term *focalizing* does not remove all the confusions ("Charac-

ters and Narrators: Filter, Slant and Interest—Focus," *Poetics Today* 7, no. 2 [1986]: 189–204), but it nonetheless remains useful.

9. See, for example, the description of a room by A. Conan Doyle cited in chapter 3, section on "types of description: representative."

10. "The Reality Effect," in *French Literary Theory Today,* ed. Tzvetan Todorov (Cambridge: Cambridge University Press, 1982), 11–18. See discussions below in chapter 3 (sections on "types of description: representative ") and chapter 16 (section on "metonymy"). Barthes also read realist details in terms of codes in *S/Z* (1970).

11. Franco Moretti, *Atlas of the European Novel 1800–1900* (London: Verso, 1998), 14–20.

12. Gérard Genette, *Narrative Discourse* [from *Figures III*], trans. Jane E. Lewin (Ithaca: Cornell University Press, 1980), 215.

13. Our concept of plot and its relation to action derives from Aristotle's *Poetics*. The chief modern discussion of this topic is in Paul Ricoeur, *Time and Narrative* (1983–85), trans. Kathleen McLaughlin and David Pellauer, 3 vols. (Chicago: University of Chicago Press, 1984–88). See also chapter 8, below.

14. The time difference continues until the end of the journal section in the novel, when Stoker moves us into a *discours* in the present tense: "As I write. . . . I am alone in the castle with those awful women. Faugh!"

15. *Time and Western Man* (London: Chatto and Windus, 1927), 445.

Part II
Description, Character, Dialogue, and Monologue

1. Anthony Trollope, *An Autobiography* [1883] (Harmondsworth: Penguin, 1996), chap. 15.

3. Description

1. See Philippe Hamon, *Du Descriptif* (Paris: Hachette, 1993), 72–75.

2. Character portraits are dealt with separately in chapter 4. This chapter concentrates on descriptions of landscapes and setting.

3. See Philippe Hamon, "What is a description?" in *French Literary Theory Today,* ed. Tzvetan Todorov (Cambridge: Cambridge University Press, 1982). Hamon suggests that narrative is *understood,* description is *recognized.*

4. G. H. Lewes in *Blackwood's Magazine* (1859), cited by Richard Stang, *The Theory of the Novel in England 1850–1870* (London: Routledge and Kegan Paul, 1959), 94.

5. Mieke Bal, *Narratology: Introduction to the Theory of Narrative*, 2nd ed. (Toronto: University of Toronto Press, 1997), 36.

6. See Denis Apothéloz, "Éléments pour une logique de la description . . ." in *La Description,* ed. Yves Reuter (Paris: Presses Universitaires du Septentrion, 1998), 19–20.

7. Apothéloz calls this an operation of "affectation" (ibid., 22–23).

8. Hamon, *Du Descriptif*, 42–48.

9. The types of description in what follows are taken from Jean-Michel Adam and André Petitjean, *Le Texte descriptif: Poétique historique et linguistique textuelle* (Paris: Nathan, 1989).

10. See Philippe Hamon, "Rhetorical Status of the Descriptive," *Yale French Studies* 61 (1981): 1–27.

11. See Rictor Norton, *Mistress of Udolpho* (London: Leicester University Press, 1999), 78–79; and Samuel H. Monk, *The Sublime* (Ann Arbor: University of Michigan Press, 1935), 226.

12. Edmund Burke, *A Philosophical Enquiry into the Origin of our Ideas of the Sublime and Beautiful* (1759), part 2, sec. 4.

13. *The Letters of James Joyce*, ed. Richard Ellmann (London: Faber, 1966), vol. 2, 134.

14. See the analysis in David Lodge, *The Modes of Modern Writing: Metaphor, Metonymy, and the Typology of Modern Literature* (London: Edward Arnold, 1977), 27–34.

15. See the section on phonetic repetition in chapter 15, below.

16. Virginia Woolf, "Modern Fiction," in *Collected Essays*, ed. Leonard Woolf (London: Hogarth Press, 1980), vol. 2.

4. Character and Character Portraits

1. Percy Lubbock, *The Craft of Fiction* (1921) (London: Jonathan Cape, 1968), 4.

2. Seymour Chatman, *Story and Discourse: Narrative Structure in Fiction and Film* (Ithaca: Cornell University Press, 1978), 118.

3. Mariko Yamaguchi, in "How Should We Treat Fictional Names?," *Tetsugaku: Philosophical Association of Japan* no 53 (2002), points out that we cannot treat both types of fictional statements in the same way as referring to abstract entities. In what follows I am much indebted to her discussion.

4. See Michael Seidel, "The Man Who Came to Dinner: Ian Watt and the Theory of Formal Realism," *Eighteenth-Century Fiction* 12, nos. 2–3 (2000): 202–3.

5. Vincent Jouve, *L'Effet personnage dans le roman* (Paris: PUF, 1992).

6. D. H. Lawrence, letter to Edward Garnett, 5 June 1914. Cited in Miriam Allott, *Novelists on the Novel* (London: Routledge and Kegan Paul, 1959), 290.

7. Characters have a role or function in the development of actions within narratives, and have been analyzed by some narratologists as *actants* (that is, as a class of actors who share a certain quality). In a *fabula* (see chapter 6) there will be a subject-actant, and the wish or intention of the subject-actant leads to an object-actant (not always a person). There may be helpers or opposition. There may be doubling of various kinds, and the question of whether the actions of the actants are truthful reflections of real intentions also comes up. This terminology derives from A.-J. Greimas; see also Mieke Bal's discussion in *Narratology: Introduction to the Theory of Narrative*, 2nd ed. (Toronto: University of Toronto Press, 1997).

8. The term *character portrait* is used here in the sense of a portrait within the

novel, and not in the sense intended by Charlotte Brontë or George Eliot (when they denied putting portraits in their novels) of a "literal portrait," taken from life, of a real person.

9. See Clair Hughes, *Henry James and the Art of Dress* (London: Palgrave, 2000).

10. Virginia Woolf, "Mr. Bennett and Mrs. Brown," in *Collected Essays,* ed. Leonard Woolf (London: Hogarth Press, 1980), vol. 1.

11. See chapter 7, below.

12. Chatman, *Story and Discourse,* 132. Chatman's discussion of Forster, and his comparison between this distinction and the actantial theory, is illuminating.

13. Umberto Eco, *The Role of the Reader: Explorations in the Semiotics of Texts* (1979) (Bloomington: Indiana University Press, 1984), 145–46.

5. Dialogue

1. Sylvie Durrer shows that the French novel gradually increases self-reference of speakers and first-person pronouns. See Sylvie Durrer, *Le Dialogue romanesque* (Geneva: Librairie Droz, 1994).

2. Gustave Flaubert, letter of 30 September 1853, in *Préface à la vie d'écrivain,* ed. Geneviève Bollème (Paris: Seuil, 1963), 151.

3. See Norman Page, *Speech in the English Novel* (London: Longman, 1973), 24–38. Monologue and free indirect discourse are also used to represent speech, and are considered separately in chapters 6 and 7.

4. Ibid., 324.

5. See Durrer, *Le Dialogue romanesque,* 31.

6. In early novels this is also sometimes done with indirect speech.

7. The term *inquit* (Latin for "he said" or "she said") is also used for "tag phrase."

8. See Durrer, *Le Dialogue romanesque,* 54.

9. Novels may, exceptionally, introduce speakers as in a play script, with their names printed above, or beside, each speech. T. L. Peacock, for example, does this in *Nightmare Abbey* (1818), as does Julian Barnes in *Love, Etc.* (2000).

10. See Durrer, *Le Dialogue romanesque,* 113–90.

11. I follow Élisabeth Ravoux Rallo in adding this category to those described by Durrer. See *L'Explication de texte à l'oral des concours* (Paris: Armand Colin, 1966).

12. Ford Madox Ford, *A Personal Remembrance* (1924), vol. 2, ii. Cited in Miriam Allott, *Novelists on the Novel* (London: Routledge and Kegan Paul, 1959), 297.

13. See Page, *Speech in the English Novel,* 51–86. There is a helpful discussion of "the phonetic representation of Cockney" in P. J. Keating, *The Working Classes in Victorian Fiction* (London: Routledge and Kegan Paul, 1971). Leech and Short point out that *wos* is sometimes used in novels to represent dialect *was.* The usage is quite illogical, since not only dialect, but standard English pronunciation is close to *wos.* In effect, illiterate spelling is being used to give the impression of dialect, a device called *eye-dialect* (168).

14. See Ann Banfield, *Unspeakable Sentences: Narration and Representation in the Language of Fiction* (Boston: Routledge and Kegan Paul, 1982), 243–53.

15. I am grateful to Akiko Kawasaki for this point about *Jane Eyre*.

6. Monologue and Stream of Consciousness

1. The term *quoted monologue* is taken from the valuable discussion in Dorrit Cohn's *Transparent Minds: Narrative Modes for Presenting Consciousness in Fiction* (Princeton: Princeton University Press, 1978), 58–98. *Embedded narrative* is one narrative contained within another; see chapter 9, section on "hierarchy of narratives."

2. The "Advertisement" to *Belinda* insists that the author does not wish it to be seen a novel, but as a "Moral Tale"—which adds further ambiguities.

3. Cohn, *Transparent Minds*, 7.

4. Ibid., 79.

5. See also "nonreflective discourse" in chapter 7, below.

6. Unless, like Philip Roth in *American Pastoral*, they decide to dream a realist novel within the frame of the first-person novel.

7. Free Indirect Discourse

1. It is quite common to separate off *free indirect speech* and *free indirect thought*. The term *discourse* is used here because it usefully covers both speech and thought, and it is not always possible to know whether speech or thought is intended. The form is often referred to as FIS (or FIT, or FID) or by its French name *style indirect libre*, or the German *erlebte Rede*, or as *represented speech and thought*. It forms the main topic of two important books: Roy Pascal, *The Dual Voice* (Manchester: Manchester University Press, 1977); and Ann Banfield, *Unspeakable Sentences* (Boston: Routledge and Kegan Paul, 1982). The problems they pose are developed in Monika Fludernik, *The Fictions of Language and the Languages of Fiction* (London: Routledge, 1993); and articles by Brian McHale and Manfred Jahn.

2. Typically we find sentences like "Now it was too late," where there is an adverb referring to the present but a verb in the past.

3. See Fludernik, *Fictions of Language*, 280–89.

4. See Manfred Jahn, "Contextualizing Represented Speech and Thought," *Journal of Pragmatics* 17 (1992): 353.

5. Mieke Bal, *Narratology: Introduction to the Theory of Narrative*, 2nd ed. (Toronto: University of Toronto Press, 1997), 50.

6. See Banfield, *Unspeakable Sentences*, 196–99.

7. See chapter 6, section on "memory monologue."

Part III
Narrative and Narrators

1. Paul Ricoeur, *Time and Narrative*, trans. Kathleen McLaughlin and David Pellauer (Chicago: University of Chicago Press, 1984–88), vol. 1, 65.

8. Narrative I

1. Roland Barthes, "Introduction to the Structural Analysis of Narratives," in *Image, Music, Text*. Ed. and trans. Stephen Heath (New York: Hill and Wang, 1977), 79-117.

2. Cf. Aristotle's requirements in *The Poetics* that a plot must have a beginning, a middle, and an end.

3. David Bordwell, *Narration in the Fiction Film* (Madison: University of Wisconsin Press, 1985), 33.

4. The terms derive from Russian formalism. See Mieke Bal, *Narratology: Introduction to the Theory of Narrative,* 2nd ed. (Toronto: University of Toronto Press, 1997), 5–10, for a clear account of how to use them in formal narratological analysis.

5. I am grateful to Stephen Clark for this analogy.

6. The concept of the kernel derives from Roland Barthes. There is a clear explanation in Seymour Chatman, *Story and Discourse: Narrative Structure in Fiction and Film* (Ithaca: Cornell University Press, 1978), 53.

7. See, for example, Bordwell, *Narration in the Fiction Film*, 50–51.

8. "Life: A Story in Search of a Narrator," in *A Ricoeur Reader*, ed. Mario J. Valdés (New York: Harvester, 1991), 426.

9. Chrétien de Troyes wrote famous examples in French verse in the twelfth century. Prose became increasingly used for romances in the thirteenth century. Works like Sir Thomas Malory's *Le Morte Darthur* (1485) and Sir Philip Sidney's *Arcadia* (1590) provide different forms of prose romance in English. French writers continued to develop the form until the mid-seventeenth century, in romances like Madeleine de Scudéry's *Artamène ou le Grand Cyrus* (1649–53).

10. Clara Reeve, *The Progress of Romance* (1785), vol. 1, Evening vii.

11. Ricoeur, "Life: A Story in Search of a Narrator," 425. The "origin" or the "rise" of the modern novel is often traced to the "realism" of these life-stories. See Ian Watt, *The Rise of the Novel* (1957) (Berkeley: University of California Press, 1964); and Michael McKeon, *The Origins of the English Novel* (London: Century Hutchinson, 1987).

12. J. Paul Hunter, *The Reluctant Pilgrim* (Baltimore: Johns Hopkins University Press, 1966), 88.

13. See Catherine Gallagher, *The Industrial Reformation of English Fiction* (Chicago: University of Chicago Press, 1985), 36–41.

14. "3 or 4 Families in a Country village is the very thing to work on." In *Jane Austen's Letters,* ed. R. W. Chapman (Oxford: Oxford University Press, 1952), 100. See also Harry E. Shaw, *Narrating Reality: Austen, Scott, Eliot* (Ithaca: Cornell University Press, 1999), 126–35.

15. See Tony Tanner, *Adultery in the Novel: Contract and Transgression* (Baltimore: Johns Hopkins University Press, 1979).

16. Kathleen Tillotson, "The Lighter Reading of the Eighteen-Sixties," introduction to *The Woman in White*, Riverside ed. (Boston: Houghton Mifflin, 1969), xv.

17. Anthony Trollope, *An Autobiography* [1883] (Harmondsworth: Penguin,

1996), 165. Trollope was not being entirely complimentary about Collins. For himself he thought plots "the most insignificant part of a tale" (84).

18. Tillotson, "The Lighter Reading of the Eighteen-Sixties," xvi.

19. *The Impressions of Theophrastus Such* (1879), cited in Miriam Allott, *Novelists on the Novel* (London: Routledge and Kegan Paul, 1959), 247–48.

20. Other readings might give a stronger focus to different plots, like the plot of integration through experience identified with the *Bildungsroman,* as described in Franco Moretti's *The Way of the World* (London: Verso, 1987); or evolutionary plots, as described in Gillian Beer's *Darwin's Plots* (London: Routledge and Kegan Paul, 1983).

21. Shaw, *Narrating Reality,* 156, 129, 126.

22. Epiphany is the Christian feast in celebration of the moment when the three Wise Men first see the infant Jesus. In the ordinary conditions of a stable, looking at the baby, the Wise Men have a sudden understanding of the meaning of their journey. Joyce talks of a "sudden spiritual manifestation, whether in the vulgarity of speech or of gesture or in a memorable phase of the mind itself" (*Stephen Hero,* chap. 24 [(1904–6), 1944]).

23. Obviously Virginia Woolf felt the passage was important and she should get the wording exactly right, since the first American edition changes the last paragraph to "'It's going to be wet tomorrow. You won't be able to go.' And she looked at him smiling. For she had triumphed again. She had not said: yet he knew."

9. Narrative II

1. Anthony Trollope, *An Autobiography* [1883] (Harmondsworth: Penguin, 1996), 153. Trollope was critical, but his own work is hardly a model. He uses digressive episodes, as when he puts a novel within the novel in *The Three Clerks* (1857).

2. Dorothy Van Ghent, *The English Novel: Form and Function* (1953) (New York: Harper, 1961), 153–70.

3. See Gérard Genette, *Narrative Discourse* [from *Figures III*], trans. Jane E. Lewin (Ithaca: Cornell University Press, 1980), chaps. 1–3.

4. Paul Ricoeur, "Life: A Story in Search of a Narrator," in *A Ricoeur Reader,* ed. Mario J. Valdés (New York: Harvester, 1991), 428.

5. See chapter 12, below.

6. Ellipsis is discussed here in relation to narrative. See also chapter 11, below, for ellipsis in the sentence.

7. Meir Sternberg, *Expositional Modes and Temporal Ordering in Fiction* (Baltimore: Johns Hopkins University Press, 1978), 50–55, 238–46.

8. See the discussion in F. Ungerer and H.-J. Schmid, *An Introduction to Cognitive Linguistics* (London: Longman, 1996), 211–17.

9. These examples are cited in ibid., 216.

10. See Gordon N. Ray, "H. G. Wells Tries to Be a Novelist," in *Edwardians and Late Victorians,* ed. Richard Ellmann (New York: Columbia University Press, 1960), 117.

11. Seymour Chatman, *Story and Discourse: Narrative Structure in Fiction and Film* (Ithaca: Cornell University Press , 1978), 72. The question of whether a novel concentrates on showing or telling has been of much concern to modern novelists. Showing is done by scenes. See ibid., 146–95.

12. Henry James, preface to *The Awkward Age,* New York ed. (1908), xvii, xiii, xvii.

13. Moore says he learned this technique from Zola's *L'Assommoir* (though it is more often identified with Flaubert and the scene of the agricultural fair in *Madame Bovary*). See *Confessions of a Young Man* (1886), 78.

14. Henry James, *Literary Criticism*, vol. 1 (New York: Library of America, 1984), 497. See also chapter 10, below, on intrusive narrators and metadiegetic commentary.

15. Viktor Shklovsky, "The Connection between Devices of Syuzhet Construction and General Stylistic Devices," in *Russian Formalism,* ed. Stephen Bann and John E. Bowlt (Edinburgh: Scottish Academic Press, 1973) and Bordwell, *Narration in the Fiction Film,* 38. Meir Sternberg's discussion of the topic is particularly helpful; see *Expositional Modes and Temporal Ordering in Fiction* (Baltimore: Johns Hopkins University Press, 1978), 159–82.

16. Sternberg, *Expositional Modes,* 161.

17. *Defamiliarization,* or "making the familiar strange," was considered by formalists to be one of the most distinctive techniques of artworks. See Viktor Shklovsky in *Russian Formalist Criticism: Four Essays,* trans. Lee T. Lemon and Marion J. Reis (Lincoln: University of Nebraska Press, 1965), 13–22, and on Sterne's novel as "the most typical novel in world literature," 25–57.

18. See the important section of Genette's *Narrative Discourse* (113–60), where he analyzes the use of frequency in the work of Marcel Proust. Textual and rhetorical repetition is discussed in chapter 16, below.

10. Narrators

1. Following Philippe Lejeune, we can make a distinction between autobiography and memoirs. An autobiography is not a series of random recollections, it is a narrative that hangs together and constructs the picture of an individual life—often around a conversion experience, or a time of mental crisis leading to self-realization. See Philippe Lejeune, *L'Autobiographie en France* (Paris: Armand Colin, 1971).

2. See the classic account in Wayne C. Booth, *The Rhetoric of Fiction* (Chicago: University of Chicago Press, 1961), 152–53. Booth points out that in a sense all first-person narrators are dramatized, but some more fully than others.

3. See Dorrit Cohn, *Transparent Minds: Narrative Modes for Presenting Consciousness in Fiction* (Princeton: Princeton University Press, 1978), 145–61; and Cohn, *The Distinction of Fiction* (Baltimore: Johns Hopkins University Press, 1999), 132–49.

4. Booth, *Rhetoric of Fiction,* 158–59.

5. Stanzel discusses the interesting case of Thackeray's *Henry Esmond,* where there is an unstable alternation between first- and third-person narrative (*A Theory*

of Narrative, 2nd ed. [1982] trans. Charlotte Goedsche, [Cambridge: Cambridge University Press, 1984], 101).

6. Narrators of this kind may be called (following Genette's terminology) *heterodiegetic,* since they stand outside the account of the fictional world (or *diegesis*) given in the main story. A narrator inside the story telling about his or her own doings may be called *homodiegetic.* See *Narrative Discourse* [from *Figures III*], trans. Jane E. Lewin (Ithaca: Cornell University Press, 1980), 245.

7. Genette introduces the useful term *metadiegetic* for such commentary.

8. The question of whether we consider the narrator in George Eliot's novels to be gendered is obviously important. See Susan Sniader Lanser, *Fictions of Authority* (Ithaca: Cornell University Press, 1992); and Harry E. Shaw, *Narrating Reality: Austen, Scott, Eliot* (Ithaca: Cornell University Press, 1999), 252–55.

9. Dorrit Cohn, *The Distinction of Fiction* (Baltimore: Johns Hopkins University Press, 1999), 148. See also Shlomith Rimmon-Kenan, *A Glance beyond Doubt: Narration, Representation, Subjectivity* (Columbus: Ohio State University Press, 1996), 14.

10. Käte Hamburger says: "Such intrusion is flourish, arabesque." See *The Logic of Literature,* 2nd ed. (1973), trans. Marilynn J. Rose (Bloomington: Indiana University Press, 1993), 156.

11. Genette, *Narrative Discourse,* 244.

12. Gérard Genette, *Figures of Literary Discourse,* trans. Alan Sheridan (New York: Columbia University Press, 1982), 141–42.

13. Ann Banfield, *Unspeakable Sentences* (Boston and London: Routledge and Kegan Paul, 1982), 250.

14. Denis Donoghue, *The Practice of Reading* (New Haven: Yale University Press, 1998), 227.

15. Elizabeth Deeds Ermarth, *Realism and Consensus in the English Novel* (Princeton: Princeton University Press, 1983), 65–66.

16. Ibid., 84, 192, 227; Elizabeth Deeds Ermarth, *The English Novel in History 1840–1895* (London: Routledge, 1997), 87.

17. Henry James, "The Art of Fiction," in *The Critical Muse: Selected Literary Criticism* (Harmondsworth, Middlesex, England: Penguin Books, 1987), 189.

18. *Joseph Conrad, A Personal Remembrance* (1924), cited in Allott, *Novelists on the Novel* (London: Routledge and Kegan Paul, 1959), 273.

Part IV
The Language of the Text

1. Quoted in Joseph Frank, *The Widening Gyre* (New Brunswick, N.J.: Rutgers University Press, 1963), 31. Frank comments that Eliot "justly observes" this.

2. Maurice Blanchot, "The Novel is a Work of Bad Faith," in *The Blanchot Reader,* ed. Michael Holland (Oxford: Blackwell, 1995), 66–67.

3. Cited in Jean-Michel Adam, *Éléments de linguistique textuelle* (Liège: Mardaga, 1990), 11.

4. I owe this example to Michael Tomasello, *The New Psychology of Language:*

Cognitive and Functional Approaches to Language Structure (Mahwah, N.J.: Lawrence Erlbaum Associates, 1998), xviii.

5. J. M. Coetzee argues that we cannot take a "naive step" from syntactic form to meaning, but we can profitably ask "what the range of meanings is that a given form accommodates in practice" (*Doubling the Point: Essays and Interviews* [Cambridge, Mass.: Harvard University Press, 1992], 149).

6. See George Lakoff and Mark Johnson, *Metaphors We Live By* (Chicago: University of Chicago Press, 1980), 165.

7. Thomas G. Pavel, *Fictional Worlds* (Cambridge, Mass.: Harvard University Press, 1986), 17.

8. "Henry James's First Interview," in *Henry James on Culture,* ed. Pierre A. Walker (Lincoln: University of Nebraska Press, 1999), 142.

9. Joseph Conrad, letter to R. B. Cunninghame Graham, cited in George Levine, *The Realistic Imagination: English Fiction from Frankenstein to Lady Chatterley* (Chicago: University of Chicago Press, 1981), 51.

11. Sentence Structure and Connection

1. See Ronald W. Langacker, "Conceptualization, Symbolization, and Grammar," in *The New Psychology of Language,* ed. Michael Tomasello (Mahwah, N.J.: Lawrence Erlbaum Associates, 1998), 4.

2. See Käte Hamburger, *The Logic of Literature,* 2nd ed. (1973), trans. Marilynn J. Rose (Bloomington: Indiana University Press, 1993), 71. Sentences of this kind are also found in nonfiction texts, but are read there as fictionalizing. See introductory section of chapter 12.

3. Elizabeth Deeds Ermarth, *Realism and Consensus in the English Novel* (Princeton: Princeton University Press, 1983), 259.

4. See Malcolm Brown, *George Moore: A Reconsideration* (Seattle: University of Washington Press, 1955), 185, for an informative account of Moore's long sentences.

5. Walter Pater, "Style," in *Appreciations* [1889] (London: Macmillan, 1910).

6. J. M. Coetzee, *Doubling the Point: Essays and Interviews* (Cambridge, Mass.: Harvard University Press, 1992), 49.

7. These are examples of relative, complement, and adverbial clauses. For an important discussion of the complex sentence with a focus on linguistics, see Ronald W. Langacker, *Foundations of Cognitive Grammar*, vol. 2 (Stanford: Stanford University Press, 1991), 417–63.

8. Peter Jones, "The Miracle of 'And,'" *The Spectator*, 8 January 2000, 17–18.

9. See Langacker, *Foundations of Cognitive Grammar*, vol. 2, 435.

10. Introduction to Penguin ed. (Harmondsworth, Middlesex: Penguin Books, 1996), xvi. Walter J. Ong suggests that women were less likely to have been educated in schools where rhetoric was taught, and so "usually expressed themselves in a different, far less oratorical voice, which had a great deal to do with the rise of the novel" (*Orality and Literacy: The Technologizing of the Word* [London: Methuen, 1982], 112).

11. Such use of phrases set off by semicolons to represent the stream of consciousness was initiated by Édouard Dujardin's *Les Lauriers sont coupés* (1887).

12. Hugh Blair, *Lectures on Rhetoric and Belles Lettres* (1784) (London: William Baynes, 1825), 129–30.

13. See Heinrich Lausberg, *Handbook of Literary Rhetoric*, trans. Matthew T. Bliss et al. (Leiden: Brill, 1998), 414–17.

14. A. S. Byatt, *On Histories and Stories: Selected Essays* (London: Chatto and Windus, 2000), 95.

15. David Bordwell, *Narration in the Fiction Film* (Madison: University of Wisconsin Press, 1985), 35.

16. See Jean-Michel Adam, *Éléments de linguistique textuelle* (Liège: Mardaga, 1990), 36.

17. See Gary Saul Morson and Caryl Emerson, *Mikhail Bakhtin: Creation of a Prosaics* (Stanford: Stanford University Press, 1990), 332.

18. Ermarth, *Realism and Consensus in the English Novel*, 81.

19. See chapter 9 for ellipsis as a narrative feature.

20. E. H. Gombrich, *The Sense of Order* (1979), 2nd ed. (London: Phaidon, 1984), 121.

21. Gertrude Stein, *Lectures in America* (New York: Random House, 1935), 210.

12. Verbs: Tense, Time, and Voice

1. See Paul Ricoeur, *The Rule of Metaphor* (1975), trans. Robert Czerny et al. (Toronto: University of Toronto Press, 1977), 15.

2. See Wallace Martin, *Recent Theories of Narrative* (Ithaca: Cornell University Press, 1986), 93.

3. Paul Ricoeur, *Time and Narrative*, 3 vols. (1983–85), trans. Kathleen McLaughlin and David Pellauer (Chicago: University of Chicago Press, 1984–88), vol. 2, 63.

4. Käte Hamburger, *The Logic of Literature*, 2nd ed. (1973), trans. Marilynn J. Rose (Bloomington: Indiana University Press, 1993), 71.

5. We might contrast such sentences with the prototypical "historical sentence" discussed by Arthur Danto: "In 1717 the author of *Rameau's Nephew* was born." In this case there is no confusion over time within the sentence, but the sentence could not have been written by someone in 1717, when Diderot was born, or indeed before the publication of *Rameau's Nephew*. It could only be written as a historical sentence. See Ricoeur, *Time and Narrative*, vol. 1, 71.

6. Elizabeth Deeds Ermarth, *Realism and Consensus in the English Novel* (Princeton: Princeton University Press, 1983), 42.

7. Seymour Chatman, *Story and Discourse: Narrative Structure in Fiction and Film* (Ithaca: Cornell University Press, 1978), 80.

8. Kathleen Tillotson, *Novels of the Eighteen-Forties* (Oxford: Oxford University Press, 1954), 94.

9. Dorrit Cohn, *Transparent Minds: Narrative Modes for Presenting Consciousness in Fiction* (Princeton: Princeton University Press, 1978), 198.

10. Geoffrey N. Leech, *Meaning and the English Verb* (1971), 2nd ed. (London: Longman, 1987), 16.

11. For example, stage-directions from *Waiting for Godot*: "They listen, Estragon loses his balance, almost falls. He clutches the arm of Vladimir who totters." It can also, of course, be read as free indirect discourse.

12. "Narrating without a Narrator," (London) *Times Literary Supplement,* 31 December 1999, 13.

13. For an analysis of the play between iterative and punctual present tenses in fiction, see J. M. Coetzee's essay on Kafka in *Doubling the Point* (Cambridge, Mass.: Harvard University Press, 1992), 210–33.

14. Quoted in Virginia Tufte, *Grammar as Style* (New York: Holt, Rinehart and Winston, 1971), 56.

15. Cited in Roderick A. Jacobs, *English Syntax: A Grammar for English Language Professionals* (New York: Oxford University Press, 1995), 159.

16. Coetzee, *Doubling the Point,* 176, 168.

17. Tufte, *Grammar as Style,* 56. To do justice to Tufte, she is pointing out that building up noun phrases at the start of a sentence (on the "left side"), makes for hard, dull reading. It is difficult to disagree: modern academic prose provides many examples.

18. Dorrit Cohn, for example, points out how James has in effect to create a new tense, a "pre-pluperfect," to communicate the complexity of decision making in his late novels. See "The Opening Episode of *The Golden Bowl* Vol. 2," *Henry James Review* 22, no. 1 (winter 2001): 7.

13. Adjectives

1. A. S. Byatt, "On the Day That E. M. Forster Died," in *Sugar and Other Stories* (London: Chatto and Windus, 1987), 133; Theodora Bosanquet, *Henry James at Work* (London: Hogarth press, 1924); Anton Chekhov, letter of 3 September 1899, in *Selected Letters and Commentary,* trans. Simon Karlinsky (London: Bodley Head, 1973).

2. Dominique Maingueneau, *Éléments de linguistique pour le texte littéraire,* 3rd ed. (Paris: Dunod, 1993). The distinction between subjective and objective adjectives is given a more complex and satisfactory elaboration by C. Kerbrat-Orecchioni, *L'Énonciation, de la subjectivité dans le langage* (Paris: A. Colin, 1980).

3. Walter Pater, "Style," in *Appreciations* [1889] (London: Macmillan, 1910).

4. Kimberley Reynolds and Nicola Humble, *Victorian Heroines: Representations of Femininity in Nineteenth-Century Literature and Art* (New York: New York University Press, 1993), 105.

5. Preface to *The Tragic Muse,* New York ed. (1908).

6. See chapter 2, section on "spaces of the incipit."

7. Anne Hollander, *Seeing through Clothes* (Berkeley: University of California Press, 1993), 423–25. Hollander suggests that the rise of photography encour-

aged vague spontaneous images, flashes of blurred camera vision, as against the previous images of clothes being made of many parts (332).

8. George Levine, *The Realistic Imagination: English Fiction from Frankenstein to Lady Chatterley* (Chicago: University of Chicago Press, 1981), 90.

14. Figures: Metaphor, Metonymy, Irony

1. George Lakoff and Mark Johnson, *Metaphors We Live By* (Chicago: University of Chicago Press, 1980), 3.

2. George Lakoff and Mark Turner, *More Than Cool Reason: A Field Guide to Poetic Metaphor* (Chicago: University of Chicago Press, 1989), 129.

3. Lakoff and Johnson, *Metaphors We Live By*, 5.

4. Cognitive linguistics uses capitals to indicate what are simply approximate names representing conceptual metaphors; they are not to be regarded as traditional word-based tropes.

5. See Gilles Fauconnier, *Mappings in Thought and Language* (Cambridge: Cambridge University Press, 1997), 9, from which I have borrowed these examples.

6. Zoltán Kövecses, in *Metaphor in Cognitive Linguistics,* ed. Raymond W. Gibbs Jr. and Gerard J. Steen (Amsterdam: John Benjamins, 1999), provides a systematic account of the different entailments from the PLANT metaphor.

7. Cited in Paul Ricoeur, *The Rule of Metaphor* (1975), trans. Robert Czerny et al. (Toronto: University of Toronto Press, 1977), 23.

8. Michele Emantian has described the same kind of sexual metaphors based on animals stalking prey in a Tanzanian language. See *Metaphor in Cognitive Linguistics,* ed. Gibbs and Steen, 206–9.

9. Lakoff and Johnson, *Metaphors We Live By*, 29.

10. Mark Turner, *Reading Minds* (Princeton: Princeton University Press, 1991), 220–22.

11. Fauconnier, *Mappings in Thought and Language*, 25.

12. *Metaphor in Cognitive Linguistics,* ed. Gibbs and Steen, 48.

13. Raymond W. Gibbs Jr., *The Poetics of Mind* (Cambridge: Cambridge University Press, 1994), 322.

14. Lakoff and Johnson, *Metaphors We Live By*, 36.

15. See David Lodge, *The Modes of Modern Writing* (London: Edward Arnold, 1979), 73–103, 109–11. Lodge's analysis is based on Roman Jakobson's contrast between metaphor and metonymy. Jakobson's dichotomy has been attacked by Gérard Genette and by Brian Vickers as an unjustifiable reduction of rhetoric (Vickers, *In Defence of Rhetoric* [Oxford: Clarendon Press, 1988], 442–52). But this does not invalidate Lodge's account of metonymy in its relation to realist fiction.

16. Raymond Carver, "On Writing," quoted in *New York Review of Books,* 12 August 1999, 54.

17. *Irony* is also used to describe actions in a narrative. Actions may represent an irony of fate when they produce the opposite result from that intended. Or they are ironic when there is a mismatch between the character's description or

idea of him or herself and the action performed. It is a *dramatic irony* when an audience of drama can see the implications and possible consequences of something that a character cannot.

18. Gibbs, *Poetics of Mind*, 360–62.

19. Not all "mentions" of language are ironic: words may be distanced from the rest of the text, or our attention drawn to them for other purposes entirely (as in quotations or when we wish to discuss the usage of the word).

20. See Gary Saul Morson and Caryl Emerson, *Mikhail Bakhtin: Creation of a Prosaics* (Stanford: Stanford University Press, 1990), 154–61.

15. Words and Meanings

1. Paul Ricoeur, *The Rule of Metaphor* (1975), trans. Robert Czerny et al. (Toronto: University of Toronto Press, 1977). See the discussion on "Metaphor and the Semantics of the Word," 101–33.

2. See J.-P. Richard, *Microlectures* (Paris: Seuil, 1979).

3. Leo Spitzer, "Linguistics and Literary History," in *Linguistics and Literary Style,* ed. Donald C. Freeman (New York: Holt, Rinehart and Winston, 1970), 32.

4. Frequency counting is sometimes done and compared to a "norm" of usage. This is less defensible, since "norms" (whether in relation to ordinary language or the writer's idiolect) are always open to question.

5. See chapter 2, section on "the narrator and the opening space."

6. A rather odd gloss is added to this reading by the fact that James allowed the paratext of the New York edition to contain a photograph of the interior of an unnamed house, which provides an image of furniture that readers could focus on and use to help them imagine (or compare with the textual descriptions of) Poynton—but it contains no images of people.

7. See the discussion of mentions and irony in chapter 14, the section on "markers of irony."

8. Calvino, *If on a Winter's Night a Traveler* (1979), chap. 8.

16. Repetition and Figures of Construction

1. See E. H. Gombrich, *The Sense of Order* (1979), 2nd ed. (London: Phaidon, 1992), 103–5, 151, 108.

2. Gertrude Stein, *Lectures in America* (New York: Random House, 1935), 167.

3. "The Connection between Devices of Syuzhet Construction and General Stylistic Devices," in *Russian Formalism,* ed. Stephen Bann and John E. Bowlt (Edinburgh: Scottish Academic Press, 1973), 53.

4. Paul Ricoeur, "Life: A Story in Search of a Narrator," in *A Ricouer Reader,* ed. Mario J. Valdes (New York: Harvester Wheatsheaf, 1991), 430.

5. Steven Connor, *The English Novel in History: 1950–1995* (London: Routledge, 1966), 166.

6. George Moore went in for extensive revision of his novels, and in the 1920

edition, chapter 46 becomes chapter 43. But Moore leaves this passage—only in the 1920 version the evening is "pale" both at the start and the end of the novel.

7. The word *isotope* is borrowed from chemistry, where isotopes have the same position in the table of elements, but different physical properties. See A.-J. Greimas, *Structural Semantics* (1966), trans. Daniele McDowell et al. (Lincoln: University of Nebraska Press, 1983), 105.

8. Cited in Richard Poirier, *A World Elsewhere* (London: Oxford University Press, 1966), 220.

9. David Bordwell, *Narration in the Fiction Film* (Madison: University of Wisconsin Press, 1985), 80.

10. See E. H. Gombrich, *The Sense of Order,* 2nd ed. (London: Phaidon, 1984), 120–26. My discussion here draws on Gombrich, though his emphasis is rather on how we spot breaks in the pattern.

11. We may well respond to motifs unconsciously. For this reason, as Leo Bersani points out, taking repetition into account is the fundamental operation in psychoanalytic readings. *A Future for Astynax: Character and Desire in Literature* (London: Marion Boyars, 1978), 17.

12. David Lodge, *Language of Fiction* (New York: Columbia University Press, 1967), 82.

13. See David Lodge, *The Modes of Modern Writing: Metaphor, Metonymy, and the Typology of Modern Literature* (London: Edward Arnold, 1977), 31–32.

14. Elizabeth Deeds Ermarth, *The English Novel in History: 1840–1895* (London: Routledge, 1997), 21–22, 27.

15. It is usual in English to refer to rhetorical devices as *figures of speech.* This book follows the French phrase *figures of construction* for this group of figures, since they do help in an important way to construct text, and speech is not in question.

16. D. H. Lawrence, foreword to *Women in Love* (1919). Brian Vickers, *In Defence of Rhetoric* (Oxford: Clarendon Press, 1988), points out that Renaissance rhetoricians advised that for anaphora the words chosen for repetition were to be important to the sense. Failure to choose such words in Graham Swift's *Waterland,* for example, produces a style that is "pleonastic" and "verbose" (383–87).

17. D. H. Lawrence was obviously not anxious on this score. And Joyce mocks the common anxiety over elegant variation on tag phrases. See chapter 5, the section on "quotation marks and tags."

18. "The First Paragraph of *The Ambassadors*: An Explication," Norton Critical Edition (1964), 465–84.

19. Adam Piette, *Remembering and the Sound of Words: Mallarmé, Proust, Joyce, Beckett* (Oxford: Clarendon Press, 1996), 45, 26.

20. See Philippe Hamon, "What Is a Description," in *French Literary Theory Today,* ed. Tzvetan Todorov (Cambridge: Cambridge University Press, 1982), 159.

21. Henry James, *Literary Criticism*, vol. 1 (New York: Library of America, 1984), 611.

17. Lists

1. *All the Names* (1997), trans. Margaret Jull Costa (New York: Harcourt, 1999), 11.

Part V
Endings

1. Frank Kermode, *The Sense of an Ending: Studies in the Theory of Fiction* (New York: Oxford University Press, 1967), 55.

2. Jorge Luis Borges, *The Aleph: Including the Prose Fictions from "The Maker,"* trans. Andrew Hurley (London: Penguin, 1999), 19.

18. Endings

1. Frank Kermode, *The Sense of an Ending: Studies in the Theory of Fiction* (New York: Oxford University Press, 1967), 17–18.

2. Anthony Trollope, *An Autobiography* (1883) (Harmondsworth, Middlesex, England: Penguin, 1996), 165.

3. Henry James, "The Art of Fiction," in *The Critical Muse: Selected Literary Criticism* (Harmondsworth, Middlesex, England: Penguin, 1987), 190.

4. George Levine, *The Realistic Imagination: English Fiction from Frankenstein to Lady Chatterley* (Chicago: University of Chicago Press, 1981), 23.

5. See Claude Duchet, "Fins, finition, finalité, infinitude," in *Genèses des fins,* ed. Claude Duchet and Isabelle Tournier (Saint-Denis: PUV, 1996).

6. Richard D. Altick shows how this often leads to dubious tricks with the chronology of the narrative. See *The Presence of the Past* (Columbus: Ohio State University Press, 1991), 172–77.

7. It should, however, be added that the novel does actually end with a return to St. John Rivers, and with Jane's premonition of his death.

8. "Vanity of vanities, saith the Preacher, vanity of vanities; all is vanity" (Ecclesiastes 1.2).

Appendix 1
Film and the Novel

1. It should be pointed out that some theorists of film are deeply hostile to the use of novels: "The contemporary film narrative is gradually liberating itself from the constraints of the literary or pseudo-literary forms that played a large part in bringing abut the 'zero point of cinematic style' that reigned supreme during the 1930's and 1940's and still remains in a position of some strength today" (Noël Burch, *Theory of Film Practice* [Princeton: Princeton University Press, 1981], 15.

2. David Bordwell, *Narration in the Fiction Film* (Madison: University of Wisconsin Press, 1985); Bordwell, *Making Meaning: Inference and Rhetoric in the Interpretation of Cinema* (Cambridge, Mass.: Harvard University Press, 1989); Brian McFarlane, *Novel to Film: An Introduction to the Theory of Adaptation* (Ox-

ford: Clarendon Press, 1996); Jakob Lothe, *Narrative in Fiction and Film: An Introduction* (Oxford: Oxford University Press, 2000).

3. Lothe, *Narrative in Fiction and Film,* 151.

4. McFarlane, *Novel to Film,* 139–68.

5. See Roger Shattuck, *Proust's Way* (London: Allen Lane, Penguin Press, 2000), 192–206.

Appendix 2
Stereotype and Cliché in the Novel

1. See Ruth Amossy and Elisheva Rosen, *Les Discours du cliché* (Paris: Sedes, 1982); Amossy, *Les Idées reçues* (Paris: Nathan, 1991); Jean-Louis Dufays, "Stéréotype et littérature," in *Le Stéréotype: Crise et transformations,* ed. Alain Goulet (Caen: Presses Universitaires de Caen, 1994). Martin Amis in *The War Against Cliché* (London: Jonathan Cape, 2001) provides a good example of muddled attack.

2. See Amossy and Rosen, *Les Discours du cliché,* 27–39.

3. Peter Brooks, *The Melodramatic Imagination* (New Haven: Yale University Press, 1995), 11–20.

Works of Fiction Cited

Austen, Jane. *Sense and Sensibility*, 1811.
——. *Pride and Prejudice*, 1813.
——. *Emma*, 1816.
——. *Northanger Abbey*, 1818.
Auster, Paul. *City of Glass*, 1985.
Banville, John. *Dr. Copernicus*, 1976.
——. *The Book of Evidence*, 1989.
Barnes, Julian. *Flaubert's Parrot*, 1984.
Beckett, Samuel. *Murphy*, 1938.
——. *Watt*, 1953.
——. *Molloy*, [Fr. 1951] 1955.
——. *The Unnamable*, [Fr. 1953] 1958.
——. *How It Is*, [Fr. 1961] 1964.
Behn, Aphra. *Love-Letters between a Nobleman and His Sister*, 1684–87.
——. *The History of a Nun*, 1689.
Bennett, Arnold. *The Old Wives' Tale*, 1908.
——. *Clayhanger*, 1910.
Bowen, Elizabeth. *The Last September*, 1929.
——. *The House in Paris*, 1935.
——. *The Heat of the Day*, 1949.
Bowles, Paul. *The Sheltering Sky*, 1949.
Braddon, M. E. *The Doctor's Wife*, 1864.
——. *Phantom Fortune*, 1883.
Brontë, Charlotte. *Jane Eyre*, 1847.
Brontë, Emily. *Wuthering Heights*, 1847.
Brookner, Anita. *A Private View*, 1994.
Brown, Charles Brocken. *Wieland*, 1798.
Bunyan, John. *The Life and Death of Mr. Badman*, 1680.

Byatt, A. S. *Sugar and Other Stories*, 1987.
Calvino, Italo. *If on a Winter's Night a Traveler*, 1979.
Carroll, Lewis. *Alice in Wonderland*, 1865.
Carver, Raymond. "Preservation," 1983.
Cather, Willa. *My Mortal Enemy*, 1926.
Coetzee, J. M. *Dusklands*, 1974.
——. *Boyhood: Scenes from Provincial Life*, 1997.
Collins, Wilkie. *The Woman in White*, (1859–60) 1861.
Compton-Burnett, Ivy. *Two Worlds and Their Ways*, 1949.
Conan Doyle, Arthur. *A Study in Scarlet*, (1887) 1888.
Conrad, Joseph. *Lord Jim*, 1900.
——. *Nostromo*, 1904.
——. *Victory*, 1915.
Deane, Seamus. *Reading in the Dark*, 1996.
Defoe, Daniel. *The Life and Strange Surprizing Adventures of Robinson Crusoe*, 1719.
Dickens, Charles. *Pickwick Papers*, (1836–37) 1837.
——. *Barnaby Rudge*, 1841.
——. *A Christmas Carol*, 1843.
——. *Martin Chuzzlewit*, (1843–44) 1844.
——. *David Copperfield*, (1849–50) 1850.
——. *Bleak House*, (1852–53) 1853.
——. *Hard Times*, 1854.

———. *Little Dorrit,* (1855-57) 1857.

———. *A Tale of Two Cities,* 1859.

———. *Great Expectations,* (1860–61) 1861.

———. *Our Mutual Friend,* (1864–65) 1865.

Doyle, Roddy. *Paddy Clarke: Ha Ha Ha,* 1993.

Dreiser, Theodore. *Sister Carrie,* 1912.

Edgeworth, Maria. *Castle Rackrent,* 1800.

———. *Belinda,* 1801.

———. *Ormond,* 1817.

Eliot, George. *Scenes of Clerical Life,* (1857) 1858.

———. *Adam Bede,* 1859.

———. *Felix Holt: The Radical,* 1866.

———. *Middlemarch,* (1871–72) 1872.

———. *Daniel Deronda,* (1874-76) 1876.

———. *The Mill on the Floss,* 1860.

Faulkner, William. *Light in August,* 1932 [1985].

———. *The Reivers,* 1962.

Fielding, Henry. *Shamela,* 1741.

———. *Jonathan Wild,* 1743.

———. *Tom Jones,* 1749.

Flaubert, Gustave. *Sentimental Education,* 1869 [tr. 1964].

Forster, E. M. *Howards End,* 1910.

———. *A Passage to India,* 1924.

Freud, Esther. *Hideous Kinky,* 1992.

Gaskell, Elizabeth. *Mary Barton,* 1848.

———. *Cranford,* (1851-53) 1853.

Gissing, George. *The Nether World,* 1889.

———. "One Way of Happiness," 1898.

Godwin, William. *Caleb Williams,* 1794.

Golding, William. *Darkness Visible,* 1979.

Green, Henry. *Living,* 1929.

———. *Loving,* 1945.

———. *Back,* 1946.

Greene, Graham. *The End of the Affair,* 1951.

Hardy, Thomas. *Tess of the d'Urbervilles,* 1891.

———. *Jude the Obscure,* 1895.

Ishiguro, Kazuo. *An Artist of the Floating World,* 1986.

———. *The Remains of the Day,* 1989.

James, Henry. *Daisy Miller,* 1878 [1909].

———. *The Portrait of a Lady,* 1881 [1908].

———. *The Spoils of Poynton,* 1897.

———. *The Awkward Age,* 1899 [1909].

———. *The Golden Bowl,* 1904 [1909].

———. "Crapy Cornelia," 1909.

Johnson, Samuel. *The History of Rasselas, Prince of Abissinia,* 1759.

Joyce, James. *Dubliners,* 1914.

———. *Portrait of the Artist,* 1916.

———. *Ulysses,* 1922 [1960].

Kelman, James. *The Burn,* 1991.

Kipling, Rudyard. "Baa Baa, Black Sheep," 1888.

Lawrence, D. H. *Lady Chatterley's Lover,* 1928 [1960].

———. "Daughters of the Vicar," 1914.

———. *The Rainbow,* 1915.

Le Fanu, J. S. *Uncle Silas,* [1865] 1899.

Lessing, Doris. *The Grass is Singing,* 1950.

———. *The Good Terrorist,* 1985.

McEwan, Ian. *First Love, Last Rites,* 1975.

———. *Amsterdam,* 1998.

Melville, Herman. *Moby-Dick,* 1851.

Meredith, George. *The Egoist,* 1879.

———. *Diana of the Crossways,* 1885.

Moore, Brian. *The Lonely Passion of Judith Hearne,* 1965.

Moore, George. *A Mummer's Wife,* 1885 [1922].

———. *Esther Waters,* 1894 [1920].

———. *A Drama in Muslin,* 1886.

———. *The Lake,* 1905 [1921].

Murdoch, Iris. *The Philosopher's Pupil,* 1983.

Nabokov, Vladimir. *The Real Life of Sebastian Knight,* 1941.

Norris, Frank. *McTeague,* 1899.

Orwell, George. *Coming Up for Air,* 1939.

Parks, Tim. *Destiny,* 1999.

Poe, Edgar Allan. "The Tell-Tale Heart," 1845.

Powell, Anthony. *A Buyer's Market,* 1952.

Pym, Barbara. *A Few Green Leaves,* 1981.

Radcliffe, Ann. *The Mysteries of Udolpho,* 1794.

Reeve, Clara. *The Progress of Romance,* 1785.

Roth, Philip. *American Pastoral,* 1997.

Roubaud, Jacques. *The Great Fire of London,* 1989 [tr. 1991].

Salinger, J. D. *The Catcher in the Rye,*
1951.
Schreiner, Olive. *The Story of an African
Farm,* 1883.
Shelley, Mary. *Frankenstein,* 1818.
Spark, Muriel. *The Driver's Seat,* 1970.
——. *Aiding and Abetting,* 2000.
Stein, Gertrude. *Ida,* 1940.
Sterne, Laurence. *The Life and Opinions of
Tristram Shandy, Gentleman,* 1759–67.
Stevenson, R. L. *Dr. Jekyll and Mr. Hyde,*
1886.
——. *The Master of Ballantrae,* 1889.
Stoker, Bram. *Dracula,* 1897.
Thackeray, W. M. *Vanity Fair,* (1847–48)
1848.
Tóibín, Colm. *The Heather Blazing,* 1992.
Trevor, William. *Felicia's Journey,* 1994.

Trollope, Anthony. *The Three Clerks,*
1857.
——. *Castle Richmond,* 1860 [1873].
Waugh, Evelyn. *Decline and Fall,* 1928.
——. *A Handful of Dust,* 1934.
——. *Officers and Gentlemen,* 1955.
Wells, H. G. *The Time Machine,* 1895.
——. *The History of Mr. Polly,* 1910.
——. *The New Machiavelli,* 1911.
White, Patrick. *The Aunt's Story,* 1948.
Wilde, Oscar. *The Picture of Dorian Gray,*
1891.
Woolf, Virginia. *Jacob's Room,* 1922.
——. *Mrs. Dalloway,* 1925.
——. *To the Lighthouse,* 1927.
——. *The Waves,* 1931.
Wroth, Mary. *Urania,* 1621.

Select Bibliography

Adam, Jean-Michel. *Éléments de linguistique textuelle*. Liège: Mardaga, 1990.

———. *Le Texte narratif: Traité d'analyse pragmatique et textuelle*. Paris: Nathan, 1994.

———. *Les Textes: Types et prototypes*. Paris: Nathan, 1997.

Adam, Jean-Michel, and André Petitjean. *Le Texte descriptif: Poétique historique et linguistique textuelle*. Paris: Nathan, 1989.

Albou, Nathalie, and Françoise Rio. *Lectures méthodiques*. Paris: Ellipses, 1995.

Allott, Miriam. *Novelists on the Novel*. London: Routledge and Kegan Paul, 1959.

Amossy, Ruth. *Les Idées reçues: Sémiologie du stéréotype*. Paris: Nathan, 1991.

Amossy, Ruth, and Anne Herschberg Pierrot. *Stéréotypes et clichés: Langue, discours, société*. Paris: Nathan, 1997.

Amossy, Ruth, and Elisheva Rosen. *Les Discours du cliché*. Paris: Société d'Édition d'Enseignement Supérieur, 1982.

Apothéloz, Denis. "Éléments pour une logique de la description." In *La Description*, ed. Yves Reuter. Paris: Presses Universitaires du Septentrion, 1998.

Bacry, Patrick. *Les Figures de style*. Paris: Belin, 1992.

Baguley, David. *Naturalist Fiction: The Entropic Vision*. Cambridge: Cambridge University Press, 1990.

Bal, Mieke. *Narratology: Introduction to the Theory of Narrative*. 2nd ed. Toronto: University of Toronto Press, 1997.

Banfield, Ann. *Unspeakable Sentences*. Boston: Routledge and Kegan Paul, 1982.

Barthes, Roland. "Introduction to the Structural Analysis of Narrative." In *Image, Music, Text*. Ed and trans. Stephen Heath. New York: Hill and Wang, 1977: 79-117.

Benveniste, Émile. *Problèmes de linguistique générale*. Paris: Gallimard, 1966.

Blair, Hugh. *Lectures on Rhetoric and Belles Lettres*. 1784. London: William Baynes, 1825.

Blanchot, Maurice. *The Blanchot Reader*. Ed. Michael Holland. Oxford: Blackwell, 1995.

Booth, Wayne C. *The Rhetoric of Fiction*. Chicago: University of Chicago Press, 1961.

Bordwell, David. *Making Meaning: Inference and Rhetoric in the Interpretation of Cinema*. Cambridge, Mass.: Harvard University Press, 1989.

———. *Narration in the Fiction Film*. Madison: University of Wisconsin Press, 1985.

Brooke-Rose, Christine. "Narrating without a Narrator." London *Times Literary Supplement*. 31 December 1999, 13.

Brooks, Peter. *The Melodramatic Imagination*. New Haven: Yale University Press, 1995.

Charaudeau, Patrick. *Grammaire du sens et de l'expression*. Paris: Hachette, 1992.

Chatman, Seymour. "Characters and Narrators: Filter, Center, Slant, and Interest-Focus." *Poetics Today* 7 (1986): 189–203.

———. *Story and Discourse: Narrative Structure in Fiction and Film*. Ithaca: Cornell University Press, 1978.

Coetzee, J. M. *Doubling the Point: Essays and Interviews*. Cambridge, Mass.: Harvard University Press, 1992.

Cohn, Dorrit. *The Distinction of Fiction*. Baltimore: Johns Hopkins University Press, 1999.

———. "The Opening Episode of *The Golden Bowl* Vol. 2." *Henry James Review* 22, no. 1 (winter 2001): 1–10.

———. *Transparent Minds: Narrative Modes for Presenting Consciousness in Fiction*. Princeton: Princeton University Press, 1978.

Connor, Steven. *The English Novel in History: 1950–1995*. London: Routledge, 1966.

Culler, Jonathan. *Structuralist Poetics: Structuralism, Linguistics and the Study of Literature*. London: Routledge and Kegan Paul, 1975.

Downie, J. A. "Mary Davys's 'Probable Feign'd Stories.'" *Eighteenth-Century Fiction* 12, nos. 2–3 (January 2000): 309–26.

Duchet, Claude, and Isabelle Tournier. *Genèses des fins*. Saint-Denis: PUV, 1996.

Dufays, Jean-Louis. "Stéréotype et littérature." In *Le Stéréotype: Crise et transformations*. Ed. Alain Goulet. Caen: Presses Universitaires de Caen, 1994.

Durrer, Sylvie. *Le Dialogue romanesque*. Geneva: Librarie Droz, 1994.

Eco, Umberto. *The Role of the Reader: Explorations in the Semiotics of Texts*. 1979. Bloomington: Indiana University Press, 1984.

———. *Six Walks in the Fictional Woods*. Cambridge, Mass.: Harvard University Press, 1994.

Ermarth, Elizabeth Deeds. *The English Novel in History 1840–1895*. London: Routledge, 1997.

———. *Realism and Consensus in the English Novel*. Princeton: Princeton University Press, 1983.

Fauconnier, Gilles. *Mappings in Thought and Language*. Cambridge: Cambridge University Press, 1997.

Fludernik, Monika. *The Fictions of Language and the Languages of Fiction*. London: Routledge, 1993.

———. "Pronouns of Address and 'Odd Third Person Forms." In *New Essays in Deixis*. Ed. Keith Green. Amsterdam: Rodopi, 1995.

Forster, E. M. *Aspects of the Novel*. 1927. Harmondsworth, Middlesex, England: Penguin Books, 1971.

Frank, Joseph. *The Widening Gyre*. New Brunswick, N.J.: Rutgers University Press, 1963.

Fromilhague, Catherine. *Les Figures de style*. Paris: Nathan, 1995.

Fromilhague, Catherine, and A. Sandier-Chateau. *Introduction à l'analyse stylistique*. Paris: Dunod, 1996.

Furst, Lilian R. *All Is True: The Claims and Strategies of Realist Fiction*. Durham, N.C.: Duke University Press, 1995.

Gallagher, Catherine. *The Industrial Reformation of English Fiction*. Chicago: University of Chicago Press, 1985.

Genette, Gérard. *Fiction and Diction*. 1991. Trans. Catherine Porter. Ithaca: Cornell University Press, 1993.

———. *Figures II*. Paris: Seuil, 1969.

————. *Figures of Literary Discourse*. Trans. Alan Sheridan. New York: Columbia University Press, 1982.

————. *Narrative Discourse*. [From *Figures III*]. Trans. Jane E. Lewin. Ithaca: Cornell University Press, 1980.

————. *Narrative Discourse Revisited*. 1983. Trans. Jane E. Lewin. Ithaca: Cornell University Press, 1988.

————. *Paratexts: Thresholds of Interpretation*. 1987. Trans. Jane E. Lewin. Cambridge: Cambridge University Press, 1997.

Gibbs, Raymond W., Jr. *The Poetics of Mind*. Cambridge: Cambridge University Press, 1994.

Gibbs, Raymond W., Jr., and Gerard J. Steen. *Metaphor in Cognitive Linguistics*. Amsterdam: John Benjamins, 1999.

Gombrich, E. H. *The Sense of Order*. 2nd ed. London: Phaidon, 1984.

Goulet, Alain, ed. *Le Stéréotype: Crise et transformations*. Caen: Presses Universitaires de Caen, 1994.

Greimas, A.-J. *Structural Semantics*. 1966. Trans. Daniele McDowell et al. Lincoln: University of Nebraska Press, 1983.

Grésillon, Almuth. *Éléments de critique génétique: Lire les manuscrits modernes*. Paris: PUF, 1994.

Hamburger, Käte. *The Logic of Literature*. 2nd ed. 1973. Trans. Marilynn J. Rose. Bloomington: Indiana University Press, 1993.

Hamon, Philippe. *La Description littéraire: Anthologie de textes théoriques et critiques*. Paris: Macula, 1991.

————. *Du Descriptif*. Paris: Hachette, 1993.

————. "Rhetorical Status of the Descriptive." *Yale French Studies* 61 (1981): 1–27.

————. "What Is a Description?" In *French Literary Theory Today*. Ed. Tzvetan Todorov. Cambridge: Cambridge University Press, 1982.

Herschberg Pierrot, Anne. *Stylistique de la prose*. Paris: Belin, 1993.

Hollander, Anne. *Seeing through Clothes*. Berkeley: University of California Press, 1993.

Hughes, Clair. *Henry James and the Art of Dress*. London: Palgrave, 2000.

Hunter, J. Paul. *The Reluctant Pilgrim*. Baltimore: Johns Hopkins University Press, 1966.

Iser, Wolfgang. *The Fictive and the Imaginary: Charting Literary Anthropology*. Baltimore: Johns Hopkins University Press, 1993.

Jahn, Manfred. "Contextualizing Represented Speech and Thought." *Journal of Pragmatics* 17 (1992): 353.

————. "Frames, Preferences and the Reading of Third-Person Narratives: Towards a Cognitive Narratology." *Poetics Today* 18, no. 4 (winter 1997): 441–68.

James, Henry. "The Art of Fiction." In *The Critical Muse: Selected Literary Criticism*. Harmondsworth, Middlesex, England: Penguin Books, 1987.

————. *Literary Criticism*. 2 vols. New York: Library of America, 1984-85.

Jouve, Vincent. *L'Effet personnage dans le roman*. Paris: PUF, 1992.

Keating, P. J. *The Working Classes in Victorian Fiction*. London: Routledge and Kegan Paul, 1971.

Kerbrat-Orecchioni, Catherine. *L'Énonciation: De la subjectivité dans le langage*. Paris: Armand Colin, 1980.

Kermode, Frank. *The Sense of an Ending: Studies in the Theory of Fiction*. New York: Oxford University Press, 1967.

Kincaid, James R., and James Phelan. "What Do We Owe Texts? Respect, Irreverence, or Nothing at All?" *Critical Inquiry* 25, no. 5 (summer 1999): 758–83.

Lakoff, George, and Mark Johnson. *Metaphors We Live By*. Chicago: University of Chicago Press, 1980.

Lakoff, George, and Mark Turner. *More Than Cool Reason: A Field Guide to Poetic Metaphor*. Chicago: University of Chicago Press, 1989.

Langacker, Ronald W. "Conceptualization, Symbolization, and Grammar." In *The New Psychology of Language*. Ed. Michael Tomasello. Mahwah, N.J.: Lawrence Erlbaum Associates, 1998.

———. *Foundations of Cognitive Grammar*. Stanford: Stanford University Press, 1991.

Lausberg, Heinrich. *Handbook of Literary Rhetoric*. Trans. Matthew T. Bliss et al. Leiden: Brill, 1998.

Leech, Geoffrey N. *Meaning and the English Verb*. 1971. 2nd ed. London: Longman, 1987.

Leech, Geoffrey N., and Michael H. Short. *Style in Fiction: A Linguistic Introduction to English Fictional Prose*. London: Longman, 1981.

Lejeune, Philippe. *L'Autobiographie en France*. Paris: Armand Colin, 1971.

Levine, George. *The Realistic Imagination: English Fiction from Frankenstein to Lady Chatterley*. Chicago: University of Chicago Press, 1981.

Lodge, David. *Language of Fiction*. New York: Columbia University Press, 1967.

———. *The Modes of Modern Writing: Metaphor, Metonymy, and the Typology of Modern Literature*. London: Edward Arnold, 1977.

Lothe, Jakob. *Conrad's Narrative Method*. Oxford: Clarendon Press, 1989.

———. *Narrative in Fiction and Film: An Introduction*. Oxford: Oxford University Press, 2000.

Lotman Yuri. *Universe of the Mind: A Semiotic Theory of Culture*. Trans. Ann Shukman. London: I. B. Tauris, 1990.

Lubbock, Percy. *The Craft of Fiction*. 1921. London: Jonathan Cape, 1968.

McFarlane, Brian. *Novel to Film: An Introduction to the Theory of Adaptation*. Oxford: Clarendon Press, 1996.

McHale, Brian. "Free Indirect Discourse: A Survey of Recent Accounts." *Poetics and the Theory of Literature* 3 (1978): 249–87.

McKeon, Michael. "Ian Watt's *Rise of the Novel* within the Tradition of the Rise of the Novel." *Eighteenth-Century Fiction* 12, nos. 2–3 (January 2000): 253–76.

———. *The Origins of the English Novel*. 1987. London: Century Hutchinson, 1988.

———, ed. *Theory of the Novel: A Historical Approach*. Baltimore: Johns Hopkins University Press, 2000.

Maingueneau, Dominique. *Éléments de linguistique pour le texte littéraire*. 3rd ed. Paris: Dunod, 1993.

Martin, Wallace. *Recent Theories of Narrative*. Ithaca: Cornell University Press, 1986.

Molinié, Georges, and Pierre Cahneé, eds. *Qu'est-ce que le style*. Paris: PUF, 1994.

Moretti, Franco. *Atlas of the European Novel 1800–1900*. London: Verso, 1998.

———. *The Way of the World*. London: Verso, 1987.

Onega, Susana, and José Ángel García Landa, eds. *Narratology: An Introduction*. London: Longman, 1996.

Ong, Walter J. *Orality and Literacy: The Technologizing of the Word*. London: Methuen, 1982.

Oz, Amos. *The Story Begins: Essays on Literature*. New York: Harcourt Brace, 1999.

Page, Norman. *Speech in the English Novel*. London: Longman, 1973.

Pascal, Roy. *The Dual Voice*. Manchester: Manchester University Press, 1977.

Pavel, Thomas G. *Fictional Worlds*. Cambridge, Mass.: Harvard University Press, 1986.

Piette, Adam. *Remembering and the Sound of Words: Mallarmé, Proust, Joyce, Beckett*. Oxford: Clarendon Press, 1996.

Pratt, Mary Louise. *Towards a Speech Act Theory of Discourse*. Bloomington: Indiana University Press, 1977.

Propp, Vladimir. *Morphology of the Folktale*. 1927. Trans. Laurence Scott. 2nd ed. Austin: University of Texas Press, 1988.

Ravoux Rallo, Élisabeth. *L'Explication de texte à l'oral des concours*. Paris: Armand Colin, 1966.

Reconsidering the Rise of the Novel. Special issue of *Eighteenth-Century Fiction* 12, nos. 2–3 (2000).

Regard, Frédéric. "Pour un retour à la 'vie de l'auteur': L'éthique du biographique." *Études anglaises* 3 (July–September 1999): 298–310.

Reuter, Yves. *L'Analyse du récit*. Paris: Dunod, 1997.

———. *Introduction à l'analyse du roman*. 2nd ed. Paris: Dunod, 1996.

Reuter, Yves, ed. *La Description: Théories, recherches, formation, enseignement*. Paris: Presses Universitaires du Septentrion, 1998.

Reynolds, Kimberley, and Nicola Humble. *Victorian Heroines: Representations of Femininity in Nineteenth-Century Literature and Art*. New York: New York University Press, 1993.

Richard, J.-P. *Microlectures*. Paris: Seuil, 1979.

Ricoeur, Paul. "Life: A Story in Search of a Narrator." In *A Ricoeur Reader*. Ed. Mario J. Valdés. New York: Harvester, 1991.

———. *The Rule of Metaphor*. 1975. Trans. Robert Czerny et al. Toronto: University of Toronto Press, 1977.

———. *Time and Narrative*. 3 vols. 1983–85. Trans. Kathleen McLaughlin and David Pellauer. Chicago: University of Chicago Press, 1984–88.

Riffaterre, Michael. *Fictional Truth*. Baltimore: Johns Hopkins University Press, 1990.

———. *Text Production*. 1979. Trans. Terese Lyons. New York: Columbia University Press, 1983.

Rimmon-Kenan, Shlomith. *A Glance beyond Doubt: Narration, Representation, Subjectivity*. Columbus: Ohio State University Press, 1996.

———. *Narrative Fiction: Contemporary Poetics*. London: Methuen, 1983.

Shaw, Harry E. *Narrating Reality: Austen, Scott, Eliot*. Ithaca: Cornell University Press, 1999.

Shklovsky, Viktor. "Art as Technique." In *Russian Formalist Criticism: Four Essays*. Trans. Lee T. Lemon and Marion J. Reis. Lincoln: University of Nebraska Press, 1965.

———. "The Connection between Devices of Syuzhet Construction and General Stylistic Devices." In *Russian Formalism*. Ed. Stephen Bann and John E. Bowlt. Edinburgh: Scottish Academic Press, 1973.

Spitzer, Leo. "Linguistics and Literary History." In *Linguistics and Literary Style*. Ed. Donald C. Freeman. New York: Holt, Rinehart and Winston, 1970.

Stang, Richard. *The Theory of the Novel in England 1850–1870*. London: Routledge and Kegan Paul, 1959.

Stanzel, F. K. *A Theory of Narrative*. 2nd ed. 1982. Trans. Charlotte Goedsche. Cambridge: Cambridge University Press, 1984.

Stein, Gertrude. *Lectures in America*. New York: Random House, 1935.

Sternberg, Meir. *Expositional Modes and Temporal Ordering in Fiction*. Baltimore: Johns Hopkins University Press, 1978.

Tannen, Deborah, ed. *Spoken and Written Language: Exploring Orality and Literacy.* Norwood, N.J.: Ablex, 1982.

Tanner, Tony. *Adultery in the Novel: Contract and Transgression.* Baltimore: Johns Hopkins University Press, 1979.

Tillotson, Kathleen. "The Lighter Reading of the Eighteen-Sixties." Introduction to *The Woman in White,* Riverside Edition. Boston: Houghton Mifflin, 1969.

———. *Novels of the Eighteen-Forties.* Oxford: Oxford University Press, 1954.

Todorov, Tzvetan, ed. *French Literary Theory Today.* Cambridge: Cambridge University Press, 1982.

Tomasello, Michael. *The New Psychology of Language: Cognitive and Functional Approaches to Language Structure.* Mahwah, N.J.: Lawrence Erlbaum Associates, 1998.

Tufte, Virginia. *Grammar as Style.* New York: Holt, Rinehart and Winston, 1971.

Turner, Mark. *Reading Minds.* Princeton: Princeton University Press, 1991.

Ungerer, F., and H.-J. Schmid. *An Introduction to Cognitive Linguistics.* London: Longman, 1996.

Van Ghent, Dorothy. *The English Novel: Form and Function.* 1953. New York: Harper, 1961.

Vickers, Brian. *In Defence of Rhetoric.* Oxford: Clarendon Press, 1988.

Walker, Pierre A., ed. *Henry James on Culture.* Lincoln: University of Nebraska Press, 1999.

Watt, Ian. "The First Paragraph of *The Ambassadors.*" Reprinted in Henry James, *The Ambassadors.* New York: W. W. Norton, 1964.

———. *The Rise of the Novel.* 1957. Berkeley: University of California Press, 1964.

Wood, David, ed. *On Paul Ricoeur: Narrative and Interpretation.* London: Routledge, 1991.

Woolf, Virginia. *Collected Essays.* Ed. Leonard Woolf. 4 vols. London: Hogarth Press, 1966–67.

———. *Women and Writing.* London: Women's Press, 1979.

Yamaguchi, Mariko. "How Should We Treat Fictional Names?" *Tetsugaku: Philosophical Association of Japan* no. 53 (2002).

Index